D1345819

2007

LORCA

LORCA

The Theatre Beneath the Sand

GWYNNE EDWARDS

MARION BOYARS

LONDON · BOSTON

First published in Great Britain and the United States 1980
by Marion Boyars Publishers Ltd
18 Brewer Street London W1R 4AS
and
Marion Boyars Publishers Inc
99 Main Street, Salem, New Hampshire 03079

Australian distribution by Thomas C. Lothian Pty Ltd
4-12 Tattersalls Lane
Melbourne Victoria 3000

British Library Cataloguing in Publication Data

Edwards, Gwynne
  Lorca.
  1. García Lorca, Federico – Criticism
  and interpretation
  862'.6'2   PQ6613.A763Z/   80-40141
  ISBN 0-7145-2698-3

Library of Congress Catalog Card Number 79-56839

Typeset by John Smith, London
Printed and bound in Great Britain by

Robert MacLehose and Company Limited
Printers to the University of Glasgow

CONTENTS

TO
GILLIAN

ACKNOWLEDGEMENTS

BLOOD WEDDING, YERMA and THE HOUSE OF BERNARDA ALBA from THREE TRAGEDIES, translated by James Graham-Luján and Richard L. O'Connell. © 1947 by New Directions Publishing Corporation, New York and Martin Secker and Warburg Ltd., London.

THE BILLY-CLUB PUPPETS, THE SHOEMAKER'S PRODIGIOUS WIFE, THE LOVE OF DON PERLIMPLÍN, DOÑA ROSITA THE SPINSTER and THE BUTTERFLY'S EVIL SPELL from FIVE PLAYS, translated by James Graham-Luján. © 1963 by New Directions Publishing Corporation, New York, and Martin Secker and Warburg Ltd., London.

Quotations from the above are published by permission of New Directions, New York, publishers and agents for the Estate of Federico García Lorca; and by Martin Secker and Warburg Ltd., London.

Excerpts from unpublished English versions in translations by Dr Gwynne Edwards are by kind permission of New Directions Publishing Corporation.

FOREWORD

With the exception of Cervantes, Lorca is for many people the most famous name in Spanish literature. His work has been translated into numerous languages; it has inspired writers, composers, choreographers, painters and film-makers; and since his death in 1936 a large number of articles and books of various kinds and varying quality, from biographies to literary studies, have consolidated Lorca's fame and reputation.

In many ways Lorca is an extremely Spanish writer, many of his poems and plays a stylized version of the image of Spain that in some degree we all possess. *The Gipsy Ballads, The Lament for Ignacio Sánchez Mejías, Blood Wedding, Yerma,* and *The House of Bernarda Alba,* inasmuch as they evoke the gipsies of Andalusia, the bullring, crumbling, sun-baked Spanish villages, and the powerful forces of passion and honour, consolidate our impression of the essential Spanishness of Lorca's work which accounts, in part perhaps, for its attraction. On the other hand, the picture must be balanced by an awareness of the extent to which much of his important writing belongs to a much broader European cultural movement. His acquaintance with surrealism, firstly through his friendship with Salvador Dalí and Luis Buñuel and later through the poetry of Walt Whitman, can be seen in the ambitious poem, *Poet in New York,* and in the two arresting plays, *The Public* and *When Five Years Have Passed.* There is nothing here to suggest the Spain of the *Gipsy Ballads* or the rural tragedies. *The Public,* in particular, in some ways echoing Pirandello and in others foreshadowing Beckett, Genet and Ionesco, is one of the most original and experimental plays in twentieth-century European theatre.

1

Whatever the subject-matter of Lorca's theatre, it has a remarkable unity of vision. From his first play, *The Butterfly's Evil Spell*, to his last, *The House of Bernarda Alba*, he dwells on the issues that haunted him throughout his life: the power of passion; frustration; passing time; and death. They are themes which, far from being particularly Spanish, touch upon us all, for these are the issues and concerns that most deeply affect us in the living of our lives. The ultimate power of Lorca's theatre lies, therefore, not in any superficial Spanish quality but in its universality, which enables his plays to transcend their settings. His characters, though heightened, are people with whose passions we can identify, mirrors in which we see ourselves. The images that linger in our minds do so because they embody our deepest fears: a man dying alone on an empty stage; women faced by the desolation of old age; figures searching for their own identity. Moreover, while Lorca lays bare the individual human soul, he exposes too man's contact with the primitive, instinctive forces of the natural world of which he is participant and sometimes victim, the roots that we all share but seek, perhaps, to forget. The major plays, and especially the rural tragedies, strip away the masks, the layers of sophistication behind which civilized man attempts to conceal his true nature.

The theatre of Lorca is also a theatre of technical advance and innovation. His stated aim of saving the Spanish theatre was part of a similar movement that, championed elsewhere by such men of vision as Edward Gordon Craig, Reinhardt and Stanislavski, altered the face of European theatre in general. For Lorca, as for them, the realistic stagecraft of the nineteenth century had to give way to a much more vital and fluid concept of dramatic action in which dialogue, song, dance, movement and staging were all important elements. The powerful themes of Lorca's plays are thus expressed in a dynamic dramatic language which, transforming ideas into memorable images, makes him one of the great communicators of our time.

This study, discussing the nature and treatment of Lorca's themes and the characteristics of his dramatic technique, seeks to make the work of this great dramatist more familiar to a wider audience. In quoting Lorca's marvellous lines in English translation, I am aware, of course, that their quality, especially in matters of rhythm, is often diminished. If, on the other hand, I succeed in stimulating in the reader some of the enthusiasm and excitement which the study of these plays has aroused in me, my purpose will have been amply justified.

INTRODUCTION

Federico García Lorca was born on 5 June, 1898, in Fuente-
vaqueros, a small Andalusian village about fifteen miles from
Granada. He was one of four children, his parents were pros-
perous landowners in the area, and, through the influence of
his mother in particular, Lorca received the benefits of a good
early education. He went to school at the age of four despite a
serious illness contracted at the age of two months, and, by all
accounts, revealed a boundless curiosity in the world around
him. His interest in drama was already clearly discernible.
From Dolores, a servant in the Lorca household, the young
Federico acquired an enthusiasm for the folklore of the peas-
ants and gipsies of Granada, and a knowledge of the traditional ballads that he would use later in his own poems and plays.
In addition, Dolores played an important part in Federico's
first dramatic ventures. With the other servants she helped
him present plays in the little puppet theatre which he had
bought in Granada and for which he designed the costumes.
As he directed the wooden and cardboard figures, issued
instructions to his helpers, and entranced his audience of
servants and children, the little boy was already the childhood
form of the dramatist-director he would become in adult life.
As a child, Federico liked too to act out the Mass for the
children and servants of the household, providing further
evidence in his passionate and emotional performances of a
precocious dramatic talent.[1]
    When the family moved from Fuetevaqueros to Granada in
1909, it marked a significant period in the young boy's life. He
attended the Colegio del Sagrado Corazón de Jesús in prepara-
tion for entry into the University of Granada, but Federico's

5

real interests lay elsewhere. Granada was itself a place of great fascination for him, for he encountered there that mixture of Arabic, Greco-Roman, and gipsy culture which gives the city its colourful, magical and haunting flavour. It was also at that particular time a city famed for its cultural activities, especially music, and here it was that yet another of Federico's prodigious talents began to emerge. At the Conservatory he studied music with Don Antonio Segura and under his patient guidance became a brilliant pianist. If as a child he had entertained his friends with a puppet show, he did so now with his pianistic virtuosity. It was, indeed, his musical ability which brought him to the attention of Manuel de Falla and which initiated between them a long and artistically rewarding friendship. Falla, like Lorca, was greatly interested in traditional Spanish music, and their researches into the subject had a clear effect on Lorca's own writing. And it was also with Falla that Lorca would present some of his puppet plays.

Granada was a meeting-place for many distinguished and cultured people. Fernando de los Ríos, Professor of Political Law in the University of Granada, was a great humanist, scholar and teacher. Martín Domínguez Berrueta, Professor of the Theory of Art at Granada, encouraged Lorca to write his first book, *Impressions and Landscapes (Impresiones y paisajes)* in 1918. Others included the sculptor Juan Cristóbal, the guitarist Ángel Barrios, the literary critic José Fernández Montesinos, the journalist José Mora Guarnido and, as well as Falla, Andrés Segovia. It was a very talented group which met regularly at the Café Alameda to spend the evening together in conversation and which welcomed as visitors to Granada such distinguished people as Wanda Landowska, Arthur Rubenstein, H. G. Wells and Rudyard Kipling. The young Lorca found artistic inspiration in such company and was already emerging as a poet of great promise. But already he was considered in Granada to be a homosexual and must have attracted that hostility meted out by Spanish males to those who fall outside their traditional concept of virility. His early poems reveal a clear sense of isolation and rejection and an identification with Granada's persecuted groups: Jews, Moors, negroes and gipsies.

In 1919 Lorca moved from Granada to Madrid to study at the University and commenced the ten-year stay at the Residencia de Estudiantes that would prove decisive in his artistic career. Founded in 1910, the Residencia was a cultural centre of international reputation which counted amongst its foreign residents François Mauriac, H. G. Wells, G. K. Chesterton and Igor Stravinsky. As far as Spaniards were concerned, Lorca found himself in the company of Juan Ramón Jiménez, Gregorio Martínez Sierra, José Caballero, Manolo Ángeles Ortiz, Salvador Dalí, and Luis Buñuel. It was stimulating company indeed, and it is little wonder that in it Lorca's genius flourished and that his knowledge of modern artistic movements – Dadaism, Ultraism, Surrealism – grew considerably. It is worth noting that Dalí was tremendously impressed by Lorca and remained a life-long friend. Above all, Lorca had in the Residencia an intelligent and perceptive audience to which he could recite his own poetry.

Between 1919 and 1929 Lorca's artistic output steadily increased. On 22 March, 1920, his first play, *The Butterfly's Evil Spell (El maleficio de la mariposa)*, was performed in Madrid. In 1921 he published his first volume of poems, entitled simply *Book of Poems (Libro de poemas)*. A second volume, *Songs (Canciones)*, appeared in 1924, and by 1925 he had completed *Mariana Pineda*. By this time poems and articles were appearing in literary magazines with great regularity. In 1926 Lorca commenced writing *The Shoemaker's Prodigious Wife (La zapatera prodigiosa)*. In 1928 he completed *The Love of Don Perlimplín (El amor de Don Perlimplín)* and in the same year published the enormously successful book of poems, *Gipsy Ballads (Romancero gitano)*. During this time Lorca also delivered a number of important lectures, notably 'The Poetic Image in Don Luis de Góngora' *(La imagen poética de Don Luis de Góngora)* and 'Imagination, Inspiration and Evasion in Poetry' *(Imaginación, inspiración y evasión en la poesía)*. His fame grew but with it he became strangely depressed, burdened perhaps by the fear that he would not be able to maintain the same artistic standards. Whether the cause of his depression lay here or in some love affair or in his awareness of his homosexuality, the fact remains that he decided to leave Spain, and in the summer of

B

1929 he arrived in New York with his friend and former teacher, Fernando de los Ríos.

Lorca enrolled to study English at Columbia University but quickly abandoned the course. His lack of English and sense of disorientation in a country with which he was totally unfamiliar augmented rather than diminished his depression, and he soon left New York to stay with friends in Newburg and Eden Mills, Vermont. He was still despondent, and only after returning to Columbia did he begin to recover, for he began now to play a greater part in social activities, to explore New York, and he lectured at Vassar and Columbia. He finally left New York in the spring of 1930 after a nine-month stay.

New York marked another important landmark in Lorca's artistic development. His experience of the enormous contrast between the steel and concrete jungle and the tranquil beauty of Granada, the terrible plight of oppressed minorities like the negroes, the frightening spectacle of a world isolated from its natural roots left its indelible mark upon him. Together with Lorca's pessimistic frame of mind at this particular point in time, it led to the composition of one of his most impressive and certainly most ambitious poems, *Poet in New York (Poeta en Nueva York)*. And to the same experience, if not the same year, belong the two important 'surrealist' plays: *The Public (El Público)* and *When Five Years Have Passed (Así que pasen cinco años)*, both written shortly afterwards. It may have been an encounter with the poetry of Walt Whitman which reawakened in Lorca the interest in surrealism which Dalí and Buñuel had fostered years before and which led now to the surrealist manner of the works of these years.

Lorca's visit to Havana in the spring of 1930 restored his spirits fully. He was again in the Hispanic world, in a setting and a way of life that he found compatible. His lectures were warmly received, and when he returned to Spain later in the year, it was to embark on the most creative and fruitful period of his career. The fall of the dictatorship of Primo de Rivera in 1930 and the appearance of a republican government in 1931 created a liberal atmosphere in which art could truly flourish. During these years, as we shall see later, Lorca became the director of the brilliant and successful itinerant student theatre company which came to be known as *La Barraca*. Here, in the performance of Spanish classical plays in many different parts of Spain, he set out to create a style of performance that, embracing settings, dialogue, movement, costume and lighting, would give old plays new life and a sense of relevance for a modern audience. It was, moreover, an approach to the theatre that he practised in his own plays which in these years dominated the Spanish stage. In December 1930 the first version of *The Shoemaker's Prodigious Wife* was performed in Madrid. In 1933 it was performed in its revised version, and in the same year *The Love of Don Perlimplín* and *Blood Wedding (Bodas de sangre)* were premièred, while *Yerma* followed in 1934 and *Doña Rosita the Spinster (Doña Rosita la soltera)* in 1935. With the performance of his plays in Spain, South America and elsewhere, Lorca became the most celebrated Spanish playwright of his day. In 1935 he made an outstandingly successful visit to Buenos Aires, attended performances of his plays, gave lectures, and was fêted wherever he appeared. At the same time he continued to produce poems: in 1934 the magnificent elegy on the sudden death of his bullfighter friend, 'Lament for Ignacio Sánchez Mejías' *(Llanto por Ignacio Sánchez Mejías)* and in 1935 and 1936 a number of single poems, including some from what was to be the *Divan del Tamarit*, a collection of poems which revealed the influence of Arabic poetry.

By July, 1936, the whole of Spain was in turmoil. The growing political unrest of the last few years finally came to a head when on 18 July Franco's troops in Spanish Morocco revolted against the Republican government and invaded the mainland. At the time Lorca was in Granada which quickly came under military rule. The city and the surrounding area lived in constant fear of the 'black squads' which, acting on military orders, initiated a reign of terror, rooting out and killing political opponents and innocent people alike. One of the first to be killed was Lorca's brother-in-law, the mayor of Granada. As for Lorca himself, his association with the Republican-supported *La Barraca* was a mark against him, as was his friendship with Margarita Xirgu, the famous actress, and other Republican supporters. Again, Lorca's reputation as

a homosexual and his enormous success as a writer were
precisely the things on which prejudice and envy, especially
fascist prejudice, could readily feed. His family lived in constant fear for his life, and on 16 August their fears were realized. He was arrested at the house of Luis Rosales, a fellow
poet, where he had been hiding, taken to the Civil Government, held there for a few days, and finally carried off to be
shot either late on the night of 18 August or in the early hours
of the following day.[2]

For the first two decades of the twentieth century the theatre in
Spain presented a spectacle of almost unrelieved superficiality.[3] The theatregoers of the time were, for the most part,
upper middle-class, seeking only entertainment, and the
dominant dramatist at the turn of the century was still José
Echegaray. In neo-Romantic plays with suitably moving subjects, passionate characters and inflated language, he satisfied the public appetite and, exploiting a well-worn formula
devoid of any real seriousness, remained the darling of the
Spanish public for many years. While in the rest of Europe
Ibsen, Chekhov, Shaw, Brecht, Pirandello and others had, or
would soon have, achieved a degree of success with their
thought-provoking and often experimental plays, Spain was
distinguished by a pattern that would prove difficult to break:
the domination of its theatre by dramatists who, on the whole,
gave an undiscerning public what it wanted, and a public
which would not tolerate serious or experimental plays.

The younger dramatists of these years, even though they
represent a movement away from Romantic drama towards a
greater realism, prove the general point. Jacinto Benavente
(1866-1954), well educated, widely travelled, knowledgeable
in the history of the European theatre and conscious too of
Spain's cultural stagnation, sought to change the Spanish
theatre only to settle for a compromise. His first play, *The Alien
Nest (El nido ajeno)*, presenting a conservative public with the
unpalatable theme of adultery and family dishonour, was
booed from the stage in 1894 and led Benavente in his second
play, *Familiar People (Gente conocida)* to temper his social
criticism. Thereafter, despite a satiric intention, his realistic

bourgeois drama, the *alta comedia* which was his principal contribution to the theatre, was distinguished by its nicely shaped plots, well-drawn characters and its witty and elegant dialogue. It was a type of drama so successful in commercial terms that other writers inevitably embraced it, and in the hands of Manuel Linares Rivas (1878-1938) and Gregorio Martínez Sierra (1881-1948) bourgeois drawing-room theatre was consolidated.

A diluted realism of a somewhat different kind, yet equally damaging to any kind of progress in the theatre, is exemplified by the plays of the immensely popular and successful Serafín and Joaquín Álvarez Quintero (1871-1938 and 1873-1944). Exploiting the tradition of the representation of popular types, the so-called *género chico*, the Quintero brothers wrote two hundred or so plays in which they projected a pleasant, colourful and charming vision of Spain, and in particular of their native Andalusia. An adoring but unthinking public was invited, and accepted the invitation, to lose itself in a world of fantasy and nostalgia, of attractive characters and witty conversation that had neither a bearing on the problems of the moment nor an intention to dislodge the theatre from its comfortable course.

Equally negative in relation to any real change was the 'poetic theatre', the third and last kind of theatre that needs to be mentioned here. Broadly speaking, it was a theatre of verse drama. The plays of Francisco Villaespesa, Eduardo Marquina and José María Pemán were in many cases set in Moorish Spain, the Medieval world, or Spain's magnificent past. In some ways they can be seen as an alternative to the bourgeois world of Benavente, but, like the drama they reacted against, they did nothing to advance in form or content the Spanish theatre of that time.

In this panorama of general stagnation Carlos Arniches (1866-1943) is a significant pointer to the way ahead. Writing, like the Quintero brothers, in the tradition of the *género chico*, Arniches placed on the stage in a vigorous and colourful style the low life of Madrid, and in his *Grotesque Tragedies (tragedias grotescas)* presented his low-life types not as picturesque but as grotesque, exaggerated characters, many of whom, nonetheless, invite compassion as well as laughter. His three-act plays *La señorita de Trevélez* (1916), *The Landowners (Los caciques)* (1920) and *The Heroic Town (La heroica villa)* (1921), portray the terrible prejudices, maliciousness and narrow-mindedness of provincial life that are both ridiculous and inhuman. In this mixture of farce and tragedy Arniches anticipates an important movement in the European drama of later years and, as far as Spain is concerned, looks forward to the themes and techniques of one of its most influential dramatists, Ramón del Valle-Inclán.

A sustained and conscious effort to shake the Spanish nation out of its long inertia, to investigate its ills and prescribe the necessary remedies, lay for the most part in the hands of the so-called Generation of '98: José Ortega y Gasset, Miguel de Unamuno, Azorín, Ángel Ganivet, Pío Baroja, Antonio Machado, Juan Ramón Jiménez, and others. Seeking to convince their countrymen of the deplorable state of Spanish life in general and of the desperate need for change, their efforts in the creative arts began a cultural renaissance of a kind and quality unknown in Spain since the glorious Golden Age of Spanish life and letters in the sixteenth and seventeenth centuries. As far as the theatre was concerned, the men of '98 signalled their protest when in 1905 they opposed a national tribute to Echegaray in recognition of his receipt of the Nobel Prize for Literature. It was with them, and in particular with Ramón del Valle-Inclán, Jacinto Grau, Unamuno and Azorín, that the initial attempt to revitalize the Spanish theatre would lie.

Ramón del Valle-Inclán (1866-1936) is one of the most significant figures in the evolution of the twentieth-century Spanish theatre and, with recent London performances of *Divine Words (Divinas palabras)*, has achieved an international recognition which in his lifetime eluded him in his own country. His importance as an innovator, which links him firmly to Lorca, lies firstly in his particular conception of theatre.[4] Rejecting the naturalistic tradition of the psychological play which concentrates on the problems of a particular individual, Valle sought instead to project through his characters a sense of the archetypal, the timeless and the universal. In addition, he aimed at achieving in a play a synthesis of its different elements of dialogue, sets, colour, movement, lighting and music, and at establishing between the stage and the audience a close rapport based not on the play's intellectual appeal but on its emotional impact, creating thereby that sense of collective experience and ritual performance that lies at the very heart of true theatre. Here, in short, was a form of theatre totally different from the refined, witty world of Benavente and his followers, and Valle's plays, in order to achieve their effect through the emotions, demanded instead of conventional plot a succession of short, self-contained scenes or visual images, as in a film; dialogue that was forceful, arresting, and often crude; a bold, open display of emotion; and broad, vigorous physical movements and actions. In his approach to the theatre, Valle-Inclán is part of that movement that was exemplified at the beginning of the century in such brilliant innovators as Edward Gordon Craig whose aim it was to replace the realistic stagecraft of the nineteenth century with a style that unified the play's different dramatic elements. There is no evidence to suggest that Valle knew Craig, friend of Stanislavski and Reinhardt and author of the authoritative *On the Art of the Theatre*, but it is significant that the revolution in the theatre in other European countries was also evident on a smaller scale in Spain.

Valle's theories are best illustrated by reference to his plays. His early plays, with their emphasis on gardens, parks, fountains and lakes, suggest perhaps that Valle was concerned with putting the aesthetic world of 'Modernism' on the stage. On the other hand, *The Head of the Dragon (La cabeza del dragón)* has a strong element of farce and in its caricature of royalty, ministers and generals looks forward to Valle's later and most characteristic manner: the technique of *esperpentismo* that in turn foreshadowed the style of other Spanish and European dramatists. In 1920, after a seven-year absence from the theatre, Valle set out his ideas in the twelfth scene of *Lights of Bohemia (Luces de Bohemia)*:

> . . . my present aesthetic is to transform classical norms by means of the mathematics of a concave mirror . . . let us deform expression in the same mirror that deforms our faces and the whole wretched existence of Spain.[5]

He observed, too, that if Carlos Arniches had used the tradition of the *género chico* to portray grotesque types, his own theatre was the *género chico* 'multiplied by four'. And in his *esperpentos* Valle-Inclán does indeed parade before us figures transformed into absurd and grotesque freaks, as though seen in a distorting mirror. *The Chaste Queen (La reina castiza)* of 1920, a parody on the nineteenth-century court of Isabel II, is peopled with grotesques, from the ridiculous figure of the queen to her highly effeminate consort and her comically named lover, Gargalito. *The Horns of Don Friolera (Los cuernos de Don Friolera)* of 1921 mocks through the technique of farce the traditionally serious theme of honour, for it is embodied in an absurd group of Spanish Army Officers. And *Lights of Bohemia* presents in a series of separate, self-contained scenes, a whole gallery of figures which, acting as a counterpoint to the central figure of Max Estrella, portrays his personal failure against the background of a general disillusionment that is that of Spain itself. In all these plays Valle combines social comment with a stage technique that in its visual qualities and its often coarse and aggressive manner becomes a brutal attack upon the emotions of the audience. Reminiscent of Alfred Jarry, Valle's theatre also looks forward to Ionesco, Genet and Arrabal.

In his reaction to the conservatism of contemporary theatre Valle had in Jacinto Grau (1877-1958) a kindred spirit. In the first place, Grau's conception of the theatre accorded with Valle's:

> To sum it up is easy: to perceive Nature in all its multiple aspects and to reflect things with the greatest possible intensity within a classical harmony. To bring to the theatre plastic, decorative and musical elements and to see the action with the eye of a painter without losing a sense of the whole, an overall interest and depth. A sense of theatre in its true meaning and a conception of tragedy in its original, noble form are, in my opinion, things which do not change with time . . .

The plays written before 1918 – including *The Prodigal Son (El hijo pródigo)* and *Count Alarcos (El conde Alarcos)* – are somewhat 'classical' in many ways, but they already exhibit Grau's use of the different elements of the stage, and in particular of scenery, costumes and lighting, in order to heighten the dramatic action. After 1918, moreover, this new and imaginative style became part of a generally more *avant-garde* manner, for Grau's plays contain more characters, a more complex action, a mixture of styles, non-realistic figures like Fate and Death, and they suggest too the sense of the futility of human effort that characterized the European scene after the First World War. Grau's best and most famous play, *Mr. Pygmalion (El señor de Pigmalión)*, written in the same year (1921) as Pirandello's *Six Characters in Search of an Author* and Karel Capek's *R. U. R.*, is a significant work in terms both of its themes and its stagecraft.[6] The main character, Mr. Pygmalion, creates a number of animated life-size puppets who have all the weaknesses of human beings and who, though loved by their creator, eventually destroy him. In a thematic sense the play voices many of the preoccupations of its period: the relationship between the artist and his characters; the true extent of human freedom; the degree to which man is himself a puppet; and the often fatal consequences of human ingenuity and progress. In terms of stagecraft it is a work that is a good example of the non-realistic European drama, for Grau employs the stage-settings, costumes, lighting, music, dance, and sound effects as an integral part of the play. The puppets dance, their costumes vividly evoke their different characters, and the sets are largely functional and simple. Like Valle-Inclán, and Lorca slightly later, Grau is part of that revitalization of the theatre exemplified in Gordon Craig's ideas and whose purpose it was to destroy bourgeois tradition and superficiality.

Despite the individual importance of Valle-Inclán and Grau, the 1920s did little to advance the cause of the theatre in Spain in general, and the commercial theatre continued to be dominated by the old favourites, most of whom were, after all, still alive: Benavente, the Quintero brothers, Linares Rivas, etc.[7] To discover productions and trends of any significance for the future we have to turn to the smaller, non-commercial theatres. These years saw, indeed, performances of works by Baroja, Valle-Inclán, Azorín, Unamuno, and Cipriano Rivas

Cherif, and of plays which, influenced by surrealism and a desire to focus on the inner lives, the dreams and obsessions of the characters, had of necessity to abandon old, traditional techniques. Claudio de la Torre's *Tic-Tac* of 1926 has as its principal character the young man who, seeking in dreams a solution to the wretchedness of his existence, discovers that the whole of his experience is a dream. Unamuno's *Dream Shadows (Sombras de sueño)* and *The Other One (El otro)* of 1926 reject the realism of the commercial theatre in favour of a symbolic, expressionist technique, for their concern is the inner life of the individual, the monologue, the soliloquy, the exploration of the divided self. And Azorín's plays, *The Invisible (Lo invisible)* of 1927 and *Angelita* of 1930, employ the resources of the stage unrealistically in expounding the themes of reality, time and death. In connection with the performance of such plays there began to emerge, moreover, young and imaginative stage-directors who would play an important part in the future development of the Spanish theatre. The most notable of these was probably Cipriano Rivas Cherif who was to direct a number of Lorca's major plays. He had studied in Italy, where he had absorbed the influence of Gordon Craig, subsequently in Paris, and had directed various theatre companies in Spain and South America. From 1928, as adviser to Margarita Xirgu, Spain's leading actress, Rivas Cherif was to develop his abilities much more fully at the Teatro Español in Madrid.[8]

The 1930's, Lorca's most creative years, were also the most important years for the modern Spanish theatre. The dictatorship of Primo de Rivera fell from Power in 1930, Alfonso XIII left the country not long afterwards, and the popular elections of 1931 brought into being Spain's Second Republic. As part of an enlightened attempt to drag Spain into the present, the newly formed Ministry of Culture and Information introduced an ambitious educational programme, ranging from the building of thousands of new schools to the formation of itinerant bands of teachers and students and of two theatrical companies whose function it would be to take the Spanish classics to the ordinary people: the 'University Theatre' *(Teatro Universitario)* under the direction of Lorca and Eduardo Ugarte, and the 'Theatre of the People', directed by Alejandro Casona. As far as the commercial theatre was concerned, these were the years which saw the performance of Lorca's *The Shoemaker's Prodigious Wife* (1930), the same play in its amplified form (1933), *The Love of Don Perlimplín* and *Blood Wedding* in the same year, *Yerma* (1934), *Doña Rosita the Spinster* (1935), and the completion of *The House of Bernarda Alba* (1936). These plays and others, notably the plays of Alberti and Casona, were the fruit of a magnificent period in Spain's theatrical history, the like of which had not been seen since the days of the great Spanish drama of the sixteenth and seventeenth centuries.

It is important to consider now the aims, the character, and the repercussions of Lorca's 'University Theatre', more commonly known as *La Barraca*. Lorca's notion for a touring theatre had occurred to him in 1931 after seeing an unimaginative performance of Zorilla's *Don Juan Tenorio*. Fired with a desire 'to save the Spanish theatre', Lorca envisaged a theatre of and for the people that would escape the financial and artistic strictures of the commercial stage. A building with a capacity for 400 people, light and portable like a hut or *barraca*, would be taken across the length and breadth of Spain. The actors would operate in the manner of the old strolling players, the *farándula*, and they would present to the ordinary people the works of the great Spanish dramatists of the past, notably Lope de Vega and Calderón. In order to reinforce the idea of a theatre of the people and to establish a closer identity with his audiences, Lorca himself designed for the company a uniform consisting of dark blue overalls, suggesting that his actors were as much labourers as artists. The actors, the stage-designers and the other members of the group were, indeed, students and therefore amateurs, for it was Lorca's conscious aim to eliminate from the outset anything which smacked of the commercial theatre.[9]

In striving 'to save the Spanish theatre' Lorca recognized the importance of presenting to his audiences plays which had relevance and meaning for them, and therefore the need to perform the classics not in an old-fashioned 'realistic' manner but in a new, interesting and 'modern' style. It was a style which would embrace all the aspects of performance, from sets to costumes, lighting, movement, gesture and speech. In speaking of his stage-designers, Lorca points to the modern, experimental nature of his productions:

> As stage-designers, I have as my collaborators the best painters of the Spanish school from Paris, of those who have studied under the direction of Picasso the most modern language of line . . .[10]

The actors should speak their lines clearly, without affectation, using movement and gesture meaningfully in order to emphasize their words and emotions. In his approach to the play as a whole and the importance of its different elements in the realization of a total effect that must be fresh and stimulating, Lorca shows himself to be another of those pioneering spirits of the twentieth century whose effect is manifest everywhere where the theatre is important.

The performances of *La Barraca* during its five-year period of operation illustrate clearly the evolution of its theatrical style. In its second tour in 1933, for example, the company presented Lope de Vega's *The Sheep Well (Fuenteovejuna)* in modern dress. The play's feudal overlord became in this production a contemporary landowner, dressed in a black suit, the vassals peasant characters in traditional provincial dress, and the old theme of the subjection of the villagers by a tyrannical overlord assumed the much more relevant meaning of the oppression of the peasant population by the wealthy landowner. But if the subject of the play acquired a greater liveliness, so did its presentation. The songs sung by the chorus had traditional Spanish melodies, and the dances, which played an important part in the action, were directed by Pilar López, the director of one of Spain's leading ballet companies. It was, in effect, a production that was full of life and colour and that, establishing a common ground with its audiences, received their rapturous support. In the same way, the 1934 production of Tirso de Molina's *The Trickster of Seville (El burlador de Sevilla)*, though performed in the costumes of the Italian Renaissance, made use of traditional Spanish ballads sung by a choir, and Spanish dancers performed a folk ballet during the play's wedding scenes. In the case of the 1935 production of Lope de Vega's

The Knight of Olmedo (El caballero de Olmedo), a greater immediacy and simplicity was achieved by presenting the action
against a plain black curtain, using simple, folding-screens for
the sets, and focusing the lighting on the characters themselves. Lorca revealed in all his productions for *La Barraca* a
consistent stylization that utilized all the possibilities of the
stage, that was intended to breathe new life and excitement
into works that in traditional performances sagged under the
weight of nineteenth-century realism. They were qualities that
enlivened for the thousands of people who saw them *La Barraca's* productions of Cervantes's *The Cave of Salamanca (La
cueva de Salamanca), The Watchful Guard (La guarda cuidadosa),*
and *The Two Gossips (Los dos habladores);* the first Act of Calderón's religious play, *Life is a Dream (La vida es sueño);* Juan del
Encina's *Eclogue of Plácida and Vitoriano,* and other plays too.
And they were performances that made *La Barraca* nationally
and internationally famous, leading to invitations to play in
France and Italy.

Lorca's experience of directing *La Barraca* was fruitfully
combined throughout these years with his activities as dramatist and director in the professional theatre itself, and the style
of performance practised in the one inevitably extended to the
other. For the professional productions of *Blood Wedding* at the
Teatro Beatriz which opened on 8 March, 1933, and of *The Love
of Don Perlimplín* and *The Shoemaker's Prodigious Wife* at the
Teatro Español on 5 April, 1933, Lorca was himself the director, and the sets and costumes were designed by another
member of *La Barraca,* Santiago de Ontañón. In the case of
Yerma, premièred in 1934 at the Teatro Español, and of *Doña
Rosita the Spinster,* premièred in Barcelona in 1935, the sets and
costumes were by Manuel Fontanals, another of Lorca's
associates in some of his private theatrical ventures. And the
style of production – and, of course, of conception – of these
plays was precisely that described already in relation to *La
Barraca.* Stage-settings, costumes, movement, music, songs
and dances were, in different degrees, a vital and integral part
of the performances of all of Lorca's plays and contributed to
their overall effect no less than in the case of the productions of
the Spanish classics by the student company. It is interesting

to note, indeed, for it throws a certain light on Lorca's
approach to the theatre as a whole, that in 1933 he directed and
designed the costumes and the sets for Manuel de Falla's ballet
suite, *Love the Magician (El amor brujo)*. In all his activities Lorca
reveals himself to be not merely an inspired and inspiring
experimenter but a man of wide and often very practical theatrical experience.

The continuing revitalization of the Spanish theatre is
evident throughout this period on many fronts. In 1933 Lorca,
supported by a wealthy Madrid socialite, Pura Ucelay, inaugurated the 'Theatre Clubs' *(Clubs teatrales)*, to be set up in
different Spanish cities and whose purpose it would be to
perform plays that would have no outlet in the commercial
theatre. At about the same time there was an active attempt by
a group calling itself 'The Proletarian Theatre' *(Teatro Pro-
letario)* to establish similar groups throughout Spain, to exchange ideas and organize theatrical performances in different
parts of the country. In the same year the influential Cipriano
Rivas Cherif was appointed Assistant Director of the Conservatory and founded the Theatre School of Art with the purpose
of running courses in dramatic art, dance and gymnastics and
the various aspects of stage design. And there also took place,
in June of 1933 and under the auspices of the Ministry of
Education, the first of a number of magnificent outdoor spectacles that were to distinguish the theatrical scene in the next
few years. The distinguished company of Margarita Xirgu and
Enrique Borrás performed Seneca's *Medea*, in a translation by
Unamuno, in the Roman amphitheatre in Mérida. Directed by
Rivas Cherif and utilizing choirs and symphony orchestra, it
proved to be a great event that was repeated subsequently in
Madrid and Barcelona. In 1934 the company performed *Medea*
and *Elektra* in Mérida, *Medea* in Salamanca and *Ifigenia* in the
Greek Theatre in Ampurias. As far as the Spanish classics are
concerned, they presented Calderón's *The Mayor of Zalamea (El
alcalde de Zalamea)* on a special stage constructed in the bullring in Madrid. In 1935, as part of the celebrations to mark the
tercentenary of Lope de Vega's death, the company performed
Lope's *The Foolish Lady (La dama boba)*, *The Peasant in his Corner
(El villano en su rincón)*, and, in particular, mounted a striking

performance of *The Sheep Well* in the main square of Fuente-ovejuna, the town from which the play took its name. When we consider the enormous burst of theatrical activity that was taking place on all sides, ranging from the commercial theatre to the resurgence of classical drama, brilliant performances of Spain's classic works, and the enlightened activities of private organizations, it is clear that during the first half of the 1930s the Spanish theatre experienced a true renaissance equal if not more splendid than that experienced by any other European country at that time.

The events of 1936 cut short the promise of those dazzling years. Through pressure of work Lorca had ceased to be the director of *La Barraca* in 1935, and although it commenced its tour of 1936 under a new director, its itinerary and its resources were affected by growing political unrest. As for Lorca himself, he completed *The House of Bernarda Alba (La casa de Bernarda Alba)* in June and subsequently gave a private reading of a play now lost, *The Destruction of Sodom (La destrucción de Sodoma)*. In July the long-feared Civil War broke out and on 19 August Lorca was brutally murdered.

La Barraca, founded by the Republican government, was kept alive by it in the early part of the war and was employed to boost the morale of Republican troops. Subsequently, as the Republicans lost ground, it declined, but its place was taken by the itinerant theatre of Luis Escobar, *La Tarumba*, and this in turn became in 1938 'The National Theatre of the Spanish Falange' *(El Teatro Nacional de la Falange Española)* which, despite the implications of its name, continued the tradition and the kind of performances given by *La Barraca*. After the Civil War the National Theatre came into being, emerging directly out of Escobar's theatre company and therefore related too to Lorca's achievements with *La Barraca*. His influence in bringing about a revitalization of the Spanish theatre in general and in establishing a new theatrical style had been decisive.

Lorca's views on and attitudes to the theatre were expressed both in his plays and in the various interviews he gave. His general aim as a dramatist is best expressed, perhaps, in an interview with Felipe Morales in 1936 when he observed that

the function of the theatre should be to communicate to people
the stark, unadorned reality of human nature:

> The theatre is poetry taken from books and made human,
> and when this is done it talks and shouts, weeps and
> despairs. The theatre requires that the characters who
> walk the stage should be dressed in poetry and that
> simultaneously we should see their bones, their blood
> . . . (p. 1634)

At one point in *The Public*, probably completed in 1930, the
First Man says to the Director: 'My struggle has been with the
mask until I have succeeded in seeing you naked.'[11] (p. 105).
Later the Director asserts that his production of *Romeo and Juliet*
is intended 'to reveal the profile of a hidden force'. The process
of communication of the true nature of human beings, however attractive or hideous or shameful or shocking, is, indeed,
the concern of the whole of Lorca's drama, from the apparent
distance of the puppet plays to the uncomfortable truths of *The
Public* and the almost tactile reality of *The House of Bernarda
Alba*. It is, of course, the baring of human passions and agonies
that often makes the experience of Lorca's plays a disquieting
and embarrassing occasion.

Since the aims of the creative artist were often stifled by the
nature of the commercial theatre, it is not surprising that many
of Lorca's observations should have been directed against it. In
an interview in *El Sol* in 1934, for example, he alludes to the
tyranny of economic factors embodied, in particular, in the
producers and impressarios:

> . . . it is intolerable and shameful that a man, by the mere
> fact of having a few millions, should be able to set himself
> up as a censor of plays and arbiter of the theatre. It is a
> tyranny that, like all others, can lead only to disaster . . .
> (p. 1630)

Economic forces had their counterpart in a public distinguished by its superficiality and lack of concern with the
theatre as an instrument of seriousness:

> . . . it is a serious matter that the people who go to the

theatre do not want to be made to think about any moral
issue. Furthermore, they go to the theatre as if they don't
really want to. They arrive late, they leave before the
performance is over, they come in and go out with no
respect . . . (pp. 1630-31)

And elsewhere Lorca refers to the creative writer at the mercy
of conceited actors:

Actors are partly to blame. It is not that they are bad
people, but . . . 'Listen, so-and-so, . . . I want you to write
me a play in which I . . . can play myself . . . I want to wear
a Spring suit. I'd like to be twenty-three years old. Don't
forget'. And theatre cannot be created like that. What it
achieves is the perpetuation of a young woman year after
year and of a young gallant in spite of arteriosclerosis.
(p. 1635)

These were the combined forces that, in Lorca's view, had
contributed to the decline of the theatre in Spain. It is a tyranny
exemplified in the puppet play, *The 'retablillo' of Don Cristóbal*,
where the Director prevents the Poet from changing the script,
orders him to do as he is told, and the Poet, acknowledging his
own betrayal of his art, asks to be paid in pieces of silver.

   Lorca's campaign in all his plays and in many of his interviews was one of outright resistance to the negative influences
that would destroy his art. He consistently asserts himself,
confronts his audience boldly, refuses to bow to their
demands. Thus, in the prologue to his first play, *The Butterfly's
Evil Spell*, he boldly offers a complacent public a play about
cockroaches and demands that they pay attention to it:

. . . And why is it that you men, full of sins and incurable
vices, are filled with loathing for the good grubs who
creep quietly along in the meadows, taking the sun of a
warm morning? What right do you have to scorn the
meanest of God's creatures? . . . Now, listen to the
play.[12] (p. 196)

In the prologue to *The Shoemaker's Prodigious Wife* the Author,
who is the playwright himself, refuses to be cowed by that fear

c.

that has stifled the poetic gifts of many writers and made them seek an outlet elsewhere:

> The poet does not ask benevolence, but attention, since long ago he leapt that barbed fence of fear that authors have of the theatre. Because of this absurd fear, and because the theatre on many occasions is run for financial reasons, poetry retires from the stage in search of other surroundings where people will not be shocked at the fact that a tree, for example, should become a puff of smoke, or that three fishes through their love for a hand and a word should be changed into three million fishes to feed the hunger of a multitude. (p. 63)

If the theatre is to communicate to its audience the true passions of men and women, and thus to survive as a living, meaningful form, writers must be free from the constraints imposed upon them; they must be free to express themselves, to be themselves; and, as part of this freedom, to be able to express the truth as they see it in whatever form seems to them appropriate for its expression.

Lorca's concern with freedom in the theatre reveals itself in almost everything he did, and above all perhaps, in his constant experimentation with different styles and techniques which took him from the insects of *The Butterfly's Evil Spell* to the puppet plays and farces, the surrealist plays, and the greater 'realism' of the later tragedies. In this respect his comments on the puppet theatre are very interesting, for they suggest that his fascination with the puppet figure lay more than anything in its capacity to express action and emotion simply, powerfully and directly: in short, with freedom and spontaneity. In a letter to the sculptor who created the puppets for *The Tragicomedy of Don Cristóbal and Miss Rosita* Lorca observes that 'Cristóbal's head is energetic, brutal, like his club'. In the prologue to *The 'retablillo' of Don Cristóbal* he speaks of 'the delicious and hard language of the puppets' and of the 'fantasy and . . . enchanting freedom' which the puppet tradition enjoys. At the end of the play, as the Director gathers up the puppets, he speaks for Lorca when he praises the spontaneity of the puppet theatre in relation to the stale tradition of bourgeois realism that stifles the Spanish stage:

> . . . The bad words are frank and fresh spoken by puppets
> . . . Let us fill the theatre with fresh wheat, and let the
> coarse words come from deep down to confront the
> tediousness and the vulgarity to which the theatre has
> been condemned . . . (p. 953)

But if the puppet figure offered Lorca freedom of expression, it offered him too freedom from the actor, the director and the impressario, for here was a theatre in which the dramatist himself controlled the action and the company. Furthermore, since it was a type of theatre in which costume, movement and music played an important part, it exemplified the concept of total theatre that Lorca practised in all his plays.

The major plays reveal precisely the same preoccupations with the theatre as the earlier puppet plays and farces. In *The Public*, in particular, Lorca reiterates in the person of the Director the need for the theatre to display true passion and, in doing so, to engage the public fully:

> . . . my characters, on the other hand, burn the curtain
> and die in the presence of the public . . . One must
> destroy the theatre or live in it! (p. 155)

The Public, When Five Years Have Passed, Blood Wedding, Yerma, Doña Rosita the Spinster, and *The House of Bernarda Alba* are in many ways puppet plays on a human scale, for in the clear, bold and direct expression of their feelings the characters are the direct descendants of the puppet figures. Having found a style, Lorca's concern was now with a greater, more challenging range of subject. In the interview with Felipe Morales quoted earlier he had observed that *The Public* and *When Five Years Have Passed* were unplayable because of their controversial subject matter but that they contained his true intention. Similarly, his comments on tragedy reveal an ever deepening purpose, as well as a darkening mood. In 1934, in an interview with Juan Chabás, Lorca spoke of his increasing interest in, and indeed need for, the writing of tragedy:

> Now I will complete *Yerma*, a second tragedy of mine.
> The first was *Blood Wedding* . . . We must go back to

> writing tragedy. We are compelled to do so by our theatrical tradition. There will be time later for comedies and farces. Meanwhile, I want to give the theatre tragedies . . . (p. 1623)

In the same year, in the interview already mentioned in *El Sol*, he suggests that, after the completion of his trilogy of tragedies, his plays will explore contemporary subjects and highly controversial themes:

> My path in the theatre . . . is something that I see very clearly. I want to complete the trilogy of *Blood Wedding, Yerma*, and *The Tragedy of Lot's Daughters*. I still have to write the latter. Afterwards I want to do something different, including modern plays on the age we live in, and I want to put on the stage themes and problems that people are afraid to face. (p. 1630)

However vague Lorca's ideas were on what he would actually write, it is clear that the way ahead was always to be one of challenge and experiment. *The Destruction of Sodom* was one of those plays which put on the stage 'themes and problems that people are afraid to face'. Described by Dr Luis Sáenz de Calzada as obscure and impossible to produce, it must have been a play in which Lorca explored again those areas already touched on in *The Public*, perhaps – though it is difficult to imagine – with an even greater boldness. [13] From beginning to end the pattern of Lorca's theatre, in terms of subject and technique, is one of constant progression and evolution in the context of which his untimely death was the greatest tragedy of all.

CHAPTER I

THE MINOR PLAYS

I

Lorca's first play, *The Butterfly's Evil Spell*, was performed at the Teatro Eslava in Madrid on 22 March, 1920, less than a year after his arrival at the Residencia. For the young writer it proved to be a disastrous introduction to the commercial theatre, for a public accustomed to the 'drawing-room plays of Benavente and the pleasant romantic pieces of the Quintero brothers reacted sharply to a play whose protagonist was a cockroach. They booed it from the stage, and it was at once withdrawn. If Lorca was bitterly disappointed, the experience taught him that the public must be educated into accepting new theatrical styles.

As far as the sources of the play are concerned, the names of Rostand, La Fontaine, Aesop, Cervantes, and, in particular, Maeterlinck, are often mentioned. Gregorio Martínez Sierra, who encouraged Lorca in the writing of the play and directed its first performance, was himself both a translator and a producer of the works of Maeterlinck, and had played an important part in making plays like *The Blue Bird (L'Oiseau bleu)* more familiar in Spain. But while Maeterlinck's plays, with their poetic and symbolist elements, may have influenced Lorca, the real source of *The Butterfly's Evil Spell*, as in the case of so many of the later plays, is to be found in Lorca's own poetry. José Mora Guarnido refers to a poem which Lorca destroyed in which a butterfly falls into a nest of cockroaches, is cared for by them until her damaged wing is healed, attracts the roach's son and, when she has recovered, deserts her lover.[1] Another poem, The Discoveries of an Adventurous Snail *(Los encuentros de un caracol aventurero)*, tells of the snail's meeting with a colony of ants. Seeing the ants dragging along

--

another member of their colony, the snail questions them and
discovers that the ant is to die because he has seen the stars. As
he dies, the ant observes a bee passing overhead and remarks
that she is the one who has come to take him to a star. The
snail, full of confused thoughts, goes on his way. Both poems
expound clearly the themes of love, illusion, frustration and
death that are central to the whole of Lorca's work. In
dramatizing them in the insect characters of *The Butterfly's Evil
Spell*, Lorca was setting out on the journey that would end with
The House of Bernarda Alba.

The opening sequence of the play presents in Doña Beetle,
an old cockroach, and Witchbeetle, the local magician, the
opposite poles of optimism and pessimism, for Doña Beetle
extols the joy of life while Witchbeetle sees in the extinction of
a star an indication of sadness and death. The initial statement
of the two contrasting themes provides an effective frame for
the expression in the second scene of the love of Silvia for
Doña Beetle's son, Boybeetle, for it is a love that is full of hope
but simultaneously doomed to disillusionment. The object of
her seeking, indifferent to her, is himself in search of something else, of an ideal that he feels strongly within him but
which he has never found:

> BOYBEETLE: Alas, my dream
> is lost in that star
> which resembles a flower
> SILVIA: And where is your star?
> BOYBEETLE: In my imagination.[2] (p. 210)

While the anguish of Silvia is experienced in the present, it is
a pointer to the future destruction of the Boybeetle's dreams
and illusions. The appearance of the scorpion in Scene Five is,
indeed, a powerful image of destruction, a mocking denial of
all things delicate and beautiful, and when he devours Silvia's
pet fly it is an ominous symbol of things to come, for in the
fly's death the lovers' own emotional and physical death is
projected.

The introduction of the wounded butterfly brings to the fore
the themes of love and beauty. The silky white of the butter-

fly's wings and its evocation of a world of light and beauty are symbolic of the perfection of dream and fantasy and find in the Boybeetle a more than willing worshipper. The butterfly becomes the focus of his dreaming, as he is the focus of Silvia's. But it is an optimism touched already by the Witch-beetle's pessimistic words:

> If you fall in love with her, alas for you!
> You'll die! (p. 221)

The Boybeetle's anguished weeping recalls Silvia's. And the scorpion, gorging flies, is never far away. In its statement of themes and situations and its suggestions of hope and despair, the first Act, like the first acts of Lorca's later plays, weaves together very effectively the dominant issues of the play.

The opening of the second Act parallels the beginning of Act I. The two cockroaches, Saintbeetle and First Fieldbeetle, represent once more the two extremes of idealism and realism. Indeed, as the butterfly's presence begins to dominate the play in the second scene, the world of illusion of which she is the symbol is always touched by darkness, sadness and death, the end of all illusion. The Butterfly sings of her beauty, but her beauty is fragile, like illusion itself, and death is always close at hand:

> For I am death
> and loveliness. (p. 228)

The scene, moreover, is illuminated by the first rays of the moon, the Lorca symbol of beauty and death. In the Butterfly's failure to fly there is an ominous pointer to her fragile perfection, while death and destruction, in the form of the scorpion's attempt to devour her, are menacingly near.

The fifth scene presents in the form of three old glow-worms the theme of love, its magical attraction and its illusory nature. The glow-worms are, in effect, in their search for love and their failure to find it, an older form of the Boybeetle:

> We old ones
> know that love
> is just like the dew. (p. 231)

In addition, inasmuch as their beauty has faded, they embody
the theme of passing time and decay that is so prominent in the
whole of Lorca's work: 'The light I once had grew dark'
(p. 232). Their anguish becomes in the play's final scenes the
anguish of the Boybeetle who now *wears a tormented look*
(p. 235). In an impassioned outburst he expresses his longing
for the butterfly, but the butterfly in turn longs only to fly to
the world from which she came. For the Boybeetle there is only
the pain of a longing which is unfulfilled, but in this respect he
is only another form of Silvia, who longs for him and is
rejected, of the glow-worms, who search for love and fail to
find it, and, indeed, of the Butterfly herself. For if she is
stronger now and will soon fly away, her beauty is fragile, her
life short, and the Boybeetle's death will soon be her own. The
Boybeetle's final, anguished words are the words of everyone
who dreams:

> Who gave me these eyes I hate?
> And these hands that try
> to clutch a love I cannot understand
> and that will end with my life?
> Who has lost me among shadows?
> Who bids me suffer because I have no wings? (p. 238)

The Butterfly's Evil Spell, despite its failure on the commercial
stage, is an interesting piece in many ways. In terms of
its dramatic presentation of the themes of passion, illusion,
frustration and death, it contains the themes of all the major
plays. In its characters and many of its settings – in the moonlight of Act II, for instance – there are clear pointers to the
later plays. Above all, perhaps, many of the characters are
seen to be like each other, linked by their desires and their
dreaming, linked too by their fate. They acquire, despite their
insect nature, human dimensions, passions with which we
can identify, and, as in the later plays, the figures on the stage
ultimately become ourselves.

II

Mariana Pineda, Lorca's second venture on the commercial stage, was performed in June 1927 at the Teatro Goya in Barcelona. It was acted by the company of Margarita Xirgu, designed by Salvador Dalí, and directed by Lorca himself. The Madrid première took place in October of the same year at the Teatro Fontalba. Its success compensated Lorca for the failure of his first play, for *Mariana Pineda* received both popular and critical acclaim.

The story of Mariana Pineda and her role in the republican opposition to Ferdinand VII was a well-known and widely celebrated one in the history and the folklore of Granada. One of the city's squares was named after her and contained her statue. The documents relating to her trial and execution were preserved in the local archives. And there were many popular ballads which told of her heroism. In approaching his subject Lorca was, indeed, confronted not by a lack but by an excess of material. His interest lay, however, less in the historical details of the story of Mariana than in the poetic possibilities offered by it, and in the elaboration of those themes which were so much part of him and which he had rehearsed already in *The Butterfly's Evil Spell*: the themes of love, frustration and death. In Lorca's play the heroine is less a martyr for the cause of liberty than for the cause of love, the human counterpart of the Boybeetle in the earlier play and a forerunner of many of Lorca's great female characters who love and hope and wait in vain. The other characters of the play – Pedro, Mariana's lover; Fernando, Mariana's admirer; and the evil and dangerous Pedrosa – are all in their different ways aspects of the themes and counterparts of the insect figure. In this sense Lorca made at an early stage in his dramatic career that step from non-human to human figures that he would repeat later in the movement from puppets to human characters.

The Prologue of the play establishes immediately its tragic tone, for it takes the form of a ballad which laments Mariana's death. The theme of death and of beauty destroyed, symbolized in the crushed lily and the rose and in the moonlight that

illuminates the scene, is projected over the action of the play
even before the action itself has begun.

In the opening sequence of Act I Mariana's association with
the liberals of Granada is linked to her love for one of them,
Pedro, but there is already a tragic portent in the sense that the
red thread with which Mariana sews the flag of liberty is
simultaneously a fatal wound, death an inseparable part of
love. The dark mood is lightened somewhat in Scenes Two
and Three by the gaiety of Amparo and Lucía, the two young
girls, but even so Mariana's melancholy is its counterpart, and
in a manner that anticipates *Doña Rosita the Spinster* Lorca
continually weaves together the joy and tears of life's contrasting faces. Amparo's evocation of the dying bull, its spilled
blood echoing the red thread, is, indeed, prophetic of
Mariana's death and gives the ending of Scene Four a tragic
colouring. The introduction of Fernando then introduces the
theme of love in another form, for if Mariana is in love with
Pedro, she is loved by Fernando, and though the theme is not
developed fully here, the anguish of unanswered love is
already hinted at in the presence of a triangle of lovers.
Mariana's joy as she receives a letter from Pedro is in Scene
Seven Fernando's sorrow:

> FERNANDO: You have cut off the road
> to all my dreaming![3] (p. 722)

But he expresses too that belief expressed in many later plays
that in relation to passion and feeling individuals are powerless to control their lives: 'But the blame is not yours . . .'
(p. 722). As the Act approaches its conclusion there is, indeed,
an increasing sense of individuals caught both in the force of
their own passions and in the affairs of other people: Mariana
in her love for Pedro, Fernando in his love for Mariana,
Mariana and Pedro in particular in the hatred of Pedrosa, the
brutal and harsh representative of the King. The ending of the
Act, reintroducing the flag of liberty, does so in a dark and
ominous form, for as Mariana's children lie on it, pretending to
be dead, the red of the flag opens up a terrible vision of spilled
blood. In the words of Doña Angustias, the adoptive mother of
Mariana, the future is one of emptiness and desolation, and,

for all the hope and yearning of love and liberty, it already has its counterpart in a deep foreboding.

The beginning of the second Act transforms the initial chatter of Mariana's children into the dark mood of the ballad that relates the tragic fate of the Duke of Lucena and the anguish of his young lover. Its implications for Mariana are clear, for she overhears the ballad, and Pedro's arrival completes the transformation of the ballad's characters into the real personages of the play. In the meeting of Mariana and Pedro the theme of love and passion acquires here a stirring, positive momentum, caught particularly in the image of blood coursing powerfully through the body. Pedro observes:

> All my blood is renewed, and you have renewed it,
> exposing your gentle heart to danger . . . (p. 738)

But love is again shown to have its darker side, for Mariana's love for Pedro is already threatened by his greater love of liberty, even though he loves her too. And both of them are threatened by external political forces that enclose them as the Act unfolds. Their dreams and illusions, of which the safety and seclusion of Mariana's house is a symbol, have their opposite in the darkness, the wind, and the swirling rain outside it. In Scene Eight, moreover, the description of the death of the liberal leader, General Torrijos, transforms the racing of the blood for love and liberty into the blood stilled by death, and, echoing and expanding earlier images and episodes, the passage becomes a 'play-within-a-play' – a favourite Lorca device – in which Pedro's death is mirrored. The arrival of Pedrosa in Scene Nine is, indeed, the introduction of the theme of death, and he is the human form of the scorpion of *The Butterfly's Evil Spell*, his clothes ominously black, his face white, his eyes penetrating, the embodiment of the harshness suggested by his name. In coveting Mariana and in seeking Pedro's death, Pedrosa deals Mariana a double blow. She is a prisoner of his tyranny and of her dreams of a lover who is now far away. As the Act concludes, Mariana is under house arrest and all the dreams of love and liberty turn into mockery. The children's initial laughter has become their weeping, Mariana's emotional death begins, and the rain that falls outside suggests a

world in which there is only desolation, the beginning for
Mariana of a spiritual death that is a prelude to her execution.

Act III, beginning with the chatter of the novices and
the curiosity of the older nun, quickly turns to Mariana's
tragic plight. She is ill and imprisoned, and her white dress,
which accentuates her paleness, is, like the moon, a symbol
of innocence and purity, but of death too. Like the female
characters of Lorca's later plays, she is a woman who, pinning
her hopes on love, is progressively stripped of hope, for
Pedro, it is now revealed, has left Spain. In Mariana's lingering
illusions, her only comfort, there is a terrible sense of pity:

> Don Pedro will come on horseback
> like a man driven mad when he learns
> of my imprisonment . . . (p.779)

The death of Mariana's dream of love is touchingly expressed
in the words and the tone of the song that floats through the
garden:

> My hope died
> by the edge of the water,
> without anyone seeing it. (p.781)

It is a dream dashed finally by Fernando's suggestion that
Pedro, despite her faith in him, never truly loved her: 'Don
Pedro will not come, Marianita, for he never loved you'
(p.795). Mariana has acquired now that terrible sense of isolation that in later plays overtakes Yerma and Doña Rosita.
Between human beings – Mariana, Pedro, Fernando – there is,
in the end, a dark and frightening void. Mariana's final heroism – her execution in the name of liberty – does not conceal
from us the fact that she has been abandoned. If she believes
that, in her final sacrifice for liberty, she will earn Pedro's love,
the Romantic heroism of the gesture has too a sense of futility
and self-deception. Her assertion of liberty rings through the
ending of the play, but it has its denial in the tolling of the bells
and the sadness of the ballad that describes Mariana's death.
Even this early and often Romantic play is permeated by
Lorca's pessimism.[4]

III

Lorca's childhood interest in the puppet theatre, reflected in the early performances at the Lorca household, matured in his adult years into his puppet plays. On 6 January, 1923, Lorca and Manuel de Falla presented a children's festival at the Lorca home in Granada, the programme consisting of *The Two Gossips (Los dos habladores)* of Cervantes, Lorca's own puppet play, *The Girl who Waters the Basil Plant (La niña que riega la albahaca)*, and a medieval mystery play, *The Three Wise Men*. The text of the Lorca play has not since come to light, but we know that he designed the settings and the miniature stage, that he manipulated the puppets, and that in the intervals between the plays he worked the puppet figure, Don Cristóbal, a Spanish Punch, engaging in impromptu dialogue with his young audience. A second puppet play, *The Billy-Club Puppets (Los Títeres de Cachiporra)*, may even have preceded *The Girl who Waters the Basil Plant* in terms of actual composition. There were plans for a production in 1932 and 1935, but the première finally took place in 1937 when, in Felipe Lluch Garín's production at the Teatro de la Zarzuela in Madrid, the play was performed as a farce, actors playing the parts of the puppets. Finally, in 1931 Lorca wrote a third puppet play, *The 'retablillo' of Don Cristóbal*, similar in some respects to the earlier piece but much shorter than it. It was first performed on 11 May, 1935 at the Book Fair in Madrid where the puppets were manipulated by Lorca himself.

The sources of Lorca's puppet plays are many. The tradition of the puppet theatre was very strong in Spain, and in the seventeenth century Cervantes himself had revealed his liking for puppets in 'Master Peter's Puppet Show' in Part Two of *Don Quixote*. In twentieth-century Spain Ramón del Valle-Inclán produced at least eight farces which he required to be played by one-dimensional, puppet-like characters. His *Farce and Licentiousness of the Chaste Queen (Farsa y licencia de la reina castiza)* is a 'farce for dolls', and in much of Valle's work the broad effects of the puppet theatre, if not puppets themselves, are used, as in the plays of Alfred Jarry, to mock the absurdity and pretentiousness of social institutions and human beings. In the 1920s Italian dramatists – including Pirandello – used the techniques of puppet theatre to suggest too the theme of human helplessness, and in Spain, of course, it was an important theme in Jacinto Grau's *Mr. Pygmalion* in 1921. As far as Lorca is concerned, the puppet figures of his early plays provided him with the opportunity of escaping from the claustrophobic realism of the traditional theatre, and of expressing himself with that vigour, freshness, directness and, of course, humour that were the essential qualities of the puppet tradition.[5]

The Billy-Club Puppets (The Tragicomedy of Don Cristóbal and Miss Rosita) begins with a comic presentation of the theme of love in conflict with parental obligation, for Rosita loves Cocoliche while, unknown to her, her father wishes to arrange her marriage to the old, but wealthy, Don Cristobita. It is the situation of *Blood Wedding* treated here in an altogether lighter manner. In the sheer ardour of the lovers, the Father's concern with money, and the old man's lust for Rosita, there is much humour. But even here there is a hint of the darker side when, for example, the clock opens up, the Hour alludes to the sunshine and the rain of life, and the ending of the scene emphasizes the sadness of Rosita. It is a mixture of laughter and tears, nicely balanced, that is sustained in the ensuing scenes. Rosita's news that she cannot marry Cocoliche draws from him a gesture of despair, expressed, however, in the weeping, stamping antics of a child. The Father's increasing reluctance to conclude the marriage has its comic counterpart in Cristobita's bullying of him, and Rosita's youthful voice in the old man's frog-like croaking.

The third scene is broadly comic. The vigorous, boisterous songs of the smugglers in Quakeboot's Tavern, the drunken antics of the love-sick Cocoliche, the insults directed at Cristobita, and Cristobita's belabouring of the innkeeper weave a pattern of lively comic action. But the scene has also introduced the Young Man, hinting at an earlier association with Rosita, and in Scene Four we see in him, as the theme of love comes to the fore again, a clear anticipation of the Young Man of *When Five Years Have Passed*, the dreamer who, having abandoned Rosita in search of an illusion, seeks her again five years later:

> You know! I used to think that the world was a place where bells were always ringing, and that white inns stood along the roads with blonde serving maids in them, wearing their sleeves rolled up to their elbows. But there's nothing like that! It's so dull! (p. 41)

In addition, Cocoliche has a dream of love that fades, and even when he awakens it is to a sad song of the lovers' separation. His own weeping underlines the point that even in Lorca's most amusing pieces the tears of broken hopes and shattered dreams are also present.

The play's final scenes build, of course, to a comic climax. Shaved by the barber, Figaro, in readiness for his wedding, Cristobita falls asleep in the barber's chair, and his painted wooden head becomes the object of the astonishment and banter of the onlookers. But it is the last scene, the longest in the play, which has all the knockabout action, the cross-purposes, and the frantic pace of puppet theatre and farce. After an initial statement of Rosita's sadness, in which there are echoes of Mariana Pineda, there is a comic sequence in which the young Man, Currito, pretending to be a cobbler, fits Rosita's wedding shoes, conveniently lifting her skirt to see her legs. It leads to a chase around the room and, with Cristobita's sudden arrival, to Currito's concealment in a wardrobe. When Cristobita leaves and Cocoliche enters, his love scene with Rosita is quickly interrupted by the second appearance of Cristobita and there follows the hasty concealment of Cocoliche in a second wardrobe. But all is not laughter, and in the sorrow of Cocoliche and Currito, when they learn of Rosita's marriage, there is that sense of love's frustration and betrayal that distinguishes the later plays. When Cristobita returns with his young and beautiful bride, the hidden lovers can barely contain themselves and Cristobita's suspicions are allayed only by Rosita's soothing words. He falls asleep only to awaken as Currito comes out of the wardrobe, and in the frantic, farcical action that ensues Currito stabs Cristobita, chases Currito from the room, returns to find Cocoliche and

Rosita embracing, fumes as they kiss before him, and falls to
the ground with a great creaking of springs. The vigorous
action of the scene, the concealments and discoveries in ward-
robes, the extremes of emotion ranging from the lovers'
anguish to the cuckolded husband's fury, have an enormous
pace and gusto, as well as a delightful sense of humour. The
comic element is sustained to the end as Don Cristóbal is
placed in his coffin, emitting a bassoon-like noise that reduces
to the sound of piccolo notes, and Rosita and Cocoliche
embrace happily as they celebrate the triumph of love, accompanied by vigorous music.

   The Tragicomedy of Don Cristóbal and Miss Rosita contains
some of the themes of Lorca's major works, notably the
themes of love and frustration, and they have their tragic
implications. In Rosita's arranged marriage and her father's
concern with money there is also a pointer to the social themes
of the later plays. The predominant emphasis is, however, a
comic one, as is to be expected in a puppet play, and in this
respect Lorca shows himself to be as much a master of the form
as he would become of the later tragedies.

   The 'retablillo' of Don Cristóbal, in some respects similar to the
earlier play, is a shorter and simpler piece. In addition, the
roles of the principal characters have changed, for Cristobita is
a doctor, though otherwise the same, and Rosita is now a girl
whose sexual appetites are never satisfied. In another sense,
inasmuch as the figures of the Poet and the Director debate the
play and its characters and intervene in the action, there are
pointers to the techniques of the ambitious and experimental
The Public. But, of course, *The 'retablillo'* remains, like *The
Tragicomedy*, a comic play, delightful in itself as well as interesting in its anticipations of the great plays that followed it.

   After an initial clash between the Poet and the Director, the
first half of the action concentrates on the greedy, bullying and
lecherous Cristobita. When he has killed a patient for his
money, the Mother is introduced, anxious to marry off Rosita,
and, inflaming the old man's passion with a description of her
daughter's 'breasts . . . like small round oranges' and 'pretty
little buttocks', quickly arranges the marriage. As in *The
Tragicomedy*, it is the comic equivalent of the arranged marriage

of *Blood Wedding*, and Rosita, indeed, when she appears, is the comic counterpart of the Bride of the later play, though her appetites are even greater:

> but I would like to lie
> on the divan
> with Juan,
> on the mattress
> with Ramón . . .[6] (p. 942)

The second half of the play is very like *The Tragicomedy*, for after the wedding Cristobita falls asleep and Rosita entertains her many lovers. The action moves rapidly to its comic climax as Rosita gives birth to quadruplets, Cristobita chases the Mother around the room, beating her with his club as he demands to know the children's parentage, and is infuriated further as Rosita bears another child. Before the old man can punish his wife's infidelity, the Director gathers in the puppets and brings the action to a close, but in the course of these events the theme of honour that is to play a vital part in the tragic conflict of the later plays is presented in a purely farcical manner.

In the puppet plays Lorca exploited fully the possibilities of that tradition, creating from its characters and situations scenes of great amusement. But, as in the case of *The Butterfly's Evil Spell* and *Mariana Pineda*, they are plays in which he was able to experiment with certain aspects of dramatic technique, in particular bold dramatic action, characters drawn in simple, broad strokes, and language that is vigorous and to the point. It is precisely these virtues, together with the more poetic and symbolic elements of his first two plays, that fused to create his mature style.

IV

Lorca had started work on *The Shoemaker's Prodigious Wife* in 1926 but he did not complete it until 1930. It was first performed before a private audience, and on 24 December, 1930, received its first public performance at the Teatro Español in Madrid where Margarita Xirgu played the heroine, Cipriano

D

Rivas Cherif directed and Picasso designed the costumes. Lorca subsequently revised and expanded the play, and the first performance of the revised version, which is the one best known today, took place in Buenos Aires on 30 November, 1933. It was performed by Lola Membrives and her company who, on 18 March, 1935, took it to the Teatro Coliseum in Madrid. Both versions were enthusiastically received by the critics, and Enrique Díez-Canedo, writing in *La Voz*, considered the play to be in no way inferior to *Blood Wedding* or *Yerma* but, of its kind, just as much a masterpiece.[7]

The Love of Don Perlimplín and Belisa in the Garden was completed in 1928 and there were plans for a performance in 1929, to be directed by Cipriano Rivas Cherif at the Sala Rex in Madrid. The performance did not take place, for the theatre was closed by the military authorities, ostensibly because the company had not observed the formal mourning for the recently deceased Queen Mother. The real cause lay probably in the military's view that the casting of a military officer in the role of Don Perlimplín could only reflect badly on the army. The play was finally premièred on 5 April, 1933 at the Teatro Español in Madrid, directed by Lorca himself and designed by Santiago Ontañón. Once more the critics recognized its merits and its striking individuality.[8]

The tradition of farce, to which both plays owe so much, was a rich and long established one in Spanish literary history. There are examples in the late fifteenth and early sixteenth centuries in some of the short pieces of Gil Vicente, Juan del Encina and Torres Naharro which reveal the influence of the *commedia dell' arte*. By the mid-sixteenth century Lope de Rueda was producing his *pasos*: accomplished comic sketches that contained well-drawn comic characters, amusing situations, and vigorous, down-to-earth language. But it was Cervantes who proved to be the master of farce and a source of inspiration for Lorca himself. In the eight *entremeses*, entr' actes, published in 1615, Cervantes turned comic types into credible and sympathetic human beings and created situations of considerable comic ingenuity. It was an achievement that in both respects anticipates Lorca, and the influence of Cervantes upon him can be illustrated by the fact that for the children's festival at his home in 1923 Lorca had adapted Cervantes's *The Two Gossips*, while a number of his *entremeses* were to be included later in the repertory of *La Barraca*. As far as later Spanish influences are concerned, Lorca would have been familiar with Alarcón's *The Three Cornered Hat (El sombrero de tres picos)*, the source of Falla's famous ballet, and, as we have seen, with the caricatured characters of Valle-Inclán's farces.

Both *The Shoemaker's Prodigious Wife* and *The Love of Don Perlimplín* deal with the traditional story of the young girl married to the old man, a favourite subject with Cervantes and Alarcón, and one which Lorca had already experimented with in his *Tragicomedy of Don Cristóbal*. For Lorca the subject provided the opportunity of sounding further those themes which in one form or another we have seen to be central to his earlier plays and which by now, of course, were the central themes of his poetry too. The theme of passion is exemplified in the shoemaker's wife and in Belisa, the wife of Perlimplín, though in an essentially light and comic manner. The former, dreaming of love and of the child she will one day have, suggests too the theme of illusion. The two husbands embody the theme of frustration, so often an integral part of love in Lorca's work, and in the case of Perlimplín it assumes that particularly anguished form that colours so many of the later female characters. And the marital relationship, unsuccessful as it is in both plays, the subject of gossip and conjecture, gives rise to an examination of the theme of honour and reputation that, treated comically here, becomes a part of the tragic conflict in the rural tragedies. While they are similar in many ways, the two farces have important differences. The mood of *The Shoemaker's Prodigious Wife* is predominantly gay and lively, while the tone of *The Love of Don Perlimplín* is darker, farce mingled with tears, comedy with tragedy, in a powerful image of things to come.

The opening sequence of *The Shoemaker's Prodigious Wife* introduces three of the play's important themes. The Wife's clash with the neighbours reveals that, as the consequence of her marriage to an old man, she is already subjected to ridicule and scorn, the victim of conventional views and attitudes.

Secondly, the Wife's frustration with her marriage is already clear:

> . . . If anybody had told me, blonde and dark-eyed – and what a good combination that is, with this body and these colours so very very beautiful – that I was going to marry a . . . I would have pulled my hair out. (p. 65)

And thirdly, the Boy who visits her is both the dream of the child for which she longs and the reality of the child she will never have. From the beginning *The Shoemaker's Prodigious Wife* is *Yerma* in another key, the intense anguish of the later tragedy expressed here in the lighter form of this 'violent farce'.[9]

The Shoemaker's first appearance sparks off a lively confrontation with his wife. In one way it is a comic scene, for in the old man's velvet suit and short trousers there is a comic incongruity, and in the exaggerated movements and the vigorous language of the couple an amusing frankness. Close to the surface of the scene there is also, though, a sadness that is all to do with the clash of illusion and reality in their lives. The Wife's description of her suitors, designed to taunt her husband, is an evocation not so much of past reality as of dreams sadly sharpened by her marriage (p. 68). It serves, too, to remind the Shoemaker of his youth, gone forever – 'I was eighteen once, too' (p. 68) – of passing time, and reveals in him a frustration just as great as hers. For all the comic appearance of the play, the Shoemaker and his wife are the prisoners of their marriage, of their age and temperamental differences, and of the values of the community in which they live.

The mixture of laughter and tears marks the Shoemaker's encounter with the Red Neighbour, for while the woman's scathing and humorous comments on the Wife strike a comic note, it has its opposite in the poor old man pleading with her, for his honour's sake, that there should be no scandal. And between the Shoemaker and the Mayor of the village there is another contrast, for in the latter's practical advice on women, born of vast experience, and the former's admission that he does not love his wife, there is all the humour of bravado offset by the pain of a sad confession.

The theme of illusion strongly colours the ending of the Act. The sound of a flute and a guitar evokes for the wife a vision of her handsome and elegant suitors, endowed with all the magic of dreams. In reality they become Don Blackbird, an absurd caricature of a lover, and the Young Man, a sad, romantic youth. Inasmuch as the Wife can respond to neither of them, she is seen to be a woman for whom illusion is more important, more stimulating than reality, and the lovers of her dreams are infinitely more attractive than her real suitors. But dreams, of course, are fleeting as well as beautiful, a truth symbolized now in the appearance of the butterfly which the Wife pursues around the room but fails to catch:

> I beg you, stay there, stay there, stay there!
> But you don't wish to linger,
> to stay there an instant . . . (p. 81)

The reality which lies in store for her, delayed by the butterfly's appearance, is the announcement of the husband's desertion of her and of the townspeople's knowledge of the fact. The ending of the Act, for all its liveliness and its many comic incidents, dashes all illusion to reveal beneath it the sadness of the husband who has run away and of the wife exposed to the malice of the villagers.

The second Act revolves to a greater extent around the theme of honour, and, as in *Yerma* in particular, distinguishes between honour as public opinion and reputation, and honour as inner virtue. The presentation of the Wife's many suitors – Don Blackbird, the Young Man, the Mayor, and others – is, of course, highly comic, for in their different ways they are all ridiculous. In addition, there is much that is amusing in the Wife's heartless treatment of them and in her flouting of convention in becoming the keeper of a public tavern. On the other hand, the Wife, left to her own devices and pursued by many men, is increasingly at the mercy of her vilifiers, and the serious theme of honour in its sense of public image is very near the surface of the comedy. In the figure of the Wife who embodies virtue and loyalty, Lorca advances his view of true honour and his condemnation of conventional morality in a way that clearly anticipates *Yerma*:

> And you might as well know, and the whole village, that
> my husband has been gone four months, but that I'll
> never give in to anybody – never! Because a married
> woman should keep her place as God commands, and
> I'm not afraid of anybody . . . (p. 85)

The unfolding of the Act is, indeed, at almost every step the
portrayal of the Wife placed at the centre of pressures which
accumulate and combine to test her virtue. Alone with the
Boy, she indulges in a dream-like vision of her first meeting
with her husband but it is immediately juxtaposed with the
reality with which she must contend in the form of the song
which mocks her honour:

> Now she's courted by the Mayor,
> now it is Don Blackbird's turn,
>
> Mistress Cobbler, Mistress Cobbler,
> Mistress, you have men to burn . . . (p. 88)

The arrival of the Shoemaker in disguise, initiating a highly
ingenious and amusing sequence, increases her difficulties.
On the one hand, his story of a quarrelsome wife who plotted
with her lover to kill her own husband – a kind of 'play-
within-a-play' – serves to condemn the Wife in the public
view, for they identify her with the woman of the story. On the
other, the Wife's defence of her loyalty and virtue to a man she
does not know to be her husband convinces him of her worth.
He is himself transformed from someone cowed and inhibited
by public opinion into a man who, seeing that honour is
more than that, becomes his wife's defender. In a delightfully
spirited final scene husband and wife are reunited, recognize
their differences, resolve to live their life together and, in the
knowledge of their acceptance of each other, defy the tongues
that will continue to malign them:

> And now, come ahead, come ahead if you want to.
> There are two of us now to defend my house.
> Two! Two! My husband and I. (p. 107)

By the play's conclusion the underlying sadness of its first Act
is transformed, the deceitful nature of illusion banished, and

reality accepted for what it is. If between *The Shoemaker's Prodigious Wife* and *Yerma* there is a similarity in themes, their trajectory is finally very different, for the forces that in the later play combine to overwhelm the characters are the forces that in this farce the principal characters succeed in overcoming. It is Lorca in a happy, optimistic mood and farce at its highest and most accomplished level.

The Love of Don Perlimplín is a farce in which the theme of the old man married to a young girl is treated in a progressively serious way. The Prologue establishes a predominantly comic note, for it stresses in particular the ridiculous contrast between Perlimplín, fifty years old and inexperienced in love, and the young and beautiful Belisa, half naked on her balcony, dreaming of young lovers:

> Ah love, ah love.
> Tight in my thighs imprisoned
> There swims like a fish the sun. (p. 112)

Their arranged marriage, facilitated by Perlimplín's scheming servant and Belisa's grasping and materialistic mother, promises the burlesque that a farcical treatment of the juxtaposition of youth and age, sensuality and frustration implies. Yet even now, in the old man's fear and inexperience as he embarks upon the marriage, there is an element of pathos that points to the conception of his character in terms that will go beyond caricature:

> What does she mean, Marcolfa? What does she mean?
> [MARCOLFA *laughs.*]
> What is happening to me? What is it? (p. 115)

Scene One, set on Perlimplín's wedding night, strikes a beautiful balance between the comic implications of the situation and its more serious and touching aspects. The scene with its great marriage bed and the exotically dressed Belisa is one in which the presence of the impotent old man seems absurdly out of place. That he, who has never experienced love, should suddenly be fired by love, is even more absurd. And that in his bed and on their wedding night his wife should take five lovers is supremely funny. On the other hand, if Perlimplín's awakening to love is comic, it is also touching, for through love he is transformed from a man who was satisfied with books into someone suddenly made aware of the magic and beauty of the world around him:

> I have never seen the sunrise.
>
> It is a spectacle which . . . this may seem an untruth . . . thrills me! (p. 121)

In addition, Perlimplín, though happy in his new-found love, knows that it has come too late, for he can never satisfy his young and ardent bride. His discovery of love, together with his knowledge of his impotence, is thus his tragedy, and the words of his song that conclude the scene contain a deep sadness:

> Love, love
> that here lies wounded.
> So wounded by love's going;
> so wounded,
> dying of love. (p. 122)

Scene Two is largely concerned with Perlimplín's acceptance of reality and the deepening of his personality. His revelation that he is aware of Belisa's infidelity and that, despite it, he is happy in his love of her, shows Perlimplín to be a man who has accepted his limitations and thereby overcome them. He has grown in his understanding of himself and of Belisa, and while she remains unchanged, Perlimplín has been transformed from the timid and inexperienced bridegroom of the play's beginning into someone full of understanding who can accept Belisa's lovers and rise above the petty condemnation of society:

> Look . . . I know everything! I realized immediately.
> You are young and I am old . . . what can we do about it!
> But I understand perfectly . . . (p. 124)

Indeed, in the mysterious episode that concludes this second scene Don Perlimplín actively encourages Belisa in her dream of a young and handsome lover who writes her beautiful letters but whom she has never seen.

If the second scene marks Perlimplín's acceptance of reality,
Scene Three portrays his triumph over it. He is again seen to be
a man transformed:

> It seems to me that a hundred years have passed. Before,
> I could not think of the extraordinary things the world
> holds. I was merely on the threshold . . . Now I can close
> my eyes and . . . I can see what I want. (pp. 126-27)

But the same is true of Belisa now, for as she waits in the
moonlit garden for the lover who fascinates her so, she admits
to Perlimplín:

> I love him! Perlimplín, I love him! It seems
> to me that I am another woman! (p. 130)

Inasmuch as Perlimplín has encouraged Belisa to love a man
she has never seen, an ideal of love rather than its physical
presence, he has, of course, triumphed over the reality of her
sensual nature, deepened her personality as well as his own.
But his greatest triumph comes when Belisa discovers that
her lover, dying from a stab-wound apparently inflicted by
Perlimplín, is Perlimplín himself. It is his triumph not merely
to have accepted the reality of Belisa's nature and his own
impotence, but to have made her believe in a vision of love,
and, beyond that, to have made her love him by becoming
himself the embodiment of that vision. Perlimplín's conquest
is, of course, inspiring, but it also has a tragic pathos. The
illusion created by him, for all its beauty and brilliance, is,
like all illusion, fleeting, its death implicit in its creation.
Perlimplín's triumph can only survive, paradoxically, if it is
stopped in time, frozen, suspended with his own death. It is a
wonderfully moving ending in which the farcical figure of the
early part of the play has completely disappeared. Indeed, the
elements of farce that remain in this final scene – of disguise
and mistaken identity – have ceased to be used for comic
effect. Lorca has moved away from the broad effects of *The
Shoemaker's Prodigious Wife* along that path towards *The Public*
and *When Five Years Have Passed* where the techniques of farce
are often used for very different and much more subtle ends. [10]

V

Between 1925 and 1928 Lorca produced three short plays – the *teatro breve* – of considerable interest. *Buster Keaton's Spin (El paseo de Buster Keaton)* was written in 1925 and published in 1928 in Lorca's own journal *El Gallo*. The title reflects, of course, that interest in the cinema that became an important influence in many of the plays that Lorca wrote during this period of his life, notably in *The Public* and *When Five Years Have Passed*. Some critics, indeed, have considered the piece to be not merely influenced by the cinema or to reveal a knowledge of cinematic techniques, but to be itself a film scenario. It is a view which does not bear close examination, for *Buster Keaton's Spin* is, despite its visual qualities, a highly literary piece. Lorca seems to have been attracted in particular by the figure of Buster Keaton and by the tragic possibilities suggested by that sad face in an absurd world. He becomes in this short but expressive work the central image around which a series of associated images are unfolded, their complexity literary rather than cinematic. *Buster Keaton's Spin* is, indeed, an unfolding of themes that are typically Lorquian.

The action begins with Keaton's murder of his four children whom he kills with a wooden knife. The incident is, of course, partly comic, but beneath the element of slapstick, so characteristic of the Keaton films, there are more serious undertones. Keaton's words after he has killed his children point to a deep sadness within him: 'My poor little children'[11] (p. 803). He counts their bodies in an automatic way which suggests already a kind of numbness: 'One, two, three and four' (p. 803). These suggestions are accompanied by the evocation in a stage direction of an oppressive urban landscape in which man is constantly degraded and dehumanized: *(Amongst old tyres and gasoline cans, a* NEGRO *eats his straw hat)* (p. 803). The jungle of the negro's ancestors has become the jungle of the city, his devouring of his straw hat as incongruous as it is expressive of futility. The urban landscape is also strangely disquieting. A parrot flies through a neutral sky and a night owl hoots in the middle of the day (pp. 803-804). In this setting

Keaton's remarks on the beauty of the afternoon (p. 803) and the pleasant songs of the birds (p. 804) are both comic and incongruous, the observations of someone who is out of touch with the reality around him. He is, indeed, an innocent in a hostile world, a quality reflected in his bicycle which is described as *full of innocence* (p. 804). As such he searches for the realization of dreams but fails to achieve them. His pursuit of the butterflies which elude him (p. 804), symbolic of his search for love, recalls the illusions of the shoemaker's wife. His words reflect a sad acceptance of his failure – 'There is nothing I want to say. What can I say?' (p. 804) – and in his eyes there is reflected both the longing of illusion and the numbed awareness of inevitable failure: (. . . *His eyes, immense and sad like those of a newly born animal, dream of irises, angels and sashes of silk. His eyes that are like the bottom of a glass. His eyes like the eyes of a silly child* . . .) (p. 804).

Reality presents itself in the form of the prostitute with her 'celluloid eyes', so different from his, and her crude and direct propositioning of him. She is, with her shoes of crocodile leather, the product of a civilization which both corrupts and destroys Nature for its own ends and, in their pursuit, blunts the sensibilities of human beings. Buster himself, the innocent in whom there is already evidence of the numbing effect of the world around him, reveals before the prostitute a resigned acceptance of the inevitable loss of his own innocence, closing the eyes that are its symbol as he accepts her terms. It is only one example of the way in which his purity is threatened by the world in which he lives, represented by the *Waltz, the moon and the canoes*, the seductive attractions of the urban world. As the piece draws to its conclusion, Keaton is alone, full of sadness, dreaming in vain:

> I would like to be a swan. But I cannot even though
> I would like to be it . . . (p. 805)

The final allusion is to the flashing lights of police cars against the sky-line of Philadelphia – lights which seem to have taken the place of the stars. It is a final evocation of the urban landscape, of people distanced from Nature and their own innocence and menaced by forces outside themselves. The comic Keaton of the cinema screen, usually pursued by the police in a frantic and hilarious chase, has been transformed by Lorca into the tragic dreamer, the innocent, the outsider in a hostile world.[12]

The Girl, the Sailor and the Student (La doncella, el marinero y el estudiante) appeared, like *Buster Keaton's Spin*, in the second issue of *El Gallo* in 1928. Less original than *Buster Keaton* it deals, nevertheless, with the favourite Lorca themes of passion, illusion and passing time, and as far as the major plays are concerned, anticipates in particular the central issues and the tragic tone of *When Five Years Have Passed*.

There is an initial contrast between the Girl and the Old Woman, not merely in the years that separate them but in the opposing worlds of illusion and reality that they inhabit. The Old Woman has no dreams, only the reality of the snails she sells, her rags and the basket of crusts. The Girl, on the other hand, dreams of love as she embroiders, recalling the fantasies of the Gipsy Nun in the *Gipsy Ballads* and looking forward too, in a sense, to the daughters of Bernarda Alba. Embroidering each letter of the alphabet so that her lovers may call her by any name they choose, she transforms herself in the world of her imagination into the woman her lovers wish her to be, and them into the idealized form in which she would have them. But it is a vision which all the time has the Old Woman as its companion, an image of youth and the fantasies of love destroyed, and the light and often comic tone of the piece is seen to have its darker implications.

When the Girl closes the windows to the balcony, it is an action which seeks in effect to deny the reality that threatens her, and the closed world of her room becomes now both the symbol and the location of her dreaming. Like the Young Man, the Secretary and the Bride of *When Five Years Have Passed*, the Girl indulges in a fantasy of love of which the Sailor and the Student are now a part. The Sailor longs for her, she for him, but their desire for each other is frustrated by the authority of the young man's captain and the Girl's mother, their dreams denied by the reality with which they must contend. The Student, moreover, introduces another form of frustration –

the reality of passing time. Like the Friend of *When Five Years Have Passed*, he attempts to escape its hold, and like the Second Friend he lives in fear of its consequences:

STUDENT: *(Entering)*: It goes too quickly.
GIRL: Who goes quickly?
STUDENT: The age.
GIRL: You are afraid.
STUDENT: I am running away.
GIRL: From whom?
STUDENT: From next year. (pp. 810-11)

The Student embodies too the passion and the longing for love that is exemplified in so many of Lorca's characters – the Secretary, the Bride, the Mannequin of *When Five Years Have Passed*, the Bride and Leonardo in *Blood Wedding*, Yerma, and, of course, Adela who in the last Act of *Bernarda Alba* expresses her yearning in precisely the same image as does the Student here:

Give me water.

For I am dying of thirst. (p. 811)

But, as in their case, the search for love is unfulfilled, the illusion of love dissipated by the reality in which the lovers find themselves. The Girl's dreams fade as she comes to the letter Z. The final suggestion is one of despair as she thinks of suicide. The sea, the symbol of death, dominates the ending of the play. And the reference to the three fog horns which deceive the coastguards, evoking the Sirens of classical mythology through the double meaning of the Spanish word *sirenas* (fog horns/Sirens), points to the deceptive nature of illusion and dream, so attractive and yet so fatal. In its characters and themes, as well as in its final pessimism, *The Girl, the Sailor and the Student* is a rehearsal for the major plays that were soon to follow it and, for all its brevity, an effective piece.

The third playlet, *Dream (Quimera)*, was to have appeared in the third number of *El Gallo* but the magazine was discontinued. Like *The Girl, the Sailor and the Student*, this is a piece which in its themes seems to anticipate in particular *When Five Years Have Passed*. Of the three short plays it is the least successful, less inventive than *Buster Keaton's Spin* and less memorable as an image than *The Girl, the Sailor and the Student*.

Enrique's departure from his wife and his six children suggests at once the theme of a journey and of passing time, an idea reinforced by the presence of the familiar Lorquian figure of the Old Man. In the dialogue between Enrique and the Old Man the allusions to time form an unbroken thread. The reference to the train's departure indicates that time passes remorselessly:

> ENRIQUE: Let's go quickly. I am to catch the train at six. (p. 815)

And again:

> ENRIQUE *(Annoyed)*: Come. It will be six at any moment. (p. 816)

The Old Man himself refers to the relentless march of time: '. . . It is worse still that things move on and that the river rushes by . . .' (p. 816). In addition, as in other plays, the Old Man is for the younger a living reminder of the passage of time and of what in time he will himself become. He is thus a mocking presence, a persistent annoyance to the younger man in the latter's efforts to forget time's passing:

> ENRIQUE: I do not want to joke. You are always the same. (p. 816)

In relation to Enrique and his wife, and indeed to his children too, parting means sadness, and the themes of life's inevitable pain and anguish and of the loneliness and isolation of the individual are closely allied to the theme of passing time. Enrique observes to the Old Man: 'It is true, but this absence saddens me' (p. 816). The Wife expresses the same idea in more passionate terms:

> I, on the other hand, will be alone in my bed. I will be cold . . . Goodbye, goodbye . . . Enrique. Enrique . . . I love you . . . (p. 819)

As far as the children are concerned, their feelings are altogether more instinctive, less consciously expressed, but their repeated demands for presents and, in particular, their spitefulness towards each other, are the expression in their terms of an insecurity and a sense of loss as keenly felt as their mother's:

> GIRL *(Quickly)*: Daddyyy! Daddyyy! Bring me the squirrel. I don't want the stones. The stones will cut my nails. Daddyyy!
>
> BOY *(At the door)*: He can't hear you. He can't hear you. He can't hear you.
>
> GIRL: Daddy, I want the squirrel. *(Starting to cry.)* Please, God! I want the squirrel.

It is a desolate ending, suggestive of the final pessimism of many of the major plays where the curtain falls on the spectacle of man alone in an empty and meaningless existence. Looked at in a broader sense, Enrique's journey is, indeed, the final journey that for all of us leads to death. His wife and children face the terrible loneliness of the widows and the fatherless children of *Blood Wedding*. About their lives there blows a cold wind and upon them there descends a darkness that are as symbolic as they are literal – the chill and the blackness of despair in which the Lorquian tragic figure is inevitably cast adrift:

> WIFE: Don't go outside. The wind has become cold . . .
> *(The light fades.)* (p. 819)

VI

A consideration of Lorca's use of the stage and his handling of the different dramatic elements in the plays under discussion here reveals that in them and the later plays his approach to the theatre is essentially the same.[13] An examination of the stage settings of these plays suggests, for example, that they have the same simple, direct, and often symbolic character as the sets of the later works, their function to set or to underline the mood of the ensuing action. In *The Butterfly's Evil Spell*, for

instance, the setting for Act II, Scene Two is essentially stylized, the glint of the water and the whiteness of the daisies
emphasized in order to evoke a world of beauty, the approach
of darkness to suggest that beauty is always threatened:

> *A garden. At the back of the stage there is a great cascade of ivy.
> And all the ground is to be planted with gigantic daisies. It is a
> real forest, but of little flowers. On Stage Left, and where it is
> partly lost amid the thickets, a spring's water glints. All the
> plants are bathed in the gentle light of deep twilight.* (p. 222)

The play is, of course, highly poetic in character, and the
stage settings are themselves part of its poetic character. In a
farce, on the other hand, as in *The Shoemaker's Prodigious Wife*,
the sets have the boldness that distinguishes the action itself,
and they act as an effective backdrop to the uncomplicated
emotions of the characters, harmonizing or contrasting with
them. Such is the setting for Act I:

> *The* SHOEMAKER'S *house. Shoemaker's bench and tools. A
> completely white room. Large window and door. The backdrop
> seen through the large window is a street, also white with some
> small doors and windows in grey. To the right and left, doors.
> All this scene shall have an air of optimism and exalted happi-
> ness to the smallest details. The soft orange light of afternoon
> pervades the scene.* (p. 65)

When the Shoemaker's Wife appears against this background,
the mood is set before a word is spoken:

> [*When the curtain rises the* SHOEMAKER'S WIFE *enters furi-
> ously from the street and pauses at the door. She is dressed in
> angry green, and wears her hair drawn back tight and adorned
> with two big roses . . .*] (p. 65)

It is, indeed, a small step from sets like these to the great wood
of *Blood Wedding* or the female characters of *The House of
Bernarda Alba* starkly outlined against the walls of the house.

In the later plays the characters are often, through the nature
of their costumes, self-explanatory images. It is a technique
that owes much, of course, to puppet play and farce, and there
are many examples of it in Lorca's earlier work. The *angry green*

(p. 65) of the Shoemaker's Wife's dress speaks for itself. In Act Two her resolve and vigour are reflected in *a burning red dress with wide skirts* (p. 84). The Shoemaker's inexperience is suggested in his little boy's suit, *with silver buttons, short trousers and a red tie* (p. 67). In *The Love of Don Perlimplín* Belisa's physical appearance, as in Scene One, is invariably an image of her sensuality:

[. . . BELISA *appears, dressed in a great sleeping garment adorned with lace. She wears an enormous headdress which launches cascades of needlework and lace down to her feet. Her hair is loose and her arms bare.*] (p. 116)

Perlimplín, on the other hand, *magnificently dressed* (p. 115) on his wedding night, is a comic spectacle, for his dress is an attempt to conceal the reality of his impotence. And what is true of the farces is also true of the other plays. In the insect world of *The Butterfly's Evil Spell* Sylvia's appearance is a visual statement of the beauty and perfection of youth:

[. . . *She gleams like jet and her legs are quick and delicate. . . . She is carrying as a parasol a tiny daisy with which she plays charmingly and wears on her head deliciously a ladybug's golden shell.*] (p. 201)

In contrast, Scorpy's grotesque nature personifies the danger which he represents for others. Similarly, in *Mariana Pineda* Pedrosa's black clothes and his white face are an image of death (p. 759), while in the last Act Mariana's pale face and her white dress are the visual representation of innocence, purity, and the proximity of death too. In all these plays Lorca's capacity for creating images of the kind which make the later plays so visually striking is already very evident.

If settings and costume are used to create mood and signify meaning, the emotional character of a given moment is sharply underlined by the physical movements of the characters. It is a technique that is again, of course, part and parcel of the tradition of farce and puppet play where the exaggerated movements of the figures are themselves expressive of emotion, and in these plays Lorca learned to the full the theatrical effectiveness of movement on the stage. In Scene Two of *The*

E

Tragicomedy of Don Cristóbal, for example, Cocoliche's disappointment when Rosita informs him that she cannot marry
him is conveyed – for comic effect here – not simply by his
anguished cries but by the vigorous, childlike stamping of his
feet:

> COCOLICHE [*shouting and stamping his feet*]: Oh, no, no,
> no, no! (p. 32)

In Act I of the *Shoemaker's Prodigious Wife* the Wife accompanies
her feeling of frustration by striking herself on the forehead,
while the Shoemaker reveals his in his violent hammering of
the shoes:

> WIFE: Oh, fool, fool, fool! [*Strikes her forehead.*] . . .
> SHOEMAKER [*hammering furiously*]: Will you be quiet?
> (p. 68)

The puppet plays and farces also display the frenetic activity of
chase and general confusion that is inherent in the genre. But
in the other plays too, like *Mariana Pineda*, physical movement
is tellingly used. In Act I, Scene Four, Mariana's agitation is
expressed in her restless movement about the room, her rising
from her chair, her crossing to the window (pp. 699-705). By
the final Act despair has overtaken her and it is reflected in
Scene Four in her motionless, seated posture: [*She sits on a
bench and rests her head in her hands.*] (p. 781). Here is a moment
that will be repeated many times in Lorca's later drama, to
convey the despair of Yerma, of the daughters of Bernarda
Alba and of Bernarda too. In the plays as a whole there is thus
a language of movement that is as important as any other
element, and in this particular respect it is worth recalling that
for Lorca ballet and dance had an enormous fascination.

Of the plays discussed here, *The Butterfly's Evil Spell* and
Mariana Pineda are in verse, while the puppet plays and farces
are mainly in prose. A consideration of Lorca's use of dialogue
is largely limited, therefore, to that special kind of dialogue –
direct, forceful, stylized – which is appropriate to the genre of
farce and puppet play. There is a good example in *The
Tragicomedy of Don Cristóbal* where Rosita expresses her feelings for Cocoliche, and Lorca indicates how the lines should be

spoken: 'Oh, but I love, love, love and double love him!'
[*This is spoken very rapidly.*] (p. 26). At the end of the play
Cristobita's rage is conveyed in short, sharp phrases which are
the linguistic equivalent of his vigorous, threatening gestures:

> I'll kill you, I'll run you through a grinder, I'll pulverize
> your bones! You'll pay for this, Miss Rosita, fallen
> woman! And you cost me a hundred coins! Br-r-r-r!
> Smash, bing, bang! I'm choking with rage! Bing! Bang!...
> (p. 57)

But there are many examples too of greater tenderness, of the
expression of love and illusion, expressed in a very different
kind of language. In *The Shoemaker's Prodigious Wife*, for instance, the Wife's words to the Boy have an altogether quieter
tone: 'My child! My treasure! I'm not angry at you! [*Kisses
him.*] Take this doll. Do you like it? Well, take it.' (p. 66). When
she evokes her suitors, the repeated phrases evoke her rapture: 'And what a cape he had for winter! What sweeps of blue
broadcloth and what trimmings of silk!' (p. 68). Similarly, in
Scene One of *The Love of Don Perlimplín* the broken pattern of
Belisa's words conveys her almost breathless ecstacy: 'Oh,
what music! Heavens, what music! Like the soft warm downy
feathers of a swan! Oh! Is it I? Or is it the music?' (p. 116).
We will see how in the later plays the dialogue is similarly
patterned and shaped to express the emotions and obsessions
of the characters. In the puppet plays and farces, partly
through the nature of the genre, Lorca acquired a mastery of
the kind of dialogue whose purpose is to transmit emotion
with spontaneity and which he would use to greater effect
later.

As far as poetry is concerned, the verse of *The Butterfly's Evil
Spell* and *Mariana Pineda* functions for most of the time as
dialogue and has much of the character of prose. It is the
moments in these and the other early plays when poetry is
used to underline and intensify particular dramatic moments
that are typical of Lorca's mature technique. In *The Butterfly's Evil Spell* there are, for example, many expressions of
anguish for which the concentrated simplicity of poetry proves
especially effective:

SYLVIA: Where lies the water,
            tranquil and serene,
            where I may still
            my questing thirst? (p. 203)

There are many occasions in *Mariana Pineda* when Mariana's
feelings are expressed in poetry whose allusive nature, extending the range of reference, deepens the impact of the moment
itself. Thus in Act I, Scene Five, Mariana's longing for and fear
of approaching night are expressed in a powerful image which
goes beyond her immediate feelings to anticipate the final
tragedy:

Night feared and dreamed of;
for you wound me from afar
with your long swords! (p. 706)

In *The Shoemaker's Prodigious Wife* the child's lines which at the
end of Act I express the Wife's illusions are as isolated in the
surrounding dialogue as are her dreams in an uncomprehending world, and are thus the more effective for it, their simple
yet expressive images and their urgent, repeated patterns
highly evocative of her deep yearning:

Butterfly of the breezes,
wind creature so lovely;
butterfly of the breezes,
wind creature so lovely;
butterfly of the breezes,
so green, so golden,
a candle's flame;
butterfly of the breezes,
I beg you, stay there, stay there, stay there! (p. 81)

Occurring at key moments in the plays, poetry reveals the
inner conflict of the characters. It is not difficult to see how it is
an integral part of Lorca's dramatic art and how the early
plays, in their use of poetry, anticipate the major works.

   For Lorca the lighting of the stage was an essential part of his
aim to create total theatre. Like poetry, lighting is used to
emphasize mood and atmosphere and to draw attention to

especially important moments. The second Act of *The Butter-fly's Evil Spell*, presenting the destruction of the Boybeetle's hopes, suggests that process through its evocation of a grow-ing physical darkness touched only by the chilling, silvery light of the moon. Similarly, in the final scene of *The Love of Don Perlimplín* the moonlight that fills the garden where Belisa awaits her mysterious lover is simultaneously romantic and death-like, a symbol of the opposites that are for Lorca juxta-posed in human experience. At the beginning of *The Shoe-maker's Prodigious Wife*, on the other hand, the *soft orange light of afternoon* (p. 65) creates a mood of optimism, while later in the Act the growing darkness (p. 79) suggests the Shoemaker's sorrow as he leaves his Wife and his village. In *The Tragicomedy of Don Cristóbal* Cocoliche's dream of Rosita is suggested in the eerie, blue light that fills the stage: [*The yellow palm tree fills with little silver lights and everything takes on a theatrical blue tinge.*] (p. 48). And in *Mariana Pineda*, in both Acts I and III, Mariana's anxiety and her final sense of desolation have their outward sign in the progressive darkening of the stage. In his use of lighting, no less than in his use of sets and costume, movement and language, Lorca reveals in his early plays that concern with and, very often, that mastery of the various dramatic elements that in his mature works were fused into a powerful and distinctive dramatic language.

CHAPTER II

THE PUBLIC
(EL PÚBLICO)

The Public, of which only an incomplete version is available to us, seems to have been conceived in New York during the years 1929-30 and nearly finished in Havana in 1930, for the manuscript was written in part on paper bearing the name of the Hotel Union where Lorca stayed.[1] He returned to Madrid in the summer of 1930 and either in late autumn or at the beginning of 1931 read the play to a small group of friends at the home of Carlos Morla Lynch. Rafael Martínez Nadal, one of the group, observes that both *The Public* and *When Five Years Have Passed* were received 'with coldness by his friends. A lack of understanding quite comprehensible considering the difficulties of these texts and, to a lesser degree, of all the poetic work written in America. I still remember the reserve, often the half-veiled hostility with which some friends listened to his first readings of the poems of *Poet in New York*.'[2] Mildred Adams provides the following account:

> . . . Soon after he returned to Madrid from South America, Federico read an early version to three friends, Carlos Morla Lynch and his wife Bebe, and Rafael Martínez Nadal. The French writer, Marcel Auclair, a friend of all of them, tells the effect of this surrealist drama on that sophisticated group. 'Raphael had a very disagreeable memory of that evening,' she says. 'Carlos and Bebe, disconcerted by the first speeches, more and more bothered by the violence, the declared homosexuality of those first acts, let Federico read his play from start to finish without saying a word. At the end, Bebe was almost weeping, not from emotion, but from dismay.
> "Federico, you are not going to have that played! It is

impossible! Apart from the scandal, it is unplayable."

Lorca did not try to defend his piece. Down in the street he told Rafael, "This is for the theatre years from now. Until then, let's say no more about it." '3

Lorca, as his observation to Rafael Martínez Nadal makes clear, regarded *The Public* as unrepresentable at the time of its composition, principally on grounds of public taste and attitudes. In 1933, during his visit to Buenos Aires he explained to a reporter form *La Nación* that no one would dare to produce the play, and the public, seeing itself mirrored in the action, would react violently to it:

> . . . for I believe there is no company which would be moved to put it on the stage and no public which would endure it without indignation. It is the mirror of the public. That is to say, it puts on the stage what each spectator may be thinking while, unawares, he is watching the performance. And since the drama within each of us is intense and usually shameful, the audience would rise up in anger and stop the performance. Yes. My play is not to be performed, but, as I have stated, it is 'a poem to be booed at.'4

In the same year Lorca published two scenes of the play, the Roman Ruin and Scene V, in the Madrid literary magazine *Los Cuatro Vientos*, and in July 1936 invited Rafael Nadal to attend a reading of the final version. Nadal tells us that he arrived late and heard only some of the last scene, but he saw the text of the play which was typed on foolscap with a good many corrections in ink.5

The first recorded attempt to stage *The Public* is, perhaps, that mentioned by Mildred Adams as taking place at the University of Texas in the early spring of 1972 when 'Rafael Nadal, lecturing there, described it in some detail. Students were wildly enthusiastic, declared *The Public* to be "Our play!" – insisted on producing the fragments that were given, and created scenes of real excitement over it.'6 The publication of the text was delayed for many years because the only version, which was in the possession of Nadal, that could be found had one scene missing. This text has now been published in Spain by Seix Barral. In the early Spring of 1978, as part of the seventy-fifth birthday celebrations of the foundation of the University of Puerto Rico, the play, as we know it, was performed by the student theatre company.

In considering the sources of and the influences upon *The Public*, one must, of course, consider the impact of surrealism on the play. André Breton had advocated 'automatic writing', the spontaneous and uninhibited expression, without the control of reason, of everything that passed through the mind, the revelation of the unconscious, the true and superior reality which lies within us. His surrealist manifesto, *Manifeste du surréalisme*, appeared in 1924, and his views were enthusiastically embraced by many others like Louis Aragon, Antonin Artaud, and, amongst painters, Max Ernst, and, of course, Salvador Dalí, himself an intimate friend of Lorca. Dalí, however, and Joan Miró and Luis Buñuel too, were later expelled from the surrealist camp championed by Breton for falsifying its ideals, and Rafael Nadal has, indeed, suggested that, in speaking of the surrealist aspects of their work 'it will be difficult to speak of "automatism of dreams without any control of reason" '.[7] Dalí himself, though seeking to be more surrealist than the surrealists, developed his 'paranoiac-critical method' which allowed him in the painting of dreams and unconscious images to remain in control of what was going on. Lorca, in a letter of 1928 to his friend, Sebastián Gash, denies the truly surrealist nature of the poems which he is sending him and asserts instead their poetic logic:

> They correspond to my new *spiritualist* manner, pure disembodied emotion, free of the control of logic, but, take note!, with absolute poetic logic. This is not surrealism. Beware! A very clear awareness shines through them.[8] (p. 1594)

In another letter to Gash, Lorca spoke of the need to protect himself against the danger of allowing himself to be fascinated by the unconscious, and in his famous lecture on 'The Poetic Image in Don Luis de Góngora' (*La imágen poética en Don Luis de*

Góngora) refers to the ultimate need of the poet to control his material:

> I do not believe that any great artist works in a state of frenzy. . . . One returns from inspiration as from a foreign land. The poem is the account of the journey.[9] (pp. 78-79)

Rafael Nadal, indeed, sees the influence of French surrealism as a less important influence on Lorca than the intellectual circles of Barcelona and Madrid in which, as well as Dalí, Miró and Buñuel, the poets Alberti, Aleixandre and Neruda were prominent figures.[10] Their work embraces the world of dreams and the unconscious, is often visionary and prophetic, but beneath much of it lies a strong foundation of Spanish cultural tradition in terms of which much of its surrealist and outlandish appearance may be quite clearly and rationally explained.

Two painters, in particular, with whose pictures Lorca was perfectly familiar, depicted scenes which, in their suggestion of confusion, transformation, violence, pain and anguish, anticipate many elements present in *The Public*. Hieronymus Bosch, the fifteenth-century Flemish painter, portrayed in many of his pictures, and notably in *The Garden of Delights* which hangs in the Prado, scenes of the most nightmarish character. In the central section of the picture a group of figures is covered by the leaves of a large flower; a man's legs, raised in the air and wide apart, hold a large fruit between them, from which a bird appears; men carry a horn of plenty containing three men, and a bear walks on its surface. In the right-hand panel of the picture the torments of Hell include a monstrous bird devouring a man, ears and bodies pierced by knives, and men and women subjected to the most terrible sufferings. *The Garden of Delights*, like many of Bosch's other paintings, contains precisely that vein of unreality that in a modern work would be termed surrealist.

Goya has often been called a forerunner of Impressionism, Expressionism and even of Surrealism, and the dark pictures of his later life, the *Disasters of War* and *The Caprichos*, must have made a deep impression on Lorca, given his own interest in painting. Here, indeed, are uncompromising images of man's inhumanity to man and, of particular relevance to one of the themes of *The Public*, the exposure of the reality beneath the mask in the forms of old and hideous women seeking to beautify themselves, men who carry donkeys on their backs, and a whole society comprised of savage monsters expressing their savagery in the name of something else. Again, in his seventies, Goya painted on the walls of his country house near Madrid the famous 'Black Series', pictures of suffering dominated by *Saturn Devouring one of his Children*, a symbol of the annihilation of man by man. And at the same time he completed a series of twenty-two etchings, *Los Disparates* – Hieronymus Bosch, interestingly enough, was known to his contemporaries as *El Disparate* – which represented in their portrayal of monsters and phantoms yet another vision of Hell. When we realize that many of the surrealist pictures which we regard as expressing the essence of that movement were painted after 1930 it seems less fanciful to take into account the visual impact on Lorca of the painters whose work hung in the Prado, and whose vision of the world, as presented in their pictures, defies logic and normality.

The films of the 1920s and 30s had their impact too as C. B. Morris has observed.[11] The cinema, which proved to be enormously influential in Spain, became a subject of serious study in the literary journals of the time. Ernesto Giménez Caballero, director of *La Gaceta Literaria*, founded the Cineclub Español in 1928 and invited Luis Buñuel, then living in Paris, to edit the cinema section of the journal. In the 1920s both critics and film-makers spoke of the close association between poetry and the cinema, and Charlie Chaplin and Buster Keaton were particular favourites with Spanish writers. The tastes of Spanish cinemagoers were very catholic, ranging from American comic films to adventure and romantic sentimentality, but film-makers like Buñuel proved, in films like *L'Age d'or* and *Un chien andalou*, that on the screen all kinds of effects could be achieved in terms of the presentation of reality and unreality, unusual camera angles, changing tempo, and unusual and unexpected association. As for Lorca, sections of the 'surrealist' poem *Poet in New York* are highly reminiscent of the startling and incongruous visual images of Buñuel's films –

a lame dog smoking, or a bird on crutches. And it was in New York that Lorca wrote a screenplay, *Trip to the Moon (Viaje a la luna)*, inspired by Buñuel's *Un chien andalou*, in which in seventy-eight scenes images of violence and extreme cruelty – a hand squeezing a fish, a background that fades into a male sex organ and then into a screaming mouth – pass before us in an unbroken sequence of transformations that defy all physical laws and suggest to us that things and people are never what they seem to be.[12] And the cinema also inspired, as we have seen, *Buster Keaton's Spin*. If, in the composition of *The Public* the influence of painters, past and present, was important, so was the impact of the film with its new and startling techniques. In its power to express visually the most powerful and complex emotions, Lorca discovered a true source of inspiration.

In the action of *The Public* the characters of Romeo and Juliet figure prominently, and it is interesting to note in this respect that *Romeo and Juliet* was one of Lorca's favourite plays. In Lorca's drama there are many echoes of Shakespeare's text and also indications that Lorca, knowing the work well, was writing without the Shakespearean work at hand. And yet, Raphael Nadal argues convincingly that, despite the frequent references to *Romeo and Juliet*, 'the theme of *The Public*, the accidental nature of love, is more closely connected with another Shakespeare play which had always haunted Lorca: *A Midsummer Night's Dream*.'[13] Lorca, in a discussion of the play with Nadal, and especially of the love scenes involving Titania and the ass, had observed that love, which is independent of the free will of the individuals concerned, exists at all levels and with the same intensity, be it between man and woman, man and man, creature and creature. What in Shakespeare's play was happening in a forest near Athens happens everywhere in the real world. This is precisely the theme of *The Public*, the revelation of love in its different forms and the revelation of the characters both as facets of each other and, beyond that, of ourselves.

The principal themes of *The Public* had, for the most part, been rehearsed in Lorca's earlier poems and plays and continued to be the dominant issues of his later work. The theme

of love occurs, of course, from the beginning, in many poems
and plays, but the theme of homosexual love, though latent in
Lorca's earlier work, really came to the forefront during his
stay in New York and is expressed powerfully in such poems
as the 'Ode to Walt Whitman' *(Oda a Walt Whitman)*, dated 15
June, 1930, when Lorca was also working on *The Public*. For
Lorca, Whitman was the embodiment of the virile man, the
man in search of a pure, total love, to be distinguished from the
corrupt, debased homosexuals, the pansies who degrade such
feelings. The theme is present too in other poems of this
period, such as 'Your Childhood in Menton' *(Tu infancia
en Mentón)* and 'Fable and Round Dance of the Three Friends'
(Fábula y rueda de los tres amigos), but after Lorca's return
from New York it ceased to be a prominent theme and the
relationships between men and women became once more the
principal subject of concern.

The close connection between love and death had obsessed
Lorca from his earliest writings. In *The Butterfly's Evil Spell*, for
example, the Prologue contains these lines:

> Because Death disguises itself as Love. How many times
> that huge skeleton carrying a scythe – which we see
> portrayed in prayer books – takes the form of a woman in
> order to deceive us and to open the door into darkness.
> Cupid himself, it almost seems, sleeps in the skull's
> hollow round chambers. In how many ancient tales does
> a flower, a kiss or a glance do the terrible office of a
> dagger.[14] (p. 196)

In the early *Book of Poems* the theme occurs in the 'Ballad of the
Little Square' *(Balada de la placeta)* when the children ask the
poet:

> What do you feel in your red
> and thirsty mouth?

And he replies:

> The taste of the bones
> of my great skull.[15] (p. 178)

The equation of love and death was one that was to give
Lorca's later love poetry its note of deep seriousness, and some
lines from one of the *Gacelas* of the *Divan del Tamarit*, though

the book itself was not published until 1936, illustrate the point well:

> There is no night that, when I give a kiss,
> I do not feel the smile of people without faces,
> Nor is there anyone who, when touching a new-born
>   baby,
> Can forget the still skull of the horses. (p. 493)

The joy of life, which Lorca felt so intensely and of which love is a supreme example, had for him as its constant companion the reverse side of the coin, the inevitability of death, whose shadow touches indiscriminately both men and women.

Closely allied with this theme is, of course, the frustration of love. Lorca had expressed it in many poems ranging from the *Book of Poems*, through *Songs*, to the *Gipsy Ballads*. The spinsters who dream of love and the women who wait in vain are the subjects of many of these poems, and in the plays, too, from *Mariana Pineda* to *The Shoemaker's Prodigious Wife*, the heroines' dreams of love are shattered. The figure of Juliet in *The Public*, lamenting the deceitful nature of love, is a more powerful form of those earlier women. But the theme of frustrated love in women had its counterpart, if on a smaller scale, in the theme of frustrated love in men.[16] In *The Shoemaker's Prodigious Wife* the old shoemaker is in many respects a comic figure, but he is also very human, and his frustration lies in his inability to satisfy the needs of his young and romantic wife. The impotent Don Perlimplín is a still more touching figure, conscious of his impotence as, on his wedding night, he sees through the keyhole the beautiful body of his naked wife. These earlier examples of the theme of frustrated love in men find a much more powerful, even tragic expression in those figures in *The Public* – the Director and the Three Men – who seek and do not find.

Another theme, inherent in the inevitability of death, is the theme of change, decay and passing time. In the third scene of *The Public* Juliet describes the slow destruction of buildings, eroded by time, while she, lying in the tomb, is the embodiment of love and beauty cruelly extinguished. In much of his earlier poetry Lorca was obsessed with the relentless march of time exemplified in ruined buildings, broken columns, and the slow advance of grass, moss and weeds. In *Poet in New York* he presents a vision of the city as a 'pyramid of moss' in times to come. It is passing time which destroys the dreams and illusions of the women who in the poetry and the plays wait for love – the gipsy nun, Soledad Montoya, Mariana Pineda. And, as time passed for Lorca and death came nearer with every passing day, it was a theme which, closely interwoven with the associated themes of love and death, acquired an increasingly serious and prophetic expression in *When Five Years Have Passed, Blood Wedding, Yerma* and *The House of Bernarda Alba*.

The title *The Public*, stark and unadorned, is, like some of its settings and not a little of its dialogue, a puzzle to make us think and ponder on. On the one hand, in terms of the theatre, stage and auditorium, actors and spectators, the public is something separated from the stage, observers of the action played upon it. On the other hand, in the sense that a play is an image of life, a metaphor of man's experience, it is also a mirror in which we see ourselves, the actors on the stage forms of the observers of the action. Furthermore, inasmuch as we, in relation to our fellow men, assume appearances and masks with which we conceal ourselves, we are as much actors in the process of our lives as any actors upon a stage. In *The Public* there is no separation between its action and its audience. The playgoer, observing on the stage episodes and incidents that, often painful, embarrassing and shameful, seemingly have no relevance to himself, is made aware that he is looking at an actor who is, in fact, himself, and that the play is merely a reflection of the larger stage of life.

In the striking setting for Scene I there is an immediate statement of one of the play's main themes:

> [*The Director's room. The Director is seated. He wears a cut-away. The décor is blue. A great hand is printed on the wall. The windows are X-ray plates.*] (p.33)

In particular, the juxtaposition of the hand, covered with flesh, and the X-ray plates, revealing the bones beneath the flesh, vividly suggests the play's intention to expose the truth that lies beneath appearances and façades. The setting of the room, repeated in the final scene in an almost identical way, conveys too the idea of enclosure, imprisonment and escape cut off, and, through the predominance of blue, the proximity of death, the ultimate truth. In this bold and concise image Lorca announces the play's principal concerns.[17]

The appearance on stage of four White Horses is in part a startling surrealist dramatic device, but in thematic terms the encounter develops an idea stated already in the stage-setting. The horses, representing as they usually do in Lorca's writings the reality of passion, suggest an unequivocal statement of things, the truth of passion. The Director, in contrast, an advocate of the Open Air Theatre (Teatro al aire libre), a form of theatre that is concerned only with the presentation of the pleasant appearance of things, rejects all that the horses stand for and angrily dismisses them from his presence.

The Director's confrontation with the horses becomes in turn a confrontation with three men *dressed identically and with identical long black beards* (p. 39). Horses and men are linked, for the words that introduce the latter have also introduced the former:

SERVANT: Sir.
DIRECTOR: What is it?
SERVANT: The public.
DIRECTOR: Let them come in. (p. 37)

And secondly, the men, echoing the horses, allude to the Open Air Theatre: 'FIRST MAN: Are you the Director of the Open Air Theatre?' (p. 39). Between one man and another there is no difference because in the nature of our passions we are all the same. And between men and horses, or the human and the natural world, the differences are of form and appearance rather than of substance, for, stripped of all pretensions, those forces that work in men, at the very centre of our being, are those forces that operate in Nature too, a favourite Lorca theme.[18]

The encounter between the Director and the three men is, in its first half, a vigorous discussion of the nature of Theatre, and in its second half a dramatization of that theme. Denouncing a

Theatre that is merely superficial, inhibited by the requirements of public taste and morality, the three men, voicing
Lorca's views on contemporary Spanish theatre, demand
instead a form of Theatre that presents the public with the
truth, stripping away the layers of flesh in order to expose the
skeleton that lies beneath the surface: 'THIRD MAN: So that the
truth of the tombs be known.' (p. 41). The First Man reiterates
the theme: 'FIRST MAN: . . . the true theatre, the theatre beneath
the sand.' (p. 41). The debate itself begins, indeed, to become a
dramatization, a revelation of the loves of the Director and the
three men, a process in which they take part not in the enactment of a plot but in an exploration of themselves as individuals and in relation to each other. The First Man proposes this
drama of real life: 'Can you think of a newer play than ourselves with our beards . . . and you?' (p. 45). But inasmuch as
they, being men, are like each other and we like them, their
exploration of themselves becomes our own. At the beginning
of the scene the three men – the public – have been invited into
the Director's room (p. 37). They were the public who saw the
Director's production of *Romeo and Juliet*. Now, in a manner
which anticipates many later influential modern plays, they
participate in a drama of their own, are both actors and public,
while we, the observers of this new stage action, are witnesses
to our own exposure, exemplified in them. In the words of the
First Man to the horses: 'Come inside, with us. You have a
place in the play. Everyone does.' (p. 45).

The introduction of the screen, a kind of portable X-ray
machine behind which the characters will pass to emerge in
another form of themselves, marks the beginning of a series
of startling revelations, the stripping away of appearances
announced at the beginning of the scene. Between the three
men, despite an initial formality, an intimate, homosexual
relationship is slowly revealed. The Director, attempting to
conceal his homosexuality, calls on Helen, the archetype of
woman, but is forced by the Second and Third Man to reveal
himself for what he is:

> [*Men 2 and 3 push the Director. He passes behind the screen
> and appears the other side as a young boy dressed in white satin
> with a ruffle around his neck. . . .*] (p. 47)

In turn, the First Man's earlier, aggressive manner falls away in the presence of this cold and aloof young lover, Enrique, who dominates his Gonzalo. But now the Second Man, exposing the Director, is himself exposed as an effeminate homosexual:

> [*The Director pushes the Second Man roughly and he appears from behind the screen as a woman dressed in black pyjama trousers. . . . In her hand a lorgnette with a fair moustache which she will raise to her lips at certain moments in the play.*]
> (p. 49)

The Third Man, like the Director, proclaims his love of woman, of Helen, but is denounced by her as a sadistic homosexual who has been the Director's lover too: [*He passes quickly behind the screen and emerges without a beard, with a very pale face and a whip in his hand . . .*] (p. 51). All the characters are shown, through their protests and denials of the truth, to conceal themselves, consciously or otherwise, behind façades. Seeking a form of Theatre which reveals uncomfortable truths and discusses complex matters, the three men, and the Director with them, have become the characters in the enactment of their own drama, witnesses to the presentation of the truth about themselves. They are their own public, as it were, while we, facets of them as they are facets of each other, are as much the public of their exposure as of our own, observing a play that, reminiscent of Pirandello in some of its techniques, has the effect of diminishing the distance between the actors and their audience.[19]

Scene II, an episode that has puzzled many critics, is set in a Roman ruin, and presents in its first half a strange ballet-like encounter between two figures, one covered with vine leaves, the other covered with bells, and in its second half their meeting with the Roman Emperor who, it emerges, is looking for the One. The setting of the ruin with its broken arches and encroaching grass evokes a typical Lorca theme – the theme of passing time and, in conjunction with it, inevitable change, decay and death. The two figures, the Figure with Vine Leaves seated and playing a flute, the Figure with Bells dancing, embark on a game of love in which the roles and moods of the

F

participants in relation to each other are themselves seen to change and shift continually. The exchanges begin teasingly, the Figure with Vine Leaves adapting to his beloved's needs:

> FIGURE WITH BELLS: If I were to turn into a cloud?
> FIGURE WITH VINE LEAVES: I would turn into an eye.
> FIGURE WITH BELLS: If I were to turn into dung?
> FIGURE WITH VINE LEAVES: I would turn into a fly. (p. 56)

But in this teasing attitude there is also an element of domination and the roles are soon reversed, revealing beneath the façade of love more vicious and destructive elements. As the game continues, its playfulness becomes instead a Pinteresque process of alternating domination and submission, threats and counter-threats, pleading and rejection. The Figure with Bells grows stronger, the Figure with Vine Leaves weaker, the former submissive, the latter assertive, the one aggressive, the other defensive:

> FIGURE WITH BELLS: [*Timidly.*] And if I turned into an ant?
> FIGURE WITH VINE LEAVES: [*With energy.*] I would turn into earth.
> FIGURE WITH BELLS: [*More strongly.*] And if I turned into earth?
> FIGURE WITH VINE LEAVES: [*More weakly.*] I would turn into water.
> FIGURE WITH BELLS: [*Forcefully.*] And if I turned into water?
> FIGURE WITH VINE LEAVES: [*Very weakly.*] I would turn into a moon-fish.
> FIGURE WITH BELLS: [*Trembling.*] And if I turned into a moon-fish?
> FIGURE WITH VINE LEAVES: [*Rising.*] I would turn into a knife . . . (p. 59)

The encounter in its accumulating tension is an arresting, stylized, almost balletic treatment of the theme of homosexual love, and the two figures are doubles in their relationship towards each other of the men presented to us in Scene I. Here the Figure with Bells dominates the Figure with Vine Leaves. There the Director (Enrique) dominated the First Man coldly and sadistically. The Figure with Bells, like the Director, speaks of a love affair with Helen (p. 63). Here the Figure with Bells whips his beloved. There the Third Man whipped the director. Inasmuch as they are observers of this scene, the men are watching a theatrical enactment of their own relationships, the revelation of the truth about themselves in the kind of theatre they have demanded.

The arrival of the Roman Emperor in search of the One, a perfect homosexual love, initiates another clash. If the encounter between the Figure with Vine Leaves and the Figure with Bells has been an attempt by one to dominate the other, the new encounter, involving another individual, is another stage in the previous struggle. The Figure with Vine Leaves, dominated earlier by the Figure with Bells, seeks revenge through an association with the Emperor, but in so doing submits to his domination: '. . . If you kiss me I will open my mouth and your sword will pierce my neck.' (p. 71). The search for love is the discovery of anguish, one relationship echoed and repeated in another. And if the Emperor, in embracing eagerly the Figure with Vine Leaves, thinks that his search for the One is ended, the Figure with Vine Leaves knows that it is not: 'He has it because he will never be able to have it.' (p. 71). The experience of love, as in the rest of Lorca's drama, is shown to be a shifting, uncertain process in which the only certainty is, like the passing of time itself, change and, in conjunction with it, anguish.

The ending of the scene establishes once more the relationship between its characters and the Director and the three men, for the screen is cleverly introduced again and they appear from behind it:

> [*The Figure with Bells pulls one of the columns and this unfolds into the white screen of the first scene. Behind it the three bearded men and the Director appear.*] (p. 73)

Indeed, the words of the Figure with Bells, the Director and the First Man echo each other:

FIRST MAN: Treason!
FIGURE WITH BELLS: He has betrayed us!

74   LORCA

DIRECTOR: Treason!
[*The Emperor embraces the Figure with Vine Leaves.*] (p. 73)

In the desertion of the Figure with Bells by the Figure with Vine Leaves, the Director seems to see the possibility of his own desertion by the First Man, Gonzalo, his own cruelty perpetrated on him. The observers of the stage action again become the participants in it, the costumes only masks, the edges between the actors and the public blurred imperceptibly.

The setting for Scene III, like a modern abstract painting, is reminiscent, in a somewhat different way, of the setting for Scene I:

[*Wall of sand. On the left, and painted on the wall, a transparent moon, like jelly. In the centre a huge green leaf.*] (p. 75)

The transparent moon, the leaf in close-up, and the sectional cut of a tree (deleted by Lorca), suggest, like the hand and the X-ray plates of Scene I, the intention of the scene to see through things to the reality that lies beneath the surface. And the wall of sand, echoing a phrase used earlier – the theatre beneath the sand (p. 41) – indicates that we are now the observers in a theatre where nothing will be concealed.

In the first section of the scene we are presented with a series of struggles, both physical and emotional, that expose further the relationships of the Director and the three men towards their homosexuality and towards each other. The First Man states immediately, in language amazingly bold for the Spain of the 1930s, the theme of homosexuality and the shame associated with it: 'But the arse is man's punishment. The arse is man's failure, his shame and his death . . .' (p. 75). Like the others, he longs to be free from his obsession but he knows too that man, since he cannot change his nature, must accept it, face up to it, and recognize himself for what he is: 'Can a man ever cease to be what he is?' (p. 77). As in *Blood Wedding* and other plays, Lorca affirms that men must follow their inclinations. The Third Man, unlike the First, seeks to deny and conceal the truth about himself, pursuing his pleasures in secret, and is denounced by the First Man for what he is:[20]

That's the man who loves the Emperor in silence and seeks him out in the dockside pubs. Enrique, look deeply into his eyes. (p. 79)

In the subsequent exchanges truths about the others are revealed too, consolidating our earlier impressions. The Director, for example, would be rid of his homosexual obsession, of his attraction to the First Man, but, faced with the possibility of losing him in a conflict with the Emperor, whom the First Man would symbolically destroy, cannot face that possibility and seeks to divert him from his task: [*The Director and the First Man struggle silently.*] (p. 83). Equally, if the Director and the First Man destroy each other, the Third Man would be free of them. But freedom for him would for the Second Man be its opposite:

> THIRD MAN: We must separate them.
> SECOND MAN: So that they do not destroy each other.
> THIRD MAN: Though I would gain my freedom.
> SECOND MAN: But I would find my death. (p. 83)

The struggle between the Director and the First Man has its counterpart in them: [*They struggle. The Second Man pushes the Third Man . . .*] (p. 85). In the series of encounters the shifting and complex relationships of the four men are revealed to us fully, as is fitting in this theatre that strips away appearances.

From its focus on the theme of love, the emphasis moves, with the appearance of Juliet, to another central Lorca theme: the frustration of love through death, symbolized in the figure of Juliet herself. This is not the Juliet of the action of Shakespeare's play but the Juliet after the action of the play has ended; not the Juliet who has lived for and been fired by love's magic, but the Juliet of the tombs, awakened, paradoxically, to the truth of the transience and thus the terrible anguish of love. The moonlight that floods the scene, the whiteness of her garments, the ivy that grows and spreads around her tomb, all is evocative of death and passing time:

> [. . . *there is revealed the tomb of Juliet in Verona. Realistic décor. Rose-trees and ivy. Moonlight. Juliet is lying in the tomb. She is wearing an operatic white dress . . .*] (p. 85)

The episode that now ensues, blending reality and fantasy, human and non-human figures, expounds familiar Lorca themes in a bold surrealist manner. The First White Horse, appearing before Juliet, is the voice of idealized Romantic love, for, like the ardent lover immersed in the dream and beauty of love, he has waited for her in the garden, the archetypal setting for all young lovers: 'I have waited for you in the garden.' (p.87). Juliet dispels his idealism, suggesting that love and death are inevitably juxtaposed: 'You mean in the grave.' (p.87). Love ends in death, dreams end in death, and the other side of beauty and happiness is the darkness of despair:

> FIRST WHITE HORSE: . . . When will you grasp the perfection of a day? A day with morning and evening.
> JULIET: And with night. (p.87)

When the First White Horse offers to carry Juliet away on its back, gives her, in other words, another opportunity to experience love, she evokes, in a powerful passage, the illusion of love, the destructive passage of time, the process of decay, and, at the end of it, the inevitability of death:[21]

> JULIET: [Weeping.] Enough. I will hear you no more. Why do you wish to take me with you? The promise of love is a lie, a broken mirror, a footprint in water. For then you would leave me in the grave once more . . .
> The moon pushes gently the empty houses, brings about the fall of columns . . . When I was small I saw the beautiful cows graze in Verona's meadows. Later I saw pictures of them in my books, but I always remember them as I passed by the slaughter houses. (pp.89-91)

The White Horse is, indeed, joined by the Black Horse, illusion complemented by disillusionment in an image of the opposing elements, positive and negative, that constitute life's whole. Like Juliet, the Black Horse rejects the White Horse's optimism, for while the latter transforms all that is ugly and lifeless into beauty, the former destroys it, including love, of which the dove is the symbol:

FIRST WHITE HORSE: On the shores of the Dead Sea there
flourish beautiful apples of ash . . .
BLACK HORSE: You know how well I behead doves . . .
(pp. 95-7)

The conflict between the two is taken a stage further with the
arrival of the Three White Horses who take up the song of love
and beat their sticks as an accompaniment to it and in defiance
of the presence of the Black Horse. But he is not to be denied
and asserts in opposition to their optimism the inevitability of
things and his own command of the kingdom of silence:
'However much you beat with your sticks things will happen
only as they must happen . . . (p. 97). Juliet, longing for love
but disillusioned by her experience of it, is herself placed at the
centre of the conflict as the White Horses reveal their desire to
make love to her. Torn by fear on the one hand, represented by
the warnings of the Black Horse, and growing optimism on the
other, instilled by the promptings of the White Horses, she
begins to succumb to the dream of passion and to assert again
the force of her personality: 'You wish to lie with me? You do?
Well now it is I who wish to lie with you, for I will command, I
will rule, I will mount you . . .' (p. 101). But the spell is broken
finally by the Black Horse, it fades, and she is reminded once
again of the cold reality that must destroy all dreams:

BLACK HORSE: [To Juliet.] To your place. No one will
penetrate you.
JULIET: Must I be silent then? A new-born child is beautiful. (pp. 101-103).

This middle section of the scene is one in which we have
witnessed a series of confrontations revolving around the
theme of love, the exteriorization, as it were, of the conflicting
thoughts and emotions of Lorca himself. The play is like a
dream, but unlike dreams it has the logic and consistency of
themes and ideas in the process of constant elaboration.[22]

The final section of the scene reintroduces the Director and
the three men, building to a climax technically and dramatically brilliant for its time. It begins with the appearance of the
First Man and the Director, the latter in the form in which he

was revealed to us in Scene I: [. . . *The Director appears as in Scene I, transformed into a white Harlequin.*] (p. 103). The presentation of him in the form which lies beneath the surface, in conjunction with the assertions of the characters, suggests that we are now to witness a further divesting of appearances, a shedding of masks, another search for individual identity beneath the guises with which we all conceal ourselves. The First White Horse observes: 'Now we have inaugurated the true theatre, the theatre beneath the sand.' (p. 103). The Black Horse continues: 'So that the truth of the tombs be known.' (p. 103). And the First Man asserts: [*To the Director.*] 'My struggle has been with the mask until I have succeeded in seeing you naked.' (p. 105). But the masks that we use are many and one discarded merely reveals another. The Director, discarding the white costume, the form of Enrique, appears as Guillermina, a female ballet-dancer, only to discard that form to reveal beneath it the costume of a figure with bells. The Second Man appears, as in Scene I, dressed in pyjama trousers, is courted by the Third Man, but the latter, assuming a different mask and pursuing Juliet, reveals the Second Man in a different guise. One by one the discarded and empty costumes themselves appear, as in a sequence from a film, seeking or sought by their lovers. The First Man embraces the white costume, believing it to be Enrique, but discovers it is not. The white costume seeks Enrique but cannot find him. The discarded ballet dress searches for Guillermina, and the empty pyjama suit of the Second Man beats its face in despair, a face that is significantly faceless, a white, smooth egg-shape without identity. In this astonishing scene in which the characters search in vain not only for others but even for themselves, we are left with an impression of the uncertainty of everything, of love, of individual identity, and of the treachery of appearances and the shift and flux of all reality. Voices echo in a growing void and the only sounds are the hiss of the rain and the song of the nightingale, synonymous with death: [23]

> HARLEQUIN COSTUME: [*Its voice fainter.*] Enrique . . .
> BALLET COSTUME: [*In a soft voice.*] Guillermina . . .
> FIRST MAN: [*Throwing the Harlequin costume to the ground*

and climbing the stairs.] Enrique . e . e . e . . !
HARLEQUIN COSTUME: [*On the ground and very weakly.*]
  Enrique . e . e . e . . .
[*The figure with the face like an egg beats its face incessantly
with its hands. Over the sound of the rain the true nightingale
sings.*] (p. 119)

An interpretation of Scene V, a bold and dramatically complex scene, is made more difficult by the fact that Scene IV is
missing and would, perhaps, have helped elucidate certain
aspects of subsequent events. The centre of the stage is dominated by a red nude figure on a perpendicular bed whose
death agony engages directly our attention. In the background
arches and steps lead to the boxes of a theatre and to the right is
the façade of a university building. While the death of the
Nude takes place on stage, the action of *Romeo and Juliet* is
performed off-stage, and its significance is discussed by
characters, especially students, who drift in and out of the
agony of the dying man, linking the on-stage and off-stage
actions.

The Nude, inasmuch as he is Romeo, parallels Juliet in the
previous scene. He is not the Romeo of the action of Shakespeare's play, a fictitious figure played by an actor, but the
Romeo outside the play, the embodiment of love betrayed by
death, a suffering, Christ-like figure, another form of all those
Lorca figures both in the play and out of it who dream of love
and are destroyed.[24] Here, clearly, is another scene from the
theatre beneath the sand, another example of the truth of the
tombs, while off-stage there is being performed the Director's
version of *Romeo and Juliet* whose purpose is, unlike his earlier
production of the play, to make its public aware of truths they
have failed to perceive before. The reference to the Director
seems to clarify his new function: 'THIRD WOMAN: They have
found the Director inside the tomb.' (p. 125). The women, on
the other hand, find the play to be merely pleasing and they
argue that they are satisfied with the entertaining spectacle of
the surface appearance of things:

> FIRST WOMAN . . . It was a lovely play and the revolution
> has no right to profane the tombs.

SECOND WOMAN. The words were alive and the forms too. Why must we lick the bones? (p. 127)

They are shocked only when the First Boy informs them that what they have witnessed is not the love affair of a young man and a young girl but, since the part of Juliet has been played by a boy, the amorous encounter of two males. In other words, the masks and costumes of the characters, like the masks of human beings, conceal unpalatable truths.

The debate on the nature and function of the theatre, which has formed a thread through the preceding scenes, is developed further now by the group of students who have witnessed the off-stage performance of *Romeo and Juliet*. The First Student, for example, suggests that the public, concerned only with the soothing appearance of things, has no wish to penetrate beneath the surface of the characters:

The public ought not to penetrate the silk and the cardboard constructed by the poet . . . Why should this matter to the public? (p. 129)

The idea is repeated later in the scene:

A spectator ought never to be part of the play. When people go to an aquarium they do not kill the sea serpents or the water rats or the leprous fish but gaze through the glass and learn. (p. 139)

From the Fourth Student we learn that the riot inside the theatre commenced when the public began to perceive the meaning behind the masks, to understand that the action on the stage is a mere image, a mirror in which they see their own reflections: 'The trouble began when they saw that Romeo and Juliet really loved each other.' (p. 127). And again:

People forget the costumes during the performance and the revolution started when they found the true Juliet gagged underneath the seats and covered with cotton wool so that she could not shout. (p. 129)

The students, representative of a more liberal, less prejudiced point of view, condemn the lack of understanding of the public.[25] The Fifth Student, for example, even though he did not perceive that the role of Juliet was enacted by a boy, rejoices when the truth is pointed out to him, for in the relationship that lies beneath the mask he perceives his own with the First Student, and for him, as for Lorca himself, the love of men for each other is as true as the love of man and woman:

> FIFTH STUDENT: [*Starting to laugh.*] I'm pleased. She seemed very beautiful and if it was a boy in disguise it doesn't really matter. (p. 141)

In the students is reflected the tolerant acceptance of a new generation.

But against the joy of young love, whatever its form, and intertwined with it throughout this scene, as in the greater theatre of life, is the grim reality of anguish and death:

> FIRST STUDENT: Joy! Joy of boys and girls . . .
> FIRST MAN: Agony. (p. 143)

The Nude has referred earlier in the scene to the anguish and solitude of men everywhere: 'For the agony of man alone, on platforms and in trains.' (p. 137). The action of the play being presented off-stage has as its constant and riveting accompaniment the on-stage death of the Nude. He, moreover, whom we know to be Romeo, is transformed before our eyes into the figure of the First Man:

> [*The bed turns on its axis and the Nude disappears. On the other side of the bed, stretched out, there appears the First Man . . .*] (p. 137)

He repeats the Nude's earlier cry: '[*Closing his eyes.*] Agony!' (p. 137). And he does so again and at greater length at the end of the scene as he dies:

> Agony! The loneliness of man in a dream full of lifts and trains where you reach incredible speeds. The loneliness of buildings and corners, of beaches where you will never again appear. (p. 145)

Nude, Romeo, First Man are aspects of each other and forms of all of us, and the final image of the scene, the illuminated face of the First Man's corpse, is our own death in the gathering shadows: [*The stage is in darkness. The lantern of the First Boy illuminates the dead face of the First Man.*] (p. 145). The curtain falls on a scene in which the different levels on which the action works and the frontiers between play and reality, actors and spectators, art and life, have ceased to exist.

The setting of Scene VI echoes, with small variations, the setting of Scene I, suggesting, as in other Lorca plays, that the action has come full circle:[26]

> [*The same set as in Scene I. On the left and on the ground the large head of a horse. On the right, an enormous eye and a group of trees with clouds against the wall. The Director enters accompanied by the Juggler. The Juggler wears tails, a white satin cape that reaches his feet, and a silk hat. The Director wears the same suit as in the first scene.*] (p. 151)

The eye, replacing the hand printed on the wall, reminds us of the play's intention to penetrate to the heart of things. But of the horses who have appeared throughout the play, the symbol of that purpose, only a lifeless head is left, as though the journey of exploration is over and only death remains.

The conversation between the Director and the Juggler is in some ways a repetition of the discussion in Scene I between the Director and the three men. There the three men challenged the Director to experiment with a different kind of theatre, the theatre beneath the sand, the truth of the tombs. Here, in the debate with the Juggler, the Director defends their viewpoint which he has himself accepted and which, put into practice in his production of *Romeo and Juliet*, has shocked and scandalized the public: 'My friends and I opened up the tunnel beneath the sand . . . When we reached the tomb, we raised the curtain.' (pp. 153-55). He goes on: 'I made the tunnel in order to have control over the costumes and, through them, to reveal the profile of a hidden force . . .' (p. 155). The Juggler, inasmuch as he symbolizes illusion, dexterity and sleight of hand, defends the theatre that is merely entertainment and display: 'I can effortlessly change a bottle of ink into a cut hand full of ancient rings . . .' (p. 155). 'I can change a seafarer into a sewing needle . . .' (p. 157). The Director, having shared this attitude in his own advocacy of the Open Air Theatre, rejects it forcibly now, denying that the curtain separates the actors from the public, and advancing the view, in one of Lorca's most powerful and illuminating statements on the purpose and function of the Theatre, that the play, the true drama, is an action in which the roles of actors and spectators are inseparable:

> . . . my characters, on the other hand, burn the curtain and die in the presence of the public . . . One must destroy the theatre or live in it! (p. 155)

And he continues:

> Only by breaking down the doors can the drama be justified . . . I detest the dying man who outlines a door on the wall with his finger and quietly goes to sleep. The true drama is a circle of arches where the wind, the moon, the creatures come in and out and find no resting place. (p. 159)

We, the public of *The Public*, have seen on the stage characters in the process of self-discovery, assuming and rejecting masks in an anguished search for their own identity. They, discussing the nature of the drama, have participated in the unfolding of their own drama. Side by side with the off-stage performance of *Romeo and Juliet*, the play within the play, there has been played out for us an action which has brought alive the issues of that play, so that its characters are aspects of the figures on the stage and these are forms of them. But for us, spectators of an action on a stage, of the action of *The Public*, its issues have simultaneously assumed a living form, its characters reflections of ourselves and we of them. It is a process in which boundaries and demarcations have dissolved and have become instead a series of mirrors.[27] The ending of the play, presenting the Director's death, is the final image that is common to us all. The Director's room, like the rooms we all inhabit, becomes a place from which there is no escape, the Juggler Death, the truth for which the Director has sought the final truth, the final dramatic act. Between the stage on which, alone, he encounters Death, and the stage of the great theatre of the world where we give our own performance there is no difference. We become the spectators of our own ultimate solitude, the public of our own final curtain:

> VOICE: [*Off-stage.*] Sir.
> VOICE: [*Off-stage.*] What?
> VOICE: [*Off-stage.*] The public.
> VOICE: [*Off-stage.*] Let them enter.
> [*The Voice becomes fainter and more distant. The Juggler waves the fan vigorously. Snowflakes begin to fall on the stage.*]
> (p. 165)

In its intellectual and emotional power, its daring use of dramatic techniques, and the 'modernity' of its vision, *The Public* is both Lorca's most experimental play and one of the most startling plays of the twentieth century.

In terms of its dramatic technique, *The Public* is Lorca's most ambitious play, its visual impact stunning, its mixture of realism and fantasy absorbing, its use of language imaginative and extremely powerful. Rafael Martínez Nadal has observed that 'by reason both of the theme and the technique employed this is indeed his most daring work', and that here he 'was experimenting in techniques and ways of expression similar to those which twenty or thirty-five years later were to characterize the avant-garde drama of Europe and America'.[28] Familiarity with Lorca's theatre in general – with the puppet plays and farces, with the symbolic figures of many of the plays – and with his more dense and obscure poetry, allows us to see how in *The Public* all those elements fuse and create a dazzling, highly original *tour de force* that is, nonetheless, highly characteristic of its author.

The stage settings, as in the theories of Gordon Craig and the plays of Valle-Inclán and Grau, are statements of the theme, and more so here, perhaps, than elsewhere, for *The Public* is to a large degree the dramatization of ideas. The first stage setting, for example, is extremely simple, composed of symbolic clues to the meaning of the action that ensues:

> [*The Director's room. The Director is seated. He wears a cutaway. The décor is blue. A great hand is printed on the wall. The windows are X-ray plates.*] (p. 33)

But what is the meaning of these strange and arresting symbols? Stated simply, and initially without an obvious correlation, they are images designed to startle and stimulate our minds as much as our emotions, to arouse our curiosity and focus our thoughts more sharply, as in some kind of intellectual game. Settings that in other plays are part of the emotional impact of the scene that follows are here the clues to the solution of a puzzle.

The setting for Scene II underlines the point, for now there is a new surprise, another challenge to our understanding:

> [*A figure, completely covered with red vine leaves, plays a flute and is seated on a capital. Another figure, covered with golden bells, dances in the centre of the stage.*] (p. 55)

If the action of Scene I has bewildered us with its startling transformation of characters and costumes, the setting for Scene II, seemingly unrelated to it, disorientates us further and offers us another puzzle, confronting us with questions about the meaning of its strange figures. As the scene unfolds, their meaning is, of course, revealed to us, and the setting with its broken columns is seen to be, like the setting for Scene I, entirely symbolic, a stylized evocation of passing time and its inherent change and decay.

The setting for Scene V has, on the other hand, a very different quality:

> [*In the centre of the stage, a perpendicular bed faces the audience, as though painted by a primitive, and on it there is a Red Nude, crowned with blue thorns. In the background arches and stairs lead to the boxes of a great theatre. On the right, the façade of a university building . . .*] (p. 121)

The red and blue of the central figure, like the aggressive and violent colours of a Fauve painting, are at once arresting, in contrast to the cool formality of the arches, the stairs, and the façade. If the strangeness of the central figure prompts our curiosity, it does so in an emotional more than an intellectual way, for it is a disturbing and haunting image, demanding our attention as the focal point in the picture and in the scene that follows.

The final Scene repeats, with minor but important changes, the setting for Scene I:

> [*The same set as in Scene I. On the left and on the ground the large head of a horse. On the right, an enormous eye and a group of trees with clouds against the wall. The Director enters accompanied by the Juggler. The Juggler wears tails, a white satin cape that reaches his feet, and a silk hat. The Director wears the same suit as in the first scene.*] (p. 151)

The action has come full circle and the head of the horse suggests the end of the vital passions that have been displayed to us, while the blue of the room, as in many Lorca scenarios, indicates that that end is death. The enormous eye, echoing the X-ray plates, informs us that here we are witnessing the final revelation, the end towards which, through all the struggle and anguish of existence, we inevitably make our way. The clues are easily deciphered now, and the pieces of the puzzle fall into place with a remorseless logic.

While *The Public* is largely a play of ideas, they are ideas whose meaning is conveyed to us as much by its general visual impact as by the statements placed in the mouths of its characters. In Scene I, for example, we are immediately confronted by the four White Horses which become in turn the three Men *dressed identically and with black beards* (p. 39). Later in the scene the Director passes behind the screen and emerges as *a young boy dressed in white satin* (p. 47), and shortly afterwards the Second Man appears from behind the screen as *a woman dressed in black pyjama trousers . . .* (p. 49). From beginning to end these extraordinary, stylized figures pass before us, as though from the world of circus, pantomime, puppet theatre, or *commedia dell' arte*. In one way their costumes are, of course, visually startling, demanding our attention like the sets themselves. More than in any other Lorca play, including *When Five Years Have Passed*, we are constantly dazzled by these figures and forms in a brilliant parade of whites, blacks, reds, pinks, golds and yellows.[29] But if the effect is kaleidoscopic, it is also purposeful, for the costumes of the figures express their meaning, each of them a concise and powerful image designed to convey to us the significance of a given moment. The transformation of the Director into the figure of *a young boy dressed in white satin* (p. 47) reveals to us immediately, with no need for words, his homosexuality. And the same is true of the Third Man, transformed before us into a figure *with a very pale face and a whip in his hand . . .* (p. 51). We are never in doubt that the White Horse of Scene III symbolizes hope and illusion, the Black Horse its opposite. All the figures of the play, the colours of their costumes instantly suggestive, their physical features highly stylized, are presented to us in such a way that we cannot fail to grasp their meaning.

If the figures are visually important individually, they are vastly more important in relation to each other, and their movement about the stage often conveys to us, as in a ballet or a film, the meaning of the action, its evocation of constant change, of the fluctuating attitudes of the characters towards each other, of clash and conflict, and of the search for individual identity. The movement of the characters behind the screen and their appearance in a totally different form is a good example of the way in which movement and meaning are closely integrated. In Scene II the movements of the Figure with Vine Leaves and the Figure with Bells express as eloquently as their words the constant shift in their relationship towards each other, from an initial playfulness to an alternating domination of the one by the other. The Figure with Vine Leaves threatens in movement as well as word, *rising up* (p. 59), is dominated by his partner, submits, *falling to the ground* (p. 63). In Scene III the conflict between the Director and the First Man is expressed in silent movement:[30] [*The Director and the First Man struggle silently.*] (p. 83). But it is the ending of Scene III that is the most effective and evocative sequence of the play as the Director and the Second Man discard and throw away their costumes, appear in a different guise, only for the empty, discarded costumes to appear too, and all of them move about the stage, seeking and never finding, embracing forms that are the opposite of what they seem to be. It is a haunting vision in which the movements of the figures, sinking to the ground in a final gesture of despair, express the futile searching that is our common lot. And especially evocative is the figure of the Second Man who sits

G

on the stairs throughout the conclusion of the scene and silently beats his face with his hands: [*The Costume sits on the stairs and slowly beats his smooth face with his hands, to the end of the scene.*] (p. 115). In *The Public* movement and gesture become images, and the fluid, shifting appearance of the play is itself a statement of its themes.

The language of the play has a very special quality. The dialogue of the later rural tragedies is invariably to the point, but the form of those plays is largely traditional and the language therefore plays its part in the setting and building of a scene towards its climactic point. *The Public*, on the other hand, lacking a plot as such, is a series of confrontations between its various characters, the emphasis moving from group to group while the tension is constantly maintained. In such scenes the language is often bare and the dramatic impact stems from simple and repeated structural patterns, often in the form of questions or exclamations. In Scene I the Second Man confronts the Director, his repeated questions acquiring a sustained momentum:

> SECOND MAN: Mr. Director, how did Romeo pee? Isn't it nice to see Romeo pee? How many times did he pretend to throw himself from the tower to be caught in the play of his suffering? What was going on, Mr. Director . . ., when it wasn't going on? And the grave? Why, at the end, did you not go down the steps to the grave . . .? (p. 41)

Later in the scene the Director exposes brutally the homosexuality of the Third Man:

> DIRECTOR: [*To the Third Man.*] And what about me? Don't you remember me? Don't you remember my torn nails? How would I have known other women and not you? Why have I called you, Helen? Why have I called you, my torment? (p. 51)

The two examples are typical of the often violent, face-to-face confrontations of the play.

On the other hand, *The Public* is a play which expresses the anguish of frustrated love and the destructive effect of passing time. And it does so not in verse, as is the case in many of the plays, but in prose. Thus the slow, measured rhythm of Juliet's lines in Scene III:

> The moon pushes gently the empty houses, brings about the fall of columns and offers to the grubs small torches to penetrate the cherries. The moon brings to the bedrooms the mask of meningitis, fills with icy water the bellies of pregnant women, and when I am inattentive throws handfuls of grass upon my shoulder. (p. 91)

The visual power of the images is greatly enhanced by the dragging weight of a rhythm that captures the sense of the slow, remorseless passage of time. And in the same scene, in the simple exchanges between Juliet and the First White Horse, her brief replies, countering the horse's Romantic optimism, undermine illusion with the stark truth of experience:

> FIRST WHITE HORSE: I have waited for you in the garden.
> JULIET: You mean in the grave.
> FIRST WHITE HORSE: You are as mad as ever, Juliet. When will you grasp the perfection of a day? A day with morning and evening.
> JULIET: And with night. (p. 87)

The expansive and lilting rhythms of hope run into the dull flatness of despair.

For all the dramatic effect of the language in terms of pattern and rhythm, *The Public* is a play distinguished by the difficulty of its language, a play whose meaning we often grasp intuitively rather than understand clearly. In Scene I, for example, the First Man speaks of the Director's repressed passions and concealed homosexuality:

> I recognize him still and I seem to see him that morning when he locked the hare, a prodigy of speed, in a small briefcase full of books. And another time when he stuck a rose behind each ear and discovered the centre parting. (p. 45)

We may sense that the hare, a traditional symbol of lust and even bisexualism, and the man with a rose behind each ear, the popular conception of an Andalusian pansy, point to the Director's homosexual inclinations, while the briefcase full of books is the intellectual coldness which conceals passion, but the sense of the lines in general is difficult to grasp, and more so in the short space of time it takes to speak them on the stage. There are many examples of such difficulty, and even when the meaning is more clear, its expression is often less than simple and direct. In Scene III, for instance, the threat which the homosexual poses to all women and his ultimate defeat by them is put in the following way:

> FIRST MAN: The head of the Emperor burns the bodies of all women.
> DIRECTOR: [*To the First Man.*] But you don't understand that Helen can polish her hands in phosphorous and quicklime. (p.81)

The dialogue of the play is full of expressions of an oblique nature that are, nonetheless, highly imaginative, often extremely visual, so that we are presented with a constant stream of images that, dissolving into each other, arrest the imagination, stimulate the mind, and keep the spectator of the play in a state of continual expectancy. It is not only the settings, the costumes and the movements of the players which repeatedy astonish and assault us, but the language too.

The lighting of the stage plays a significant part in certain scenes: the central section of Scene III which presents the tomb of Juliet; the final section of Scene V, involving the death of the Red Nude; and the ending of Scene VI which portrays the Director's death. Otherwise, perhaps, though we cannot be sure, the stage is lit uniformly and brightly, without dark areas, so that in the bright, flat light the figures stand out clearly in all their brilliance, as in the often open and uncluttered backgrounds of surrealist paintings.[31] The lighting itself, illuminating the figures, serves the dramatist's intention to expose them to us as they really are. The central section of Scene III, introducing Juliet, and, in conjunction with her, themes and associations of death and disillusionment, marks a moment in the play when the final and ultimate truth of everything, the knowledge of the transcience of love and all things bright and beautiful, is made clear to us. It is in every way a chilling moment, a moment when we should feel the cold touch of death, and it is therefore dramatically fitting that the stage should take on the cold, steely light of the moon and that Juliet's white dress should catch that light: [. . . *Moonlight. Juliet is lying in the tomb. She is wearing an operatic white dress. . . .*] (p. 85). The remainder of the scene is presumably dominated by the same cold light. If so, it is a truly haunting background to the figures and costumes which, as the scene draws to its conclusion, grope their way vainly about the stage in an image of life's futile seeking.

As Scene V moves towards its close and the Red Nude dies, the stage becomes darker: [. . . *The stage is in shadow* . . .] (p. 133). And when the bed on which he lies turns on its axis and the Red Nude is seen to be as well the First Man, the one merely a form of the other, the stage takes on a strong silvery-blue light:

> [*The light takes on a strong silvery tone like a cinema screen. The arches and stairs in the background are touched by a bluish light* . . .] (p. 137)

It is an earlier version of the death scene of *Blood Wedding*. As the curtain falls the darkness is almost total, symbolic of life extinguished, the moment emphasized by the patch of light from a lantern that illuminates a dead face: [*The stage is in darkness. The lantern of the First Boy illuminates the dead face of the First Man.*] (p. 145). Lorca uses lighting here as elsewhere he uses poetry: to accentuate important dramatic moments and to create in us an awareness that the haunting visual images presented to us are also the key moments in our lives.

In the final scene, which presents the Director's death and establishes, in its closing lines, our relationship with him, the lighting of the stage grows brighter and more intense:

> [. . . *The left-hand corner of the set opens up and there appears sky with long clouds, brightly lit, and there is a gentle rain of white gloves, rigid and well spaced out.*] (p. 165)

There is a cold, clinical feeling here, an indifference to the fact of the anguish and death of a human being that gives to the ending of the play that terrible sense of the emptiness of human existence that is an increasingly persistent note in Lorca's drama.

CHAPTER III

WHEN FIVE
YEARS HAVE PASSED
(ASÍ QUE PASEN CINCO AÑOS)

When Five Years Have Passed was completed on 19 August, 1931, almost a year after the completion of *The Public*, some of it written in New York, some in Granada.[1] Carlos Morla Lynch gives us a vivid and detailed account of Lorca's reading of the play on the night of 4 October, 1931, when, after dinner, he produced the play from his pocket and commenced reading it to his friends.[2] Morla's own reaction is significant. At first he was full of curiosity, then of interest, but gradually disconcerted by the play's meaning, for 'we found ourselves, unexpectedly, outside Spain, in the world of "surrealism", far from the *Gipsy Ballads*', and 'as in the case of everything that is "avant garde", a great effort is needed to understand the writer's purpose. And here lies the difficulty.' If the meaning of the play presented difficulties, Morla had no doubt about its dramatic and poetic qualities, particularly in certain scenes. He found the scene in Act I between the Dead Child and the Dead Cat to have 'a moving tenderness . . . we are made aware of the anguish of dying, the fear of being buried, the terror induced by the thought of total oblivion beneath the earth and the stone (Federico's obsession).' Similarly, the figure of the Mannequin in Act II has 'an astonishing suggestive power.' As for the work as a whole, it exhibits Lorca's genius and, as he performs it, his enormous interpretative gifts, but Morla wonders if the power of Lorca's performance can ever be recaptured on the stage, and in his general reaction to the play we feel, despite his positive response to certain scenes, a lingering doubt, at times a bewilderment, that must have been felt too by the

93

others present on that first occasion. There is nothing, though, in Morla's account to suggest, as Rafael Nadal has done, that *When Five Years Have Passed* was received 'with coldness by his friends.'[3] Despite its difficulty, it is, clearly, less obscure than *The Public*, its themes less shocking, its break with earlier plays in general less abrupt. It would have been surprising if Lorca's private audience had reacted as they had done a year earlier.

In an interview with Felipe Morales, Lorca, aware of what the public reaction to his 'surrealist' plays would be, had observed that they were 'unplayable'.[4] On the other hand, he asserted their importance by stating that 'these impossible plays contain my true intention.' There were, indeed, plans for a performance of *When Five Years Have Passed* at Madrid's 'Club Anfistora' in 1936, though the historical events of that year prevented the performance. In April, 1945, the play was performed in English at the Provincetown Playhouse in New York. The Spanish première took place in 1954 at the University of Puerto Rico. In 1956 there was a notable television production in Mexico. And in September 1978, in a climate of opinion much more ready to receive what in 1936 Lorca feared to be 'unplayable', *When Five Years Have Passed* was performed at the Teatro Eslava in Madrid, and given its due acclaim. Lorenzo López Sancho, reviewing the Madrid performance in *ABC*, observes that:

> It seems to me that in *When Five Years Have Passed* we see the true depth of the great theatrical personality that García Lorca would have become and, probably, his most original and experimental contribution to the theatre. The Teatro Estable Castellano has embarked boldly, with literary and artistic fervour, on its theatrical adventure. This first production soars above the level of mediocrity in which, with our new freedom, we see our theatre immersed.[5]

Lorca's belief in the importance of his play, whatever his doubts about the difficulty of performing it, has by now been thoroughly confirmed.

In considering the sources of the play, what has been said of

The Public is equally valid here. In terms of its general technique, *When Five Years Have Passed* reveals its debt to the cinema and painting, for its visual impact and many of its startling moments are reminiscent of Buñuel, Picasso and Dalí. In Act II the scene in which the inanimate figure of the Mannequin comes to life is ideally suited to the cinema. In Act III the figures dressed in black with faces the colour of plaster are, as C. B. Morris has suggested, like the heavily made-up figures in *The Cabinet of Dr. Caligari*, while at the end of the Act the projected image of the ace of hearts on the bookshelves of the library is again clearly cinematic.[6] In the same Act the Young Man's clothes laid out on the bed may be an echo of a similar incident in Buñuel's *Un chien andalou*, while the stylization of the characters in general, not unlike the figures in a Fellini film, is at least in part a response to the cinema.[7] As for the influence of painting, Lorca had himself shown in the exhibition of his drawings in Barcelona in 1927 a taste for the depiction of the absurd, the irrational and the disquieting, and his drawing entitled 'Cut Hands' ('Manos cortadas') possibly anticipates the episode of the severed hand in *Un chien andalou*. The nightmarish atmosphere and the dream-like quality of many of the play's scenes made us think of the paintings of Dalí, and the figure of Harlequin in the last Act had been a favourite in the 1920s with painters like Dalí and Picasso. But Harlequin was, of course, an important figure too in the *commedia dell' arte*, and its influence, together with that of farce and puppet theatre is important here, for if the stylization of the figures can be traced to film and painting, it can equally be found in these theatrical antecedents. Moreover, the actions and movements of many of the characters, notably the animated movements of the Friend and the Rugby Player and the mechanical movements of Harlequin, owe more to Lorca's puppet plays and farces than to anything else.

As far as the themes of *When Five Years Have Passed* are concerned, the Young Man exemplifies the frustration of love. He is either sexually timid or impotent, preferring the dream to the reality of love, and in some ways bears a resemblance to Don Perlimplín, though in a general sense he is the male equivalent of all the magnificent female figures who in Lorca's

poems and plays wait and dream of the love that never comes.
In this play the Secretary and the Mannequin, in particular,
look back to the frustrated women of the poems, while they
echo in the drama Mariana Pineda, the shoe-maker's wife, in
some ways Juliet in *The Public*, and they anticipate, of course,
Yerma and the ever-waiting daughters of Bernarda. The
dreams and desires of all those women are caught perfecty in
the words of the Mannequin:

> . . . This silk yearns,
> thread by thread, strand by strand,
> for a mouth that is warm.
> And my petticoats wonder
> where are the warm hands
> that grip my waist.[8] (p. 1011)

The theme of passion, on the other hand, is exemplified here
in the Bride and the Rugby Player. In Act II she expresses the
attraction which the Rugby Player has for her:

> In your breast there is a torrent where I will drown. I will
> drown . . . [*She looks at him*] and then you will go running
> off [*She weeps*] and you will leave me dead on the river
> bank. [*The* RUGBY PLAYER *puts a cigar in his mouth and the*
> BRIDE *lights it for him.*] Oh! [*She kisses him.*] What white
> heat, what marble fire leaps from your teeth! (p. 989)

He, in turn, embracing the Bride powerfully, exhaling cigar
smoke like a dragon, is the epitome of masculinity. The Bride
illustrates the theme of passion expressed in many of the
earlier poems, for instance in 'The Unfaithful Married Woman'
(*La casada infiel*) and 'Thamar and Amnon' (*Thamár y Amnón*),
and in the plays in the sensual Belisa of *The Love of Don
Perlimplín*. And she clearly is the precursor to the passionate
Bride of *Blood Wedding* and the rebellious Adela of *The House of
Bernarda Alba*. The Rugby Player, lacking a precise equivalent
in the earlier plays, anticipates the ardent Leonardo of *Blood
Wedding*.

The theme of death is symbolized in particular in *When Five
Years Have Passed* in the Dead Boy and the Dead Cat. Both the
boy and the cat evoke the joy of life in the description of the
pleasures they enjoyed:

CAT: I played!
  I went on the roof, flat-nosed,
  tin-nosed cat,
  and in the morning I went
  to catch fish in the water,
  and at noon I slept
  under the rose-tree by the wall. (p. 974)

The theme of life's enjoyment in one form or another fills the
pages of Lorca's earlier work. In the early *Songs* there is often
expressed that sense of the magic of childhood that the boy
and the cat evoke in *When Five Years Have Passed*. Child-like
innocence becomes in 'Eros with a Walking-Stick' and 'Love' a
celebration of the sensuous beauty of women and of love:

  Lucía Martínez.
  Shade with red silk.
  Your thighs like the afternoon
  move from light to shadow.
  Hidden jet
  darkens your magnolia . . . (p. 326)

And in many of the *Gipsy Ballads* Lorca extols the rapture of
physical love:

  Not nard nor snail had ever
  Texture of skin so fine,
  Nor crystal in the moonlight
  Glimmered with purer shine:
  Her thighs slipped from beneath me
  Like little trout in fright
  Half chilly (but not frigid)
  Half full of shining light.[9] (p. 31)

Against the celebration of life's pleasures is placed the constant reality of death.[10] Thus in *Songs*:

  There were three.
  (The day came with the axes)
  There were two.
  (Skimming wings of silver)
  There was one.

There was none.
(The water was left exposed.) (p. 295)

In *Gipsy Ballads* and *Poet in New York* the theme of death is more and more insistent. Antoñito el Camborio, with skin 'of olive and jasmine', dies in the flower of his youth 'like a broken stalk of wheat'. In the New York poem 'Abandoned Church' *(Iglesia abandonada)* we read:

I had a son and his name was John.
I had a son.
One Friday he was lost in the archways of the dead.
(p. 410)

And in 'City without Sleep' *(Cuidad sin sueño)*:

Life is not a dream. Awaken! Awaken! Awaken!
We fall down the stairways to taste the damp earth . . .
(p. 421)

That terror of death that in *When Five Years Have Passed* is embodied in the hand that pushes the cat into the blackness of oblivion was a terror that for Lorca became an increasing obsession.

But if there is a theme that, more than any other, permeates this play, it is the theme of passing time, its importance indicated from the outset in the subtitle: *Legend of Time in Three Acts and Five Scenes.* Throughout the poems and the plays the idea of passing time is, of course, part of the theme of frustration, for the women to whom love never comes wait day after day, year after year, their looks fading, their hopes destroyed as life passes them by. Thus in one of the *Gipsy Ballads* Soledad Montoya is addressed by the poet:

What trouble is yours,
What terrible trouble!
You weep lemon juice,
Bitter-mouthed from the waiting.[11] (p. 32)

In the earlier 'Elegy' in *Book of Poems* the spinsters of Granada are left behind by the passing seasons:

You fade into the autumn mist, virgin
like Inés, Cecilia and sweet Clara,

a bacchante who would have danced,
crowned by green vine. (p. 131)

In a more general sense Juliet evokes in *The Public* time's
relentless and destructive march:

> The moon pushes gently the empty houses, brings about
> the fall of columns and offers to the grubs small torches to
> penetrate the cherries. The moon brings to the bedrooms
> the mask of meningitis, fills with icy water the bellies of
> pregnant women, and when I am inattentive throws
> handfuls of grass upon my shoulder.[12] (p. 91)

Here are the antecedents of all the many occasions in *When Five
Years Have Passed* when the characters are seen to be conscious
of passing time. In Act I the Friend seeks to enjoy in all its
intensity the pleasure of the present moment, for in that
moment the present becomes the past. The Second Friend
embodies the magic of childhood but feels already within him
the haunting presence of old age. The Young Man, the Old
Man, the Secretary, the Girl, all of them in their different ways
are poised in time on the journey that leads, as in the Young
Man's case, to death.

Finally, as in *The Public*, the characters of *When Five Years
Have Passed* are seen to be different facets of a single individual
or the personification of different attitudes towards a given
fact. The Friend, the Second Friend and the Old Man are
different facets of the Young Man, and their varying attitudes
towards the fact of passing time are his at different stages of his
life. Moreover, in them we see ourselves, and the play, like *The
Public*, is seen to be a mirror, the distance between stage and
auditorium bridged, for the characters' preoccupations with
love, passing time and death are also ours. If the themes of the
play are those of Lorca's other plays, the play itself, like those
which preceded and followed it, is equally an image which
projects the common concerns of men in general.

The title of the play reveals unambiguously its central concern
with time and, in addition, with time's passing. It points,
indeed, from a moment in the present to a moment in the

future, to five years hence when present dreams will have become present reality. Moreover, in evoking a world of dreams the play exposes its precariousness before the advance of time and suggests in doing so that what is true of the future is true of the present too, for the future is inevitably the present, the present the past, the whole a shifting process in which, in terms of illusions, the only certainty is disillusionment, and in terms of life the only certain end is death. It is a play which, in its concerns with and its power to condense in powerful and moving images those issues which are central to our lives, is amongst Lorca's most powerful statements.

The opening scene links the Young Man and the Old Man.[13] Both are seated, their immobility reflecting the way in which they are suspended in a world of dream and illusion. The blue pyjamas of the Young Man have in the grey coat of the Old Man a more muted form, the older man a faded version of the younger.[14] And their opening dialogue, presenting the theme of time, reveals between them much greater similarities than differences. The Young Man seeks to escape the present in a world of day-dream and illusion. He has kept the sweets to eat them later, for the illusion of their taste is better than the taste itself: 'I kept the sweets in order to eat them later.' (p. 956). Similarly, he indulges in the day-dream of his sweetheart and imagines her return in five years' time in a vision that, ignoring the short hair with which she went away, endows her with all the magic of romantic fantasy:[15]

> The fact is that I am in love, and I want to be in love, as much as she is in love with me, and so I can wait five years, hoping that one night, when the whole world is asleep, I can wind those tresses of light around my neck. (p. 960)

In his leaning towards illusion the Young Man is supported by the Old Man for whom memories of the past are intolerable: 'Yes, one must remember towards tomorrow.' (p. 957). Above all, their attempt to evade the present is symbolized in the way in which they strive to keep at bay the reality outside the silent house. The Young Man observes:

> Noise, always noise, dust, heat, bad smells. It annoys me

that things from the street enter my house. [*A long moaning is heard. Pause.*] Juan. Shut the window. (p. 959)

The constant presence of reality suggests, of course, the vulnerable nature of illusion, and, in conjunction with the musings of the Young Man and the Old Man, it manifests itself throughout the scene. Even as the Young Man speaks of the future – 'Towards tomorrow' (p. 957) – the clock strikes six, reminding us of the reality of the present and of passing time: [*A clock strikes six . . .*] (p. 957). Moreover, the Secretary who appears as the clock strikes represents an attitude very different from the Young Man's, for her love for him is of the present, a passion needing to be satisfied here and now:

> What explanation can I give? There is only one explanation and that is . . . that I love you. I can still feel that blood, alive like a red serpent, trembling between my breasts. (p. 965)

And she introduces too the characteristic Lorca note of anguish that is equally relevant to the Young Man's dream. The Secretary weeps throughout the scene because her love is rejected by the Young Man in favour of his idealized dream of love. But neither is he free from anguish, for, clinging to what he considers to be the safety of his dream, he is simultaneously aware that, for all its cocoon-like isolation, it is prone to change. The Old Man extols illusion in contrast to the things that change. The Young Man's words suggest, despite his faith in fantasy, that it too is vulnerable: 'Yes, yes. What we have within is still more alive, although it changes too.' (p. 962). Moreover, the house, the symbol of the isolated world of fantasy, is continually threatened – by encroaching weeds (p. 957), by the noise and bustle of the world outside (p. 959), by storms (p. 971).[16] Neither the reality of the present nor the illusion of things to come can escape the ruthless passage of time, change, and the anguish that change brings with it. The opening scene clearly expounds the familiar Lorca themes.

The appearance of the Friend repeats the theme of the present in another form. Like the Secretary he represents an attitude that is the opposite of the Young Man's. His entrance is dynamic – [*He appears causing a great commotion*] (p. 966) – and his actions, all movement and agitation, are a total contrast to the Young Man's dreaminess. The Friend lives only for the present, rushing about, downing cocktails, throwing himself around, flitting from one affair to another, impatient with the passive dreaming of the others. For him, indeed, time is too short: '. . . for I have no time.' (p. 967). And again: 'I have no time, I have no time for anything, everything rushes by.' (p. 967). But if he is the symbol of the present, he is also another illustration of the theme of change and passing time. Before he has properly experienced something, it has changed, and, seeking to defeat time, he discovers that he is defeated by it. If illusion is no safeguard against the ravages of time, neither is the desperate pursuit of pleasure in the present: 'The moment is gone already; it is horrible, always the same.' (p. 968).

The episode of the storm occupies a central position and a central significance in the Act. It is, in effect, the reality which the Friend welcomes and which the Young Man strives to keep at bay, though its advance upon the house is, like the passage of time itself, remorseless. The appearance of the Dead Child, his face waxen, and the Dead Cat bleeding from his wounds, though strange and dream-like, bathed in a blue light, is a nightmare whose connection with the real world and the play's predominant themes is very clear.[17] Firstly, the Dead Child is the child that the Young Man will never have, the symbol of the futility of all his dreams of love and marriage. And secondly, the Dead Child and the Dead Cat, like the Secretary, underline once more that Lorca theme of life's inevitable pain and anguish, of things passing and coming to an end. Their evocation of the joy of life, of the Dead Child's happy games (p. 975) and the Dead Cat's freedom and contentment (p. 974), dissolves before the terror of death that destroys everything. There is the Dead Child's anguished cry – 'I don't want them to bury me.' (p. 975) – and his horror of being eaten by the worms, its inescapability made more horrific by his touching but hopeless longing just to be alive: 'I want to be a child, a child!' (p. 977). The scene is one in which the darkness grows more intense and both the child and the cat are lost in it, seeking escape where there is none, until in a superbly dramatic and terrifying moment they are snatched away by a hand that appears from the darkness, the Dead Cat [*with anguish*] (p.979), the Dead Child despite his desperate cry: 'Don't bury me. Wait a few minutes ...' (p.979). The march of time ruthlessly destroys young and old, present joy and future dreams, and it is no accident that this intense and dramatic scene is witnessed by the Young Man, the Old Man, and the Friend, for the Dead Child's fate will be theirs too. Despite the differences symbolized in the fans they hold – the Young Man's blue, the Old Man's black, and the Friend's red (p.979) – they are individuals, or stages in life, linked to each other by their failure to escape the ravages of time. Indeed, the point that the horror of the Dead Child's death is a reality and not a dream is impressed upon them, and on us too, by the announcement of the servant: 'The child of the Porter's wife has died and they are going to bury him. His mother is crying.' (p.980). And the same is true of the Dead Cat: 'The children threw a cat they had killed onto the roof in the garden, and it has to be taken down.' (p.980).

The incident precipitates a confrontation between the Friend and the Old Man, sharpening their conflicting viewpoints. The Young Man gravitates towards the latter when he is suddenly confronted by another, entirely different attitude in the shape of the Second Friend. His dress – [*He is dressed in white . . . with great blue buttons*] (p.982) – is symbolic of the innocence and nostalgia of childhood and it links him too to the Young Man, suggesting that he represents the latter's childhood memories.[18] The 'five years' of the Young Man's waiting has, indeed, its opposite in the memories of the Second Friend when he was five years old: 'When I was five . . .' (p.983). And the woman who for the Young Man and the Friend takes on an idealized or an actual form is echoed in the childhood world of fantasy: '. . . one year I caught one of these little raindrop women and I kept her for two days in a fishbowl.' (p.983). But the characters are linked too in other ways that are significant. The Second Friend wishes, like the Dead Child, to remain young forever, insulated against the ruthess march of time, but he realizes that he cannot, for the Old Man

H

is there before him, a witness to life's passing, and he can already feel within himself the other stages that he must go through and the change that affects already his tender skin:

> But my face is mine and they are stealing it away from me. I was young and I used to sing, and now there is a man, a gentleman [*To the Old Man.*] like you, who is inside me with two or three masks ready. [*He takes out a mirror and looks at himself.*] (p. 985)

His gesture of despair – [*He covers his face with his hands*] (p. 985) – parallels the Young Man's earlier in the Act (p. 959), suggesting that for both of them, and for the Friend and the Old Man too there is no escape. Indeed, the Old Man dispells the illusion of past and present: 'Our clothes wear out, anchors rust and we move on . . .' (p. 985). He is reminded, in turn, that the passage of time brings him nearer to death and he withdraws, followed by the Young Man, before this onslaught upon the illusion of future happiness. As the Act draws to its conclusion, it portrays the Friend feverishly drinking, the Secretary longing for the Young Man, and the latter closing his eyes to her needs in favour of his dream of his sweetheart. As for the Second Friend, he is half asleep, dreaming of childhood. All of them in their different ways reflect different and conflicting attitudes to time's passing, but it is its passing that is significant, for the clock strikes six, linking the ending to the beginning of the Act, and the ticking of the clock is echoed too in the young Man's insistent drumming of his fingertips upon the table.

The setting for the second Act is the bedroom of the Bride, exotic and romantic, while she is beautifully dressed and superbly groomed: [*She has a long train and her hair is all curls.*] (p. 988). This is, it would appear, the Young Man's dream of his reunion with the Bride in five years' time, for the description of her accords with his vision of her and the scene has about it the quality of dream. Moreover, the figure of the Rugby Player, all masculinity and animation, the Friend in another form, is the Young Man's idealized vision of himself, and also his imagining of how the Bride would like to see him. The unfolding of the scene is, indeed, the dramatic representation of the Young Man's doubts about himself, of his capacity to measure up to the fantasy he has constructed. Inasmuch as the Rugby Player never speaks but only moves, lighting and extinguishing cigarettes, kissing and embracing the Bride passionately, he is the embodiment of fantasy rather than a real person.

The Bride herself, like the Secretary, voices the Lorca theme of passion. Her attraction to the Rugby Player is expressed in purely physical terms: 'What white heat, what marble fire leaps from your teeth!' (p. 989). In contrast she describes the Young Man's lifelessness:

> My lover had frozen teeth; he used to kiss me and his lips were covered with small, withered leaves. They were dry lips. (p. 989)

It is her view of him which, to the extent that it is also his imagining of how she sees him, seems a step in the process of his own increasing disillusionment with the world of fantasy that is his growing experience throughout this Act. She, indeed, echoing not merely the Secretary but the Friend too is the voice of reality that pricks the balloon of illusion.

The Bride's father, who escorts the Young Man into her presence, is another character who underlines the themes of passing time and change. The Bride's change of heart towards the Young Man means change and anguish for the Father too, for he has waited in anticipation for the wedding only for time to dash his hopes. His question is significant: 'What change is this?' (p. 999). As the Bride suggests in her reply, she is another person now. Moreover, the disappointment of the Father in relation to his daughter has its counterpart and parallel in his failure to see the eclipse that he has dreamed of seeing. Age has dimmed his sight – [*He shows signs of being somewhat myopic*] (p. 998) – his binoculars are useless to him, and for him, as for others, there is only the pain of a changed reality that passing time brings with it:

> Now the eclipse will begin. [*He goes to the balcony*]. They have put out the lights. [*With anguish*] It will be beautiful. I have been waiting for it for a long time. And now I cannot see it. (p. 1000)

The Father is, of course, what the Old Man was in Act I, and, in the sense that the young Man and the Old Man were closely linked in their illusion, the Father's disillusionment is here a prelude to the Young Man's.

The ensuing scene between the Bride and the Young Man is, indeed, the destruction of his dream of her. That he is still immersed in it is seen in his reference to her hair; for as he comes to her he comes with a vision of her not as she is but as he has imagined her:

> . . . while I was climbing the stairs, I remembered all the songs that I had forgotten and wanted to sing them all at once. [*He approaches the Bride*]. Your hair . . . (p. 1002)

The climbing of the stairs, an idea repeated later in the play, is itself suggestive of ascent from the world of reality to the rarified atmosphere of dream. As he embraces her, he embraces not the woman who has responded with passion to the Rugby Player but a delicate and fragile image fashioned in imagination, as unreal as the shape of the woman seen in the raindrop by the Second Friend:

> For I have waited for you and now I realize my dream. Your tresses are not a dream because I will fashion them with your hair, and your waist where the blood sings is not a dream, because it is my blood . . . (p. 1004)

The Bride's words, reminiscent of the Secretary's, expose the unreality of the Young Man's view of her: 'Leave me. You could have said anything but the word dream. One does not dream here. I do not want to dream . . .' (p. 1004). He is slowly disillusioned, his shattered dream symbolized in the fans with their romantic decorations that are now broken (pp. 1007-8). But his despair – [*He covers his face with his hands*] (p. 1005) – is again linked to that of the Second Friend in the previous Act (p. 985), repeats his own (p. 959), and is, indeed, that of the Father in the previous scene. Moreover, if the Bride seems secure in her rejection of the Young Man, she is in fact equally vulnerable, for the Rugby Player is no less an idealized vision of her lover than is the Young Man's of the Bride. Her dream must fade like his, changed by time, and it is no coincidence

that here, in the reference to the cat stoned by the children
(p. 1002), the idea of inevitable pain and anguish should be
repeated, for these are things that in the plays of Lorca are seen
to affect us all.[19]

The appearance of the Mannequin, the dummy that wears
the Bride's wedding-dress, introduces a brilliantly theatrical
and poetic scene that also marks a vital moment in the play. It
is a scene that has a haunting dream-like quality, created in
part by the figure itself that, like the dead child of Act I, comes
to life, in part by the blue light that floods the stage, echoing
the earlier scene: [*The stage grows dark. The lights held by the
angels take on a bluish hue . . .*] (p. 1009). Between the two
episodes there are clear links, for if the Dead Child symbolized
both the idea of life's inevitable anguish and the child that the
Young Man will never have, the Mannequin underlines both
themes. She enters sobbing – [*A moan is heard*] (p. 1009) – and
her words to the Young Man are the words of the person
whose dreams and illusions of happiness and fulfilment in the
present, like the Secretary's, are destroyed:

> . . . This silk yearns,
> thread by thread, strand by strand,
> for a mouth that is warm.
> And my petticoats wonder
> where are the warm hands
> that grip my waist. (p. 1011)

She is, of course, the Bride too who will dream uselessly of the
Rugby Player and be equally disillusioned. But more important here is her significance for and effect upon the Young
Man, for her accusations are his accusations against himself, a
voice that within him makes him aware of the folly of living
only for the future:

> . . . You are to blame.

> You could have been a loud whinny,
> but you were a sleeping pond,
> with dry leaves and moss
> where this dress rots. (p. 1011)

He is transformed from the dreamer who, as the consequence
of his inertia, has lost the Bride into someone who, through
the impact of the Mannequin, becomes aware that with the
Secretary he may still experience the reality of love and the
child, the flesh and blood that is the living symbol of that love.
He becomes more positive, a form both of the Friend and of the
Rugby Player:

> Before the red moon
> cleans with the blood of the eclipse
> its perfect curve,
> I will bring my wife, naked
> and trembling with love. (p. 1015)

And it is significant that, as he turns his back on illusion, the
dream-like light of the scene begins to disappear until it reverts
to normality: [. . . *the stage slowly takes on its normal light* . . . *The
light grows stronger.*] (p. 1015).

The Young Man's transformation and the beginning of his
search for the reality of love is accentuated as the Act concludes with the re-appearance of the Old Man. This symbol of
illusion and dream is now a broken, bleeding figure, wounded
and abandoned by the Young Man's change of attitude: '. . .
Oh, you have wounded me! Why did you come up? I knew
what would happen.' (p. 1016). The Young Man breaks the old
man's grip on him in a physical and spiritual sense and he is
left in anguish and despair, his cries unheeded: 'Wait! Wait!
Don't leave me hurt! Wait! Wait!' [*He goes out. His cries grow
faint.*] (p. 1017). He rushes out, searching for the Young Man.
But simultaneously the Father rushes in, searching for his
daughter:

> FATHER [*Entering.*]: Daughter! Where are you? Daughter!
> (p. 1016)

The Bride has run off, seeking happiness with the Rugby
Player, and the Young Man commences his search for the
Secretary and the enjoyment of love and passion in the
present: 'I will go too. I will look, like her, for the new flower of
my blood.' (p. 1017). They are different people seeking different things, but they seem linked more than separated by the

prophetic anguish of the Mannequin who weeps and faints as the curtain falls.

The final Act contains a symbolism that clearly anticipates Act III of *Blood Wedding*. [20] From the beginning there is the sense of human beings hemmed in, firstly by their physical surroundings – [*A Forest. Huge tree-trunks*] – and secondly by the strange, menacing, dehumanized figures that from the outset make their appearance:

> As the curtain rises two figures dressed in black pass amongst the tree-trunks, their faces the colour of plaster, their hands white too. Distant music can be heard. HARLEQUIN appears. He is dressed in black and green. He has two masks, one in each hand concealed behind his back. He moves in the visual manner of a dancer. (p. 1018)

Throughout the Act, moreover, the sounds of hunting-horns are heard, confirming the impression that human beings are the helpless prey of forces greater than themselves. The theme of the helplessness, the smallness, and the ultimate insignificance of the lives of men and women comes progressively to the fore.

The Harlequin's opening lines link time and illusion and suggest clearly that tomorrow is as painful as yesterday, the weeping child and the old man indistinguishable:

> Yesterday and tomorrow devour
> the dark flowers of pain.
>
> On the same column
> sleep and time are embraced,
> and the cry of the child is woven
> with the broken tongue of the old man. (p. 1018)

The Girl, seeking her lover, dreaming of love, is a form of all the other characters in the play who have their illusions:

> My lover waits for me
> at the bottom of the sea. (p. 1019)

But like them she is disillusioned, mocked, firstly by Harlequin and then by the nightmarish, death-like figure of the Clown:

[*There appears a magnificent* CLOWN, *covered in sequins. His powdered head suggests a skull. He laughs loudly.*] (p. 1021). Between
them they ridicule and frighten her, shatter her dreams, until
the girl who entered skipping and full of hope is reduced to
tears by their inhumanity. In the sense in which Harlequin and
the Clown suggest the circus – HARLEQUIN. [*Loudly and as
though he is in the circus.*] (p. 1021) –, human beings become
the helpless victims of their merciless and deadly clowning,
pawns in the grotesque game of life.[21]

It is no coincidence that the Girl's exit should become the
Secretary's entrance, for they are linked in several ways – by
their search for love and by their failure to realize their dreams.
Indeed, the Secretary, abandoning her earlier role, is now
what the Young Man was, waiting, dreaming of love in the
future. Her words repeat his: 'When I was small, I kept the
sweets in order to eat them later.' (p. 1027). And her vision of
her tall and curly-headed lover is very similar to the Young
Man's earlier fantasy of the Bride:

> If my friend were to come – so tall, with his hair curled,
> but curled in a special way – you will pretend not to know
> him. (p. 1027)

Furthermore, the Secretary is accompanied here by the Mask
who is to her what the Old Man was to the Young Man,
encouraging indulgence in a world of romantic dream, for she
recounts the story of her affair with Count Arthur of Italy and
of his constant search for her (p. 1026). We discover later that
it is he who has abandoned her, and to this extent her self-
deception and her disillusionment are a prelude to the Secretary's futile search. But here, significantly, the Young Man is
searching too, and his way is blocked by Harlequin and the
Clown:

> HARLEQUIN: You! You can't get through here.
> YOUNG MAN: Have they blocked the way? (p. 1029)

The way in which he cannot move in any direction and is, like
the girl, mocked by them, anticipates the fact that for him, as
for all the others, there will be no escape, no solution to his
seeking except in death.

The Young Man's encounter with the Secretary is significant in a variety of ways. As she is now what he once was, immersed in a world of dream and fantasy, so he has assumed her former role, and the Friend's too, seeking not the dream but the reality of love:

> I will bear you naked,
> withered flower and clean body,
> to the place where the silk dress
> is trembling with cold.
> White sheets await you.
> Let us go now, this very moment . . . (p. 1031)

But if their roles are ironically reversed, there is the added irony that for both of them the search, be it in illusion or reality, must be in vain, for both have been changed by time. At this point in the play, indeed, the scenario of Act I is vividly evoked again in the form of the small stage that stands in the centre of the main stage and whose curtains open to reveal the Young Man's library: [*The curtains of the theatre open and the library of Act I is seen, reduced in size and paler in colour.*] (p. 1033). In one way the reappearance of an earlier setting in which the characters have changed their roles underlines the point that beneath the surface things never change. The Young Man and the Secretary are the opposite of what they were but for both of them there is in store the anguish that is the only constant thing in our experience. As though to emphasise the point, the Dead Child of Act I appears again, a haunting image linking the Young Man and the Secretary in the futility of their different aspirations: [*The Dead Child crosses the small stage. He is alone and goes out through a door on the left.*] (p. 1035). And secondly, the miniature stage inevitably suggests, especially at this point in the play, both the smallness and the helplessness of the individuals concerned. It is an impression heightened by the appearance of Harlequin and the Clown as the scene concludes, for they mock the Young Man's disappointment, confuse him, manipulate him cruelly:

YOUNG MAN: [*In desperation, to the* CLOWN.]
   Where is the way out?

YOUNG MAN: [*Trembling.*]
  Show me the door.
CLOWN: [*Mocking, pointing to the left.*]
  That way.
HARLEQUIN: [*Pointing to the right.*]
  That way. (p. 1040)

The sense of total disorientation experienced by the Young Man is accompanied ominously as the curtain falls by the sound of Harlequin's violin that anticipates the final dance of death.

The setting for the play's final scene, returning to the setting of Act I – *The same library as in the first Act* (p. 1041) – suggests a circular movement, a sense of no escape. The Young Man has indulged in day-dreams of future happiness and exchanged them for the pursuit of happiness in the present. In both directions his journey has been in vain, nothing changes, he ends where he began, and the only certainty is the destruction of his dreams, symbolized in the broken figure of the Mannequin: [*On the left, the dress of a bride on a mannequin without head and hands.*] (p. 1041). He expresses his sense of helplessness in the image of the weather-cock blown at random by the wind: 'Does the weather-cock like to be whirled around as the wind pleases?' (p. 1043). The broken figure of the Mannequin also has a parallel in the Young Man's suit laid out like a corpse on the bed, a prelude to his own spiritual and physical death. For him there remains only one journey, the journey that in the end time imposes upon us all. Momentarily he seeks to avoid it by escaping, like the Second Friend, into childhood memories:

> Yes. The bed carved in walnut. I slept so well in it. I remember, as a child, seeing the huge moon rise behind the rail at the foot of the bed . . . Or was it through the balcony railing? I'm not sure. (p. 1044)

But there remains only the reality of death from which there is no escape and for which his suit and his shoes, ominously black, are already set out for him:

> YOUNG MAN: You will have put out my leather shoes.
> SERVANT: The ones with the black silk ribbon.

YOUNG MAN: Black . . . No . . . Look for another pair.
(p. 1045)

The Young Man is increasingly beset by alien forces and even
the house that was his refuge, the symbol of the apparent
safety of illusion, is no longer so, for the air is foul and un-
welcome plants encroach upon it:

> Can it be that in this house the air will always be thin? I
> am going to cut all the flowers in the garden, above all the
> accursed rosebay that climbs over the walls, and that
> weed that comes out on its own at midnight . . .

The final invaders are, significantly, the three Cardplayers,
the Fates, who in the end invade all our lives. They echo in the
black of their evening clothes all the other allusions to black
which, symbolic of old age and death, form a thread through
the play, and in the white of their capes the white suit and face
of the Dead Child and the white faces and hands of the
menacing figures who introduce Act III:

> [*The Cardplayers appear. There are three of them. They wear
> evening suits. They have long capes of white satin which reach
> their feet.*] (p. 1045)

There is about their manner and appearance a sense of ritual,
for the scene to be enacted is, after all, the ritual of death that
terminates the game of life. The words of the Servant, introducing the Cardplayers, suggest both the idea of life as a game
and the way in which individuals are the playthings of fate, of
life, of things outside themselves: 'These are the gentlemen
who have come to play.' (p. 1045). The game is, of course, one
in which the cards are stacked, the outcome inevitable, and
thus the drama of the card-game is one in which the Young
Man is increasingly stripped of his chances of winning. The
laughter of the Cardplayers punctuates the scene from time to
time, echoing the mocking laughter of Harlequin and the
Clown. As the cards are dealt there is a fine tension created by
the calling of the cards. And there is, too, a terrible sense of
inevitability in the progressively insistent tones of the three
Cardplayers:

> YOUNG MAN [*Joyfully*]: My turn. [*He throws a card on the table*].
> FIRST PLAYER [*Forcefully*]: Mine.
> SECOND PLAYER: Mine.
> THIRD PLAYER: Mine.

It is a rhythm that reaches its most dramatic point when they demand to see the Young Man's card and he, attempting desperately to stave off the final moment by offering them drinks, is compelled to reveal the ace of hearts, the symbol of love which in different forms he has sought and failed to find:

> THIRD PLAYER [*Forcefully*]: You must play.
> FIRST PLAYER [*Forcefully*]: You must give us your ace.
> SECOND PLAYER [*Forcefully*]: Because you must win or lose . . . Come. Your card. (p.1052)

In a superbly theatrical final moment an illuminated ace of hearts is projected on the bookshelves of the Young Man's library and the First Player, drawing his pistol, shoots it through. The Cardplayers, having completed their deadly mission, exit silently and the Young Man dies alone, his futile cries echoed only by his own voice. It is a moment which, as in other plays, leaves us with that bleak and pessimistic image of the ultimate loneliness and isolation of men and women. And it is appropriate that, as the Young Man dies and the curtain falls – his own last curtain – the clock should strike to remind us of the remorseless and destructive passage of time:

> [*The* YOUNG MAN *dies. The* SERVANT *enters with a lighted candlestick. The clock strikes twelve. Curtain.*] (p.1054)

Rafael Martínez Nadal has reached the conclusion that, notwithstanding the brilliant originality of *The Public*, *When Five Years Have Passed* is still an extremely daring and adventurous play:

> Though convinced that the extant version of this play is not the final one, it is easy to realize that, even in its present form, we are in the presence of one of the most original poetical dramas in the modern theatre.[22]

Let us consider this view of *When Five Years Have Passed* in relation to Lorca's handling of the different dramatic elements.

There are four stage settings in the play, one for Act I, one for Act II and two for Act III. Of the four sets, those for Act I and Act III, Scene Two, are the same, a room in the house of the Young Man, and the stage direction suggests that this is a relatively straightforward set, for we are merely told that the Young Man and the Old Man are seated in the library. The room, simply suggested, creates the framework within which the human characters and their different forms are set, and, since the action begins and ends with the same room, anchors the incidents of the play to a world which, despite its surrealist character, we recognize and with which we can identify.

In contrast, the setting for Act II suggests the world of dream and illusion:

> *A bedroom in the style of 1900. Strange furnishings. Great curtains full of folds and tassels. On the walls are painted clouds and angels. In the centre a bed with hangings and plumes. On the left, a dressing table supported by angels who hold electric lights in their hands. The windows are open and moonlight enters. A car horn blares furiously. The* BRIDE *leaps out of bed dressed in a magnificent dressing gown adorned with lace and rose-coloured bows. She has a long train and her hair is all curls.* (p. 988)

In many ways – the evocation of the bed with its hangings and of the Bride in all her finery – the set is reminiscent of the first scene of *Don Perlimplín*. But if it is reminiscent of the exaggerated style of farce, it is used here for a different end, its extravagance introducing the heightened world of illusion. The setting, for all its exaggeration, is not so much a frame within which the characters are ridiculed as one that sets the scene for the dreams of the Bride, the Rugby Player, the Mannequin and others.

From this exotic setting we move in Act III, Scene One, to its opposite, from a world of dream and fantasy to the frightening reality of the smallness and insignificance of human lives. The stage picture is now symbolic of this, for the great trees dominate the little theatre that is the stage of human life, and

dehumanized figures symbolize the hostile and powerful
forces that manipulate the lives of human beings:

> *A forest. Huge tree trunks. In the centre, a theatre surrounded
> by baroque curtains which are closed. A small staircase links the
> little theatre to the main stage. As the curtain rises two figures
> dressed in black pass amongst the tree trunks, their faces the
> colour of plaster, their hands white too. Distant music can be
> heard.* HARLEQUIN *appears. He is dressed in black and green.
> He has two masks, one in each hand concealed behind his back.
> He moves in the visual manner of a dancer.* (p. 1018)

The figures with white plaster faces are reminiscent of the
arresting and startling figures of *The Public*. In addition, the
figures, the setting of the wood and the sound of distant music
anticipate the symbolism of Act III, Scene One, of *Blood
Wedding*. The sets of *When Five Years Have Passed* point to
the conclusion that the play marks an important moment
of transition in Lorca's dramatic style. *The Public* had been
in many ways a critical point, a bold experiment. After it
Lorca seems to pause and reflect, and out of that reflection
comes *When Five Years Have Passed*, not a step backward in his
evolution as a dramatist, but, in its echoes of earlier plays and
styles and its anticipation of later ones, a step forward towards
Blood Wedding.

The influence of *The Public* is very clear in the highly visual
presentation of the characters.[23] At the beginning of the play
the Young Man in blue pyjamas and the Old Man, *dressed in a
grey coat, white bearded and with very large gold spectacles* (p. 955),
are stylized, visual images of the two extremes of youth and
old age. The Second Friend, a childhood form of the Young
Man, expresses through the dazzling whiteness of his suit,
with its matching gloves and shoes, all the magic and fantasy
of childhood (p. 982). In Act II the Bride, *in a magnificent
dressing gown adorned with lace and rose-coloured bows* (p. 988), is
the epitome of romantic love, and the Rugby Player *in knee-
pads and helmet* (p. 988) is the physical embodiment of her
dream of a virile, forceful man. As in *The Public*, the figures are,
through the stylization of costume and appearance, arresting
and self-explanatory images. In this respect, the most striking

and moving images are those that make us almost physically aware of the reality of pain, frustration and death. In Act I the Little Boy and the Cat appear, the child *dressed in white . . . his face the colour of wax . . . his lips like dry lilies*, the Cat *with two enormous stains of blood on its grey-white breast and on its head* (p. 971). In Act II the Mannequin *with her grey face and her eyebrows and lips painted in gold* (p. 1009) is a startling image of frustrated love, the visual effect heightened by the moonlight. In Act III the Clown's *powdered head suggests a skull* (p. 1021), and the three Cardplayers *in cloaks of white satin* (p. 1045) instantly convey the terrible and sinister proximity of death. In general, the visual impact of the figures of *When Five Years Have Passed* is no less powerful than in *The Public*. And just as there the effect is not of alienation but of establishing a relationship between the characters and the audience, so here these figures, for all their puppet-like appearance, move us emotionally, for in them we see paraded before us those issues to which we cannot be indifferent, for they are the things that affect us most and that lie at the very core of our existence – joy, love, sorrow, death. In both plays Lorca has succeeded in transforming the puppets of his early plays into figures that symbolize the key issues of human experience.

The visual impact of the play is greatly enhanced by Lorca's handling of the physical movements of the characters. If, for example, the Friend lives for the pleasure of the moment, his philosophy is conveyed at least as much in movement as in word. He enters *causing a great commotion* (p. 966). He whirls the Young Man around in his arms in a manner reminiscent of *The Shoemaker's Prodigious Wife*. He sits down, stretches out on the sofa, leaps up, throws himself down again, throws a cushion in the air, downs cocktails, the almost unbroken flow of physical action an eloquent statement of his restless pursuit of life's enjoyment. In Act II the virility of the Rugby Player is suggested entirely through action, for he has no dialogue. As the Friend downs cocktails, so the Rugby Player smokes cigars endlessly: [*He carries a bag full of cigars and he lights them and stubs them out without pause.*] (p. 988). When he embraces the Bride, he does so with enormous vigour and energy: [*. . . he suggests great vitality and embraces the Bride forcefully.*] (p. 989).

Movement and action, creating a figure larger than life, emphasize the extent to which this dynamic lover is a pure figment of the Bride's imagination, their meeting her dream of a longed-for moment in her life.

When Five Years Have Passed is, despite the liveliness of some of its figures, a play in which anguish and despair loom large. The expression of these moods and attitudes have, like their opposites, their own physical language. In Act I the Young Man *covers his face with his hands* (p. 959) in a gesture of despair. At the end of the Act the Second Friend, aware of the remorseless passage of time, repeats the gesture (p. 985). In Act II the Young Man covers his face as his dream of the Bride is shattered (p. 1005). The Young Man's despair is often suggested too by his immobility, for he is often seated, as in the opening sequence, or when the Friend makes his first ebullient appearance (p. 966). Similarly, at the end of Act I the Second Friend, as though paralyzed by fear, *sits on the sofa, with his legs drawn up*, a telling image of despair. At the end of Act II the Mannequin's anguish is embodied in her prostration on the sofa: [*She collapses and lies inert on the sofa.*] (p. 1017). And at regular intervals throughout the play the Secretary crosses the stage weeping, or is echoed in other characters like the Girl or the Mask of Act III, Scene One, their movement as expressive of their grief as any words they utter.

Finally, in their mechanical, puppet-like movements, the figures of Harlequin and the Clown in Act III suggest not only the inhuman forces that manipulate men's lives but also, in their jerking, exaggerated gestures, they mock the insignificance of human beings. In the initial stage-direction we read of Harlequin: [*He moves in the visual manner of a dancer.*] (p. 1018). Later, he accompanies the violin with jerking movements of his head: [*Harlequin plays a white violin that has two golden chords. It should be large and flat. He moves his head with the rhythm of the music*]. (p. 1022). In the episode when the Young Man tries to escape and cannot, Harlequin and the Clown express their pleasure by resorting to the farcical, clownish antics of the circus:

> CLOWN: [*He strikes Harlequin in the manner of the circus*]. (p. 1029)

Lorca, falling back on his experience of the puppet theatre, uses its techniques for ends that are more than merely humorous.

The dialogue of the play is in general less difficult and obscure than the language of *The Public*. Both plays, however, express ideas and there are occasions when, in *When Five Years Have Passed*, it is the apparently odd, incongruous, even contradictory nature of a statement that draws our attention to it. [24] In Act I the Old Man, rejecting the past and living only for the future, expresses his philosophy in an arresting paradox:

> OLD MAN: Alright. That is to say [*Lowering his voice*], one must remember, but remember beforehand.
>
> YOUNG MAN: Beforehand?
>
> OLD MAN: [*Slyly.*] Yes, one must remember towards tomorrow. (p. 957)

For the most part, on the other hand, the ideas are expressed in a language that is immediately accessible and that has both the evocative and emotional power of poetry. In Act I the Old Man speaks of the destructive effects of passing time in a manner reminiscent of the simplicity of expression of Juliet's observation in Scene III of *The Public*:

> Our clothes wear out, anchors rust and we move on . . .
> Houses crumble . . .
> Eyes grow dim and a sharp sickle cuts the rushes on the river bank. (p. 985)

All the inevitability and terror of passing time lies in the rhythm and the simple yet allusive nature of these lines. Similarly, the Old Man's attempt to keep alive illusion is suggested in two graphic metaphors:

> I have struggled all my life to light a light in the darkest places. And when someone has tried to wring the neck of a dove, I have stilled his hand and helped it to fly away. (p. 982)

In Act II the Bride, describing the Young Man's failure to arouse her, uses a simple yet evocative metaphor that anticipates Yerma's allusions to the dryness of her husband: 'My

I

lover had frozen teeth; he used to kiss me, and his lips were covered with small, withered leaves . . .' (p. 989). The difference between *When Five Years Have Passed* and *The Public*, as far as the dialogue is concerned, is that the former eliminates much of the difficulty but retains the power of the latter. In this sense it is a step along the way to the clear and powerful language of the rural tragedies.

The dialogue of the play expresses, of course, much more than ideas, for it is, along with costume and movement, the essence of a given character. In Act I the Friend's restless energy is conveyed to us by the sudden switches in direction of the dialogue:

> Who was that old man? A friend of yours? And where in the house do you have the pictures of the girls you sleep with? Look. [*He draws near.*] I'm going to take you by the lapels, I'm going to paint those cheeks of wax with rouge . . . (p. 966)

In contrast, the disjointed rhythm of the Second Friend's lines reflects his terror at the thought of passing time:

> But my face is mine and they are stealing it away from me. I was young and I used to sing, and now there is a man, a gentleman [*To the Old Man.*] like you, who is inside me with two or three masks ready. [*He takes out a mirror and looks at himself.*] But not yet, for I still see myself climbing the cherry trees . . . with that grey suit . . . A grey suit that had some silver anchors on it . . . Oh, God! (p. 985)

And in Act II the Bride's almost breathless ardour for the Rugby Player is communicated to us in the accumulative, repeated patterns of her dialogue:

> Because you are like a dragon. [*She embraces him.*] I think you will crush me in your arms, because I am weak, because I am small, because I am like frost, because I am like a small guitar burnt by the sun, but you do not crush me. (p. 989)

In his handling of dialogue Lorca reveals very clearly that

instinct for the right expression at the right moment which distinguishes his later plays.

There is also a movement away from *The Public* and towards *Blood Wedding* in the use of poetry at particularly dramatic or significant moments in the play. It is used first in the episode of the Dead Boy and the Dead Cat, an episode in which the preoccupations of the other characters with passing time and death are personified in a particularly intense and concentrated form in the two figures who appear before them. The beginning of the scene suggests in its sprightly rhythms and playful associations the joy of childhood:

> DEAD BOY [*Joyfully*]:
>   And I used to go, flat-nosed,
>   tin-nosed cat,
>   to eat blackberries and apples,
>   and afterwards to the church with the boys
>   to play . . . (pp. 974-75)

A clap of thunder changes the mood from gaiety to terror and anguish, expressed in insistent, repeated lines:

>   I don't want them to bury me.
>   Tinsel and glass adorns my coffin;
>   but I would rather sleep
>   in the reeds by the water.
>   I don't want them to bury me. (p. 975)

Or repeated negatives, denying all that symbolizes life, hammer home the inevitability of death:

>   Never will we see the light,
>   nor the clouds lifting away,
>   nor the crickets in the grass,
>   nor the wind like a sword. (p. 977)

The poetry of this central section of Act I, isolating it from the events concerning the principal characters, isolates it too as an episode of special significance, and in so doing, like a 'play-within-a-play', makes its meaning all the clearer to them.

In Act II poetry is used in the important scene involving the Mannequin. It is another episode in which the preoccupations

of the main characters are embodied in a figure who, separated
from the main action of the play, is a powerful image of its
meaning. All the yearning and frustration of the various
characters, and of the Bride in particular, acquires in the com-
pressed and concentrated form of poetry its most intense
expression. The question posed five times expresses all the
futility of a seeking that, despite its urgency, is fruitless:

> Who will wear my dress? Who will wear it?

> Who will wear the fine clothes
> of a bride dark and small? (pp. 1009-15)

Or the question assumes its indirect form:

> And my petticoats wonder
> where are the warm hands
> that grip my waist. (p. 1011)

Otherwise, all the disillusionment of dreams is contained in
the sustained juxtaposition of positive and negative:

> And underclothing becomes
> frozen with dark snow . . .

> And instead of a warm sound,
> a broken body of rain . . .

> You could have been a loud whinny,
> but you were a sleeping pond,
> with dry leaves and moss
> where this dress rots. (pp. 1010-11)

Density of image, rhythm, and the formal possibilities of
poetry create a powerful lyricism.

In Act III, Scene One, the opening section, presenting Harlequin and the Clown, is entirely in verse. Here, as in the final
Act of *Blood Wedding*, the action of the play is transposed to a
more symbolic level, and poetry creates not merely a greater
intensity of expression and feeling but also, through its allusive power, the sense of universality required at this point.
Harlequin's opening lines, switching rapidly from happiness
to sadness, capture in rhythm and image the two extremes of

human experience and condense it, as only poetry can, into concise but meaningful lines:

> On the same column,
> sleep and time are embraced,
> and the cry of the child is woven
> with the broken tongue of the old man. (p. 1018)

Similarly, in the poetic dialogue that follows, the Girl with her simple, child-like dream of love, mocked by Harlequin and the Clown, becomes symbolic of the disillusionment that awaits us all, the little scene another of those poetic 'play-within-a-play' techniques that Lorca uses so often here. Indeed, later in the Act the Young Man and the Secretary are seen to be the particular participants in the universal anguish expounded earlier, and their dialogue, in verse, captures all the intensity of their vain seeking that, stated on a symbolic level, acquires in them a moving poignancy:

> I will bear you naked,
> withered flower and clean body,
> to the place where the silk dress
> is trembling with cold.
> White sheets await you.
> Let us go now, this very moment,
> before the yellow nightingales
> moan in the branches. (p. 1031)

All the poetic passages in the play indicate that Lorca, having abandoned verse in *The Public*, returned to it with renewed enthusiasm, aware more than ever of its emotional and symbolic value in the theatre.

Lighting is often used, in conjunction with the play's poetic passages, to underline the significance of certain moments. When the Dead Boy and the Dead Cat appear, the lighting of the stage changes: [. . . *the blue light of a storm floods the stage* . . .] (p. 971). The blue light emphasizes both the atmosphere of unreality and dream and the eerie, sinister feeling of death's proximity and coldness, heightening in particular the whiteness of the child's clothes and the waxen colour of his face. As in other plays, blue is symbolic of death, and since it is sustained throughout the scene, it isolates the episode, fixes it in a frame that marks it off from what precedes and follows it. But, inasmuch as the child's death anticipates the fate of all the characters, the blue light from which they hide behind a screen will touch them too.

The stage direction at the beginning of Act II indicates that moonlight enters through the open windows: [... *The windows are open and moonlight enters* . . .] (p. 988). Together with the stylized appearance and movements of the characters, the lighting enhances the effect of dream, but since moonlight is also associated with death, it is a pointer here to the ultimate futility of dreams and illusions. Indeed, it is not long before the light assumes a bluish tone as the Bride lights a lamp: [*She lights the lamp hanging from the ceiling. The light is bluer than that which comes through the windows.*] (p. 990). It firmly links the scene and the figures in it to the earlier incident of the Dead Child and the Dead Cat. And again, later in the Act, the blue light accompanies the appearance of the Mannequin:

[. . . *The lights held by the angels take on a bluish hue. The moonlight enters again through the windows and grows stronger right to the end of the Act* . . .] (p. 1009)

Enveloping the Mannequin and the Young Man, it links them to the Dead Child and the Dead Cat and anticipates the death of their respective dreams. But they are only facets of other characters, and other characters facets of them – Young Man, Friend, Second Friend, Mannequin, Bride, Secretary, Girl – and in this respect all of them are touched by the blue light of death. As a linking element in the play, lighting is particularly effective, both underlining particular dramatic moments and drawing attention to their meaning.[25]

CHAPTER IV

BLOOD WEDDING
(BODAS DE SANGRE)

Blood Wedding, possibly the best known of Lorca's plays, is the first in the trilogy of rural tragedies written in the dramatist's last years. It was read by Lorca at the home of Carlos Morla Lynch on 17 September, 1932, and received its première on 8 March, 1933 at the Teatro Beatriz in Madrid.[1] Josefina Díaz de Artigas and her company were directed by Lorca himself, by now an experienced director with *La Barraca*, and the play was enthusiastically received by both the critics and the public who saw it as Lorca's most mature and powerful theatrical work to date.[2] Indeed, the acclaim given to the play in Spain heralded its success and Lorca's growing fame abroad. It was translated into French by Marcel Auclair and Jean Prevost, though its first French performance, at the Theatre de l'Atelier in Paris, did not take place until 1938, while in New York Irene Lewisohn sought the rights to an English translation and it received its first performance at the Lyceum Theatre in 1935.[3] In September 1933 Lorca was invited to attend a special performance of *Blood Wedding* in Buenos Aires where it was already a successful play. With Lola Membrives, who headed the cast, he collaborated in an outdoor production of the tragedy. The performance, together with the success of *Mariana Pineda* and *The Shoemaker's Prodigious Wife*, generated for Lorca a rapture and enthusiasm seldom received by a Spaniard in Latin America. For several months in Buenos Aires he was the subject of general adulation, engaging in a series of theatrical productions, interviews, lectures and literary parties. Before he returned to Spain in 1934, representatives of many of the Latin American republics paid homage to him, proclaiming him 'ambassador of Spanish culture to Latin

America'. It was the triumphant ending to a triumphant tour.[4]
Blood Wedding made Lorca famous, financially independent,
and, above all, more confident in his own abilities both as
dramatist and director.

In many ways *Blood Wedding* seems to mark a new point of
departure for Lorca in relation to his earlier plays. The experiments with the techniques of puppet theatre and farce and the
bold incursions into the realm of surrealism become here the
representation of a world that is more immediately recogniz-
able, more 'real' in the sense that its settings are Spanish
houses and villages and its characters people with whose
passions, for all their power, we can identify. It is, indeed, a
play which reflects to a large extent, through the medium of a
simple, direct and powerful plot, the reality of the narrow and
crushing forces of honour and tradition that, heightened in
rural areas, were nevertheless characteristic of Spanish society
in general. One source of the play, was, indeed, a real incident
described in a Granada newspaper years before the composition of the play. Francisco García Lorca has given the following
account:

> Before *Blood Wedding* was a play, it was a short news-
> paper account in *El Defensor de Granada*, one of the local
> papers. I remember Federico reading to me an account of
> a bride from Almería who, on her wedding day, ran off
> with her former lover. The bridegroom followed them
> and the two men killed each other . . . Apparently, after
> this, the newspaper account was forgotten; yet some
> time later Federico told me of an idea he had for a tragedy
> – it was based on the incident in Almería. Then, for some
> time, the play would seem to have been forgotten again.
> This process of letting a play write itself was my brother's
> method. He never consciously wrote down a play's out-
> line.[5]

But elsewhere he has also shown how, over a period of time,
the real events and characters of the newspaper report were
transformed into an essentially poetic vision, and that, far
from being a 'realistic' play, divorced from his earlier work,
Blood Wedding is, in fact, the culmination of it:

In *Blood Wedding* there is a palpable . . . intention of taking
the play's atmosphere away from any nature of a newspaper story. From the field of the very human passions of
concrete beings he removes to an unreal world, one in
which the appearances of the mysterious and fantastic
players (as in the personification of the Moon and Death)
are possible. Then he makes the flesh and blood characters rise to a plane less real, one which converts them into
forces whose incentives are outside themselves. . . . They
have moved away from the newspaper account from
which they came but have gained in human and poetic
significance. They have been converted into anonymous
beings who possess a country's generic character, who
are opposed by a tragic personage, their fate, and who
are led by this fate among songs and premonitions
toward death . . .

Thus there is a greater abundance of poetic themes in
this work; the turning to verse in climactic situations is
frequent. Even more: the moments of the play's greatest
dramatic intensity are in verse . . .

To some critics this is the play which best achieves an
integration of poetry and drama. It is the most spontaneous and simple because the poet does not struggle
against his poetic instinct; he gives himself over to it, but
without forgetfulness of his previous experiences.[6]

If a real event provided an outline for the action of the play,
its poetic elements have their roots in other, more important
sources, notably in Lorca's own poetry and drama and in the
poetic drama of Spain's Golden Age with which he was so
familiar. In his *Poem of Deep Song (Poema del Cante Jondo)*, its
individual poems written in the 1920s and published as a
volume in 1931, the themes of fate and death are already
presented in a powerfully dramatic form, and two poems in
particular anticipate scenes in *Blood Wedding*. The first of these,
'Dialogue of the Bitter One' *(Diálogo del Amargo)*, is, as its title
suggests, a dramatic dialogue, a play in miniature, in which
Amargo, journeying at night to Granada, is met on the road by
a mysterious rider. Amargo has begun to sing a song about

death and Death, in the form of the rider, suddenly appears. She invites him to ride with her, tells him of her three brothers who sell knives, he is persuaded to go with her, she offers him a knife, and his death-cry chillingly ends the poem. The poem that follows, 'Song of the Mother of the Bitter One' (*Canción de la madre del Amargo*), is the mother's lament for her dead son:

> They bear him in a sheet,
> rosebay and palm.
> On the twenty seventh of August
> with a little knife of gold.
> The cross. Let us go.
> He was dark and bitter.
> Neighbours, give me a jar
> of brass with lemonade.
> The cross. Let no one weep.
> Amargo is with the moon.[7] (pp. 269-70)

In the last scene of *Blood Wedding* the Mother laments the death of her son in the following lines:

> Let them put on your breast
> the cross of bitter rosebay;
> and over you a sheet
> of shining silk . . .

Leonardo's wife continues:

> Ay-y-y, four gallant boys
> come with tired shoulders!

The bride:

> Ay-y-y, four gallant boys
> carry death on high!

And the mother again:

> It's the same thing.
> Always the cross, the cross.
>
> Neighbours: with a knife,
> with a little knife,
> on their appointed day, between two and three
> . . . (pp. 94-5)

The general situation, particular words and phrases and the emotional impact of the incident reveal that an episode of *Blood Wedding* already had an antecedent in poems written seven years earlier.[8] Similarly, in many of the poems in *Gipsy Ballads* the themes of love and death, passion and destruction, and the motifs of the horse and the moon, are prominent and their treatment highly dramatic. The sensuality of 'The Unfaithful Married Woman' *(La casada infiel)*, the dead girl illuminated by moonlight in 'Somnambulistic Ballad' *(Romance sonámbulo)*, the lament in 'The Death of Antonito el Camborio' *(Muerte de Antoñito el Camborio)*, anticipate elements of *Blood Wedding*. The dramatic nature and the thematic significance of the *Gipsy Ballads* have been aptly described by L. R. Lind:

> Perhaps the most remarkable characteristic of the *Gipsy Ballads* is the powerful sense of life they give forth. The moods each one creates arise from an intense feeling for the major phases of existence, love and death, which is without parallel in modern Spanish literature . . .[9]

When we turn from Lorca's poetry to his earlier plays, it is clear that many of the themes of *Blood Wedding* have an antecedent there. The theme of passion was expressed to some extent in the figure of Curianito in *The Butterfly's Evil Spell*, in the heroine of *Mariana Pineda*, and in the passionate Belisa of *The Love of Don Perlimplín*. But it is in *When Five Years Have Passed* that the theme is stated with greatest power, in the figure of the Secretary who longs for the Young Man, the Bride who sees in the Rugby Player the ideal of virility, and the Rugby Player himself who embraces her passionately, breathing smoke in her face, 'like a dragon'. Here, more than anywhere, are the earlier versions of the Bride and Leonardo of *Blood Wedding*.

The theme of frustration, so often connected with the theme of love in Lorca's writings, is, logically enough, reflected in the same characters. Thus, Curianito, Mariana Pineda, and the Secretary of the plays mentioned above are victims of love's frustration. In *The Public* Juliet expresses the theme too, but of the plays which preceded *Blood Wedding* it is clearly *When Five Years Have Passed* which develops this typical Lorca theme with the greatest consistency. The Secretary, the Mannequin, the Young Girl all have a dream of love's fulfilment which is never realized, while the Young Man, the Friend, the Second Friend, and others with them, see their hopes and ambitions ruthlessly destroyed.

Another variation on the theme of love, its frustration by death, is central to the whole of Lorca's drama. Curianito and Mariana Pineda die at the end of the plays in question, Juliet in *The Public* voices the theme of love overtaken by death, and at the end of the play the Director is confronted by death, the end of everything, in the form of the Juggler. Here, indeed, is an antecedent of the figure of Death in the final Act of *Blood Wedding*, but it is again *When Five Years Have Passed* which best anticipates this play, for in the terrible figures of Harlequin and the Clown and the three Cardplayers who pay the Young Man the fateful visit, the doom-laden final Act of *Blood Wedding* has a clear precedent.

As far as the influence of the theatre of Spains's Golden Age is concerned, *Blood Wedding* bears the particular imprint of Lope de Vega, and it is interesting to note in this connection that Lope's *The Sheep Well (Fuenteovejuna)* and *The Knight from Olmedo (El caballero de Olmedo)* were in the repertory of *La Barraca* and were directed by Lorca himself.[10] In the final Act of *The Knight of Olmedo* the protagonist, Don Alonso, travels at night along a road lined by trees and hears approaching, intoned by a mysterious stranger, the ominous refrain that tells of his imminent death:

> SINGER: They killed him in the darkness,
>   The noble knight,
>   The glory of Medina,
>   The flower of Olmedo.
>
>   Shades warned him
>   He should not go,
>   They counseled him
>   He should not go,
>   The noble knight,
>   The glory of Medina,
>   The flower of Olmedo.[11] (pp. 221-2)

In writing the first scene of his own third Act Lorca may well have been reminded of Lope's play, of the ominous atmosphere of the wood and of the song of the peasant that seems to be echoed in his own woodcutters. In any case there can be no doubt that the songs and dances that announce and celebrate the wedding in Act II, as well as the atmosphere of rural life that impregnates the play, belong to a tradition of Spanish drama of which Lope, above all, had been the greatest exponent. In *Peribáñez* the flavour of country life and, in particular, the songs and dances that accompany the wedding of Casilda and Peribáñez are highly reminiscent of similar elements in Lorca's play. It seems clear enough that the influence of Lope, in general if not in particular, was very strong. It is worth noting, too, that in *Blood Wedding*, to a greater extent than in the plays that followed it, Lorca, like Lope in so many of his plays, has no clear-cut protagonist but a number of important characters amongst whom the focus of attention is fairly evenly divided.

Ramón del Valle-Inclán had influenced Lorca's puppet farces but there are also elements in his tragic plays which may have an echo in *Blood Wedding*. In a short piece entitled *Tragedy of Illusion (Tragedia de ensueño)*, which Lorca undoubtedly knew, a Grandmother laments her dead sons:

> I had seven sons and my hands have sewn seven shrouds . . . One by one death has deprived me of the sustenance of my old age. My eyes do not weary yet of weeping for them. They were seven kings, young and handsome![12]

Similarly, in *The Bewitched (El embrujado)* Don Pedro Bolaño has lost his own sons and, at the end of the play, laments the death of the boy presumed to be his grandson while he is left to face old age alone. His cry – 'He was the flower of the land!' – once more reminds us of the Mother's anguish in Lorca's play:

> A sunflower to your mother,
> a mirror of the earth. (p. 94)

The parallels are at least suggestive.

Much has been made of the influence on *Blood Wedding* of Ibsen's *Peer Gynt* and Synge's *Riders to the Sea*. In the first of

Peer Gynt's five long Acts there is, of course, a scene in which, just after the wedding, Peer abducts the bride, Ingrid, while the beginning of the second Act focuses on their flight into the mountains and their conflicting emotions. In *Riders to the Sea* there is the figure of the mother who grieves the death at sea of her husband and her six sons and, throughout the play, that sense of the closeness of men and women to the world of Nature which is so prominent in Lorca's play. He may well have known both plays, in translation if not in the original, and it is interesting to note that *Riders to the Sea* had been translated into Spanish by no less a figure that Juan Ramón Jiménez.[13] The extent of the influence of such works is in the end, however, a matter of conjecture, for the real sources of *Blood Wedding* lie much closer at hand, in Lorca's own work, in his own land, and in the Spanish dramatic tradition.

A general influence that must also be mentioned is that of Greek tragedy. Some critics have, to a considerable degree, seen in the various elements of the play a clear Aristotelian pattern.[14] To this extent it meets the requirement that, to awaken the tragic emotions of pity and terror, the characters who suffer should be close to each other. Secondly, the catastrophe that overtakes the Mother and the Bride may, in Aristotle's terms, be attributed to their 'error', the Mother's residing in her persistent hatred of the Félix family which, in effect, makes her drive her one remaining son to an attempted vengeance that brings about his death, the Bride's in her marrying a man she does not love. Thirdly, inasmuch as the Mother brings about the opposite of what she seeks there is the 'reversal of intention' of Greek tragedy, and in her understanding of the Bride's contribution to the death of her son the Greek 'recognition'. The ultimate anguish and solitude of the Mother and the Bride, more than the deaths of the two men, awaken pity and terror. In the figures of the Moon, Death, the girls who, like the Fates, unwind and cut the thread of life, we have the equivalent of the Greek *Deus ex Machina*, the supernatural forces that intervene in human lives. And, finally, in the dirge-like pronouncements of the Woodcutters, the song of the three girls, and the final lamentations of the Mother, the Bride, Leonardo's wife, and the Neighbours, there are clear

echoes of the Greek Chorus. One might say, as a general conclusion, that Lorca, like any educated dramatist, was familiar
with the character of Greek tragic drama and that its influence
is evident in *Blood Wedding*, but it would be as wrong to over-
state that influence as to underestimate the expression in the
play of the concern with fate, with passion, with sorrow and
death that is peculiarly Andalusian.

The title of the play contains a striking element of paradox that
captures the essence of the contrary and contrasting movements of its action.[15] The wedding is suggestive of everything
creative and harmonious, of man and woman, of families
joined together in love, joy and celebration, and of their continuity in and through their children. Blood, on the other
hand, evokes the opposite of all these things: violence, death,
destruction, men and women, individually or collectively, set
against each other, and the bitter grief and anguish that are the
outcome of such conflict. The paradoxical nature of the title
suggests, indeed, the paradox of life itself which is precisely a
composite of things perpetually in opposition to each other.
But in the order of the words in Spanish – *Wedding of Blood* –
there is too a logical, deliberate progression from one set of
implications to another that, embodied in the principal characters and actions of the play, anticipates its movement from
harmony to chaos, from hope and aspiration to despair.
Furthermore, the words of the title evoke an attraction of
men and women to each other that is purely instinctive and
irrational, a marriage of the blood and of natural passion in
contrast to all that is traditional and arranged. It anticipates,
indeed, the power of instinct that in this play is a permanent
link between mankind and the natural world of which he is a
part, and which is reflected in all the major characters. The title
of the play is, then, a pointer to its predominant direction and
to the impulses that lead in that direction. And it catches too,
in its unexpectedness, the disquieting, ominous, almost
inevitable note of doom that, inherent in the play from its
beginning, progressively descends upon it.
    The opening sequence, in its powerful presentation of the
Mother, announces clearly a characteristic Lorca theme. Fail-

ing to escape the force of the feelings that oppress her, she anticipates already all the other characters – the Bridegroom, the Bride, Leonardo – who become progressively the victims of their passions. For her, as for them, her life is something that is ultimately ruled by instinct. Secondly, the theme of instinct and of Man as part of Nature's instinctive processes is reinforced early in the play by the insistence on the close proximity of Man and Nature, a relationship that distinguishes all the rural tragedies and that here is soon extended to all the other characters. The Mother expresses her deepest feelings in terms of Nature. Her husband had for her the scent of a carnation, her son the strength of a bull:[16]

> First your father; to me he smelled like a carnation . . .
> Oh, is it right – how can it be – that a small thing like a
> knife or a pistol can finish off a man – a bull of a man?
> (p. 34)

They are people who, close to the soil, are attuned to the world around them and reflect its impulses. Their lives, like the lives of animals and crops, are shown to respond to deep, instinctive patterns, and their own particular concerns with love, birth, death, are set within a broader context. And thirdly, inasmuch as Nature's patterns are inevitable, its creatures the instruments of blind and remorseless processes, so it is implied that in human lives there are movements that suggest a doomed inevitability.[17] The Mother's past will, in the course of events, become her future, her husband's death repeated in her son's. Between the beginning of the play and its conclusion there is a striking parallel, and, in between, a relentless movement of events towards a given end that conveys the sense of things determined in advance. Moreover, the Mother's experience is reflected elsewhere, in the Neighbour's. She too has lost a son, and their experience has a further parallel in the anguish of another neighbour: '. . . Two days ago they brought in my neighbour's son with both arms sliced off by the machine.' (p. 37). For them and for others the suffering of life is seen to be cyclic and inescapable. And the conclusion of the scene fixes more deeply in our minds the sense of no escape. As the Neighbour informs the Mother of the Bride's earlier association with the Félix family, she seems inexorably hounded by events, the horror of the past repeated in the present. Feelings of revulsion overwhelm her. Outside the heat relentlessly besieges her: 'Have you ever known such a hot sun?' (p. 39). As the curtain falls she is a lonely, solitary, isolated figure. But she is too, in a way that is characteristic of all Lorca's major plays, the symbol of an isolation and a helplessness that are also common to all the other major characters and that, expressed through them, become an increasingly insistent theme. The dark, brooding mood suggested visually in the black of the Mother's dress and echoed in the Neighbour's, suggests the sad and melancholy fate of other, innumerable Andalusian women, and, beyond them, of women as a whole. And the Mother's house with its bilious walls which are the silent, unfeeling witness of her solitary weeping, becomes an image of all the other bitter, empty, lifeless houses where women – and men too – will weep alone.

The lullaby that opens the second scene is theatrically effective, but it has, too, a clear symbolic and thematic meaning. It suggests the violence and pain of life of which the child is so far ignorant but to which he must grow up. Indeed, inasmuch as within the lullaby itself there is a violent transition from the flesh tints of the baby to the darker, more sinister splash of blood, the child seems already part of a harsher world. And the 'silvery dagger' in the horse's eyes, in conjunction with its bleeding legs, menacingly evokes the adult world, the loves, hatreds and violent conflicts of which the Mother's husband has already been a victim. As the lullaby ends and our attention moves to the lives and relationships of the Wife, Leonardo and the Mother-in-Law, the implications of the lullaby are transformed into the reality of their existence. Their conversation embraces, on the one hand, the ordinary domestic things that are their day-to-day concerns, but throughout the scene there is a growing, unavoidable tension that disrupts the initial mood of domesticity. The Wife is haunted by constant doubts concerning Leonardo and he is strangely agitated. In their different ways they are disturbed, the moments of happiness and tenderness destroyed by the continuing presence in their lives of the Bride, Leonardo's former sweetheart and the

K

Bridegroom's intended bride. By the conclusion of the scene
the mood of optimism has been dispelled completely and its
characters, far from being different from the Mother in their
capacity to escape life's pain and anguish, are seen to be
engulfed by it. The way in which the Bride links them all and is
a common factor in their lives establishes, in fact, that closer,
more fundamental bond between them that is all to do with
their common humanity and its inherent suffering. There is a
gradual transition through the scene to the point where the
Wife and the Mother-in-Law are, in effect, the Mother in
another form, her earlier grief now theirs:

> MOTHER-IN-LAW [*Weeping*]: My baby is sleeping . . .
> WIFE [*Weeping, as she slowly moves closer*]: My baby is rest-
>   ing . . .(p. 46)

And the theme of inevitable pain is expressed too in the figure
of the Girl whose pleasure in the description of the Bride's
wedding gifts is destroyed by Leonardo's sudden anger.
Young girl, young wife, two widows, embracing a lifetime of
experience, are, for all their differences, fused into a single
pessimistic image.

The third scene, set in the home of the Bride and her Father,
parallels initially the optimistic beginning of Scene Two.
Splashes of rose enliven the white walls and fans, jars and
mirrors add gaiety to the scene:[18]

> At the back is a cross of large rose-coloured flowers. The round
> doors have lace curtains with rose-coloured ties. Around the
> walls, which are of a white and hard material, are round fans,
> blue jars and little mirrors. (p. 47)

The simple splendour of the home reflects the constructive
efforts and instincts of the Father, and of others like him, to
fashion something of his life. He refers with pride to his
conquest of a land that was unyielding:

> When I was young this land didn't even grow hemp.
> We've had to punish it, even weep over it, to make it give
> us anything useful. (p. 48)

Earlier, the Mother, observing the parched landscape, has
suggested what her husband would have made of it:

MOTHER: Your father would have covered it with trees. (p. 47)

The parents symbolize the concern with land, property and money which, in rural communities in particular, is the deep and continuing expression of individual achievement and identity, and which, passing from one generation to another, is a comforting assurance of continuity. Thus, for the Mother marriage is a husband, children, property: 'A man, some children, and a wall two yards thick . . .' (p. 50). For the Father the greatest joy is to see the respective lands joined together:

> What's mine is hers and what's yours is his. That's why. Just to see it all together. How beautiful it is to bring things together. (p. 48)

To this extent the Mother and the Father are the voices of age-old instincts and traditions. Coming together to arrange the marriage of their children, they convey the sense of a parent's ambitions for himself and for his children achieved within a social framework, of which, especially for a conservative and Catholic Spain, marriage is the symbol and the sustenance.[19] The scene is, indeed, marked by its formality and sense of ritual. The Mother and the Bridegroom wear their finest clothes. They are greeted with ceremony by the Father:

> [*The* BRIDE'S FATHER*enters. He is very old, with shining white hair. His head is bowed. The* MOTHER *and the* BRIDEGROOM *rise. They shake hands in silence.*] (p. 48)

The exchange of gifts, the correctness of the conversation, all the mannered and formal aspects of the encounter call attention to it as the performance of a social rite.

In contrast, the conclusion of the scene pinpoints again the theme of passion. The Bride, alone with the Servant, reveals that her real feelings lie with Leonardo, and, as she does so, all the formality that has gone before is dramatically thrown aside. For her the only reality is her continuing desire for Leonardo. But in this respect she is no different from the Mother whose obsessive grief for her husband overwhelms her constantly, or from Leonardo who is continually haunted by the Bride's memory. The first three scenes illustrate, in effect, the clash between the demands of passion, which seeks to satisfy itself, and society, in the interests of which men must subordinate their instincts. The clash is, moreover, progressively one-sided in its outcome. In Scene I the Mother attempts to dominate her feelings, accepting the Neighbour's advice that her son's happiness is more important. In Scene Two Leonardo, though tormented by his passion for the Bride, seeks to assert instead his duty towards his wife and child. In Scene Three the Bride strives to conform to her father's wishes for her marriage to the Bridegroom: 'I'm happy. I've said "yes" because I wanted to.' (p. 50). All of them seek to deny their natures in the interests of a greater good, but of the three only the Mother is in any way successful, her fears yielding to resigned acceptance. Leonardo and the Bride confirm, in contrast, the unmitigating rule of passion and personify the clash between the individual and society that in Lorca's rural tragedies is its outcome. The Act is a movement towards individual and collective harmony, but it is also, disturbingly, a movement away from it. The Father and the Mother, for all their good intentions, cannot in the end contend with the passions that, disrupting already the lives of Leonardo and the Bride, will soon disrupt the lives of others, and the social striving of the Act becomes the spectacle of individuals divided within themselves and from each other. There exists for the Bride only the dark, chaotic world of her longing for Leonardo, its growing, suffocating hold upon her caught and expressed in the descent of night as the Act concludes.

The sense of isolation and enclosure dominates the beginning of the second Act. The exchanges between the Bride and the Servant evoke a world in which there is no escape from Nature's tyranny. At night the heat is suffocating:

BRIDE: It's too warm to stay in there. (p. 53)

The dawn brings no relief. The land in which these people live is harsh and inhospitable, a place where crops and individuals wither and die, and where the fate of one is the fate of another, and no one will be spared:

BRIDE: As we're all wasting away here. The very walls give off heat. (p. 53)

We are presented here, as elsewhere in Lorca's rural plays, with a vision of men and women set in a hostile world and subjected to Nature's unrelenting domination.[20] And if there are suggestions of a different world – the land from which the Bride's mother came, the fertile vineyards of the Bridegroom – it is the harsh, oppressive landscape of the beginning of this second Act that becomes the focal image, the central, dominating landscape of the play. The other, more comfortable areas of experience are left progressively behind. The Bridegroom's journey takes him into the burning, destructive heat of 'the wastelands' and the Mother and Leonardo are, metaphorically, his companions. There is conveyed to us quickly and intensely both the particular and the more general sense of human beings beset by forces that are alien and irresistible.

From the theme of Nature's broader, external tyranny, we move immediately to its inner counterpart: the tyranny of passion. The Servant's words evoke the reality of physical love: 'Oh, lucky you – going to put your arms around a man; and kiss him; and feel his weight.' (p. 53). On one level the scene presents the surface appearance of marriage, its traditional image reflected in the ritual of all the elaborate preparations – the dressing of the bride, the combing of her hair, the choice of appropriate flowers. In contrast, the Servant's words expose the reality beneath it:

> But, child! What is a wedding? A wedding is just that and nothing more. Is it the sweets – or the bouquets of flowers? No. It's a shining bed and a man and a woman. (p. 54)

And it is this to which the Bride increasingly, and despite herself, responds, though not in relation to the Bridegroom. On the one hand, the theme of parental and social obligation is steadily developed, for the Bride herself acknowledges both the necessity of obedience and the truth of her love of the Bridegroom:

SERVANT: You love your sweetheart, don't you?
BRIDE: I love him.
SERVANT: Yes, yes. I'm sure you do.
BRIDE: But this is a very serious step.

SERVANT: You've got to take it.
BRIDE: I've already given my word. (p. 54)

To this extent she is part of the positive, affirmative movement
of the play. Indeed, as the Servant begins to intone the song
in celebration of the bride and the wedding that will grow in
its insistence as the scene unfolds, there appears to open up
a whole new world of hope and optimism, caught in the
allusions of the song to the morning, the flowing rivers, the
flowering laurel:

> Awake, O Bride, awaken,
> On your wedding morning waken!
> The world's rivers may all
> Bear along your bridal Crown!
>
> Awake,
> with the fresh bouquet
> of flowering laurel.
> Awake,
> by the trunk and branch
> of the laurels! (p. 55)

The song, with its fertility associations, sets in motion the
theme of love and marriage as part of the harmony of the
universe, of men and women fused into the pattern of creation.

This positive direction, no sooner stated, is confronted by a
second, more powerful statement of the theme of passion,
exemplified in Leonardo. He arrives at the Bride's house, and
what for her was the image of passion etched by the Servant's
words becomes the unavoidable fact of Leonardo's presence.
The positive momentum of the Act dissolves before the spectacle of human beings and human passions which, far from
being part of a greater social and cosmic harmony, suggest its
discord. Leonardo and the Bride, despite their efforts to set
aside their feeling for each other, discover that they cannot do
so. The horse has been mentioned in Act I by Leonardo's
mother-in-law:

Well! Who's been racing the horse that way? He's down

there, worn out, his eyes popping from their sockets as
though he's come from the ends of the earth. (p. 43)

The frenzied beast, driven against its will, is an eloquent if
traditional symbol of the instinctive force that equally drives
Leonardo, negating his will, to the object of his instinctive
seeking. There is, indeed, in this characteristic Lorca vision of
things that terrible, destructive power that is everywhere part
of the tension of the natural world.

Against this, the refrain intoned by the Servant draws
nearer as the wedding guests approach, bringing to the fore
the theme of creative and collective harmony:

VOICES: Awake, O Bride, awaken,
On your wedding morning waken! (p. 56)

It slowly envelops Leonardo and the Bride, weaving around
them its positive and optimistic rhythms:

[VOICES *are heard singing, nearer.*]
VOICES: Awake, O Bride awaken,
On your wedding morning waken! (p. 58)

Even in them there are impulses that are affirmative, for the
Bride asserts her self-respect and her duty to her husband, and
Leonardo, for all his bitterness, vows that he will never speak
to her again. In one way they are driven apart, their hostility
towards each other paradoxically healing and creative. But, in
contrast, Leonardo states once more the essence of the
immovable force that, denying the existence of all else, links
him inexplicably to the Bride:

What good was pride to me – and not seeing you, and
letting you lie awake night after night? No good! It only
served to bring the fire down on me! You think that time
heals and walls hide things, but it isn't true, it isn't true!
When things get that deep inside you there isn't anybody
can change them. (p. 57)

His violent outburst encapsulates the illogical yet undeniable
reality, the core of passion that, deep within his being, no one
can eradicate. And it has its counterpart in the Bride who

responds to Leonardo's words as though her reason and her will were nothing:

> I can't listen to you. I can't listen to your voice. It's as though I'd drunk a bottle of anise and fallen asleep wrapped in a quilt of roses. It pulls me along, and I know I'm drowning – but I go on down. (pp. 57-8)

They are, as the scene unfolds, less individuals than the helpless and pitiful pawns of Nature's violence.

The conclusion of the scene transforms its disruptive elements into a hymn of joy, an incantation and celebration of all that in life is vital and creative. The darkness of night that accompanies Leonardo's visit and is the symbol of his passion becomes the radiance of the dawn: [*Day begins to break.*] (p. 58). And the dawn in turn announces the awakening to a new life of the bridal pair. In the songs that precede the Bride's appearance are contained images of bursting, flourishing life and of Nature's vitality:

> FIRST GIRL [*Entering*]:
> Awake, O Bride, awaken
> the morning you're to marry;
> sing round and dance round;
> balconies a wreath must carry. (p. 58)

The sense of ritual that earlier distinguished the formal agreement of the Mother and the Father to the marriage of their children is caught and intensified now in the stylized performance of song and dance that is the collective expression of those deep and primitive instincts that are all to do with marriage, procreation and birth.[21] Young men and women enter singly, intoning a stanza or a couplet, and the song is passed from one to another, expanded, echoed and repeated, its rhythms and the movements of the participants weaving patterns that are themselves expressive of the harmony of Nature. At the centre of the song are the bridal couple, celebrated as part of Nature's splendour. And, as in ancient fertility rites the myth that celebrates the lovers in song and dance gives way to the appearance of a human couple, so here the bride of the song becomes the Bride herself, resplendent in all her finery:

[*The* BRIDE *appears. She wears a black dress in the style of 1900, with a bustle and large train covered with pleated gauzes and heavy laces. Upon her hair, brushed in a wave over her forehead, she wears an orange-blossom wreath. Guitars sound. The* GIRLS *kiss the* BRIDE.] (p. 61)

She is succeeded by the Bridegroom, both of them at the centre of the outpouring of a communal joy that is both a desire for their happiness and a prayer for the life-force which, in marriage, they represent.

In the case of other individuals too there is the suggestion of the cleansing and purification of disruptive and discordant elements in the interests of a greater harmony. The Mother's grief and fear are reawakened by Leonardo's presence, but she is encouraged by the Father to put the past behind her:

MOTHER [*to the* FATHER]: Are these people here, too?
FATHER: They're part of the family. Today is a day of
    forgiveness! (p. 62)

The Bride attempts to cling, in both a physical and metaphorical sense, to her vows to the Bridegroom, and the Father's words are an affirmation of a new dawn, a new cycle in the lives of the Mother, the Bridegroom, the Bride and himself, all of them freed from the shadows of the past:

FATHER: Quick now! Round up the teams and carts!
    The sun's already out. (p. 62)

But even now into the individual and collective optimism, the intoxicating magic of the accumulating rhythms of the scene, there intrude persistent discords. The Mother's fears return: 'And go along carefully! Let's hope nothing goes wrong.' (p. 63). And the Wife, knowing that Leonardo does not love her, cannot escape her sorrow:

I don't know what's happening. But I think, and I don't
want to think. One thing I do know. I'm already cast off
by you. But I have a son. And another coming. And so it
goes. My mother's fate was the same. (p. 64)

The impulse of the scene towards all that is positive in human life is seen again to be tied to its opposite, ominously present

still in the grief and fear of the women and the continuing
presence of Leonardo.

For the second scene the curtain rises on a setting and a
mood that seems to underline these pessimistic implications.
Outside the Father's home the colours are the whites, greys,
cold blues and dull browns of the dreary desert landscape of
'the waste-land', the outlines hard and disquieting:

> The exterior of the BRIDE's Cave Home, in white, grey and cold
> blue tones. Large cactus trees. Shadowy and silver tones.
> Panoramas of light tan tablelands, everything hard like a land-
> scape in popular ceramics. (p. 65)

The landscape, moreover, has its inner counterpart in the
gloom that descends on the Mother as she learns of Leonardo's
arrival at the wedding feast. Within her there appear again
those feelings that in Act I rose up to choke her: 'Always in my
breast there's a shriek standing tiptoe that I have to beat down
and hold in under my shawls.' (p. 66). Even the Father,
attempting to turn her thoughts to more pleasant things,
evokes a picture of man's unending battle with the weeds, the
thistles and the stones that are the constant enemies of fertile
land, and the symbols of all those things that in this play choke
and spread insidiously within the being of its characters. And
if Man's closeness to the world of Nature runs throughout the
scene in a positive sense, it invariably has its negative counterpart. The Mother, alluding to her son and his bride, observes:
'My son will cover her well. He's of good seed.' (p. 67). The
Servant sings the song in which the love-making of the newly
married couple is part of the vitality of Nature's processes, the
virgin's blood a source of joy and celebration:

> for the bridegroom is a dove
> with his breast a firebrand
> and the fields wait for the whisper
> of spurting blood. (p. 66)

But the Mother transforms the image into the more persistent
and haunting vision of the spilled blood of her eldest son and
its accompanying sense of waste and devastation:[22]

That's why it's so terrible to see one's own blood spilled

out on the ground. A fountain that spurts for a minute, but costs us years. (p. 67)

And this, in turn, is linked to another kind of blood – the bad blood that runs through the veins of the Félix family, from one generation to another, a kind of blight, an infected breeding that affects the world around it:

> What blood would you expect him to have? His whole family's blood. It comes down from his great-grandfather, who started in killing, and it goes on down through the whole evil breed. (p. 66)

From its pessimistic opening the scene begins to open out again into the increasing animation of the wedding celebrations, from individuals to the colourful tapestry of their interplay in chatter, movement and dance. Characters engage in lively conversation, move from group to group, young men and women excitedly appear and disappear, and the stage is filled with lively movement. The general sense of happiness and animation is concentrated too in some of the principal characters. The Bridegroom's joy is emphasized. The Father is overjoyed by his new-found happiness. And the Mother's initial pessimism is again alleviated, to the point where her habitual melancholy becomes her joyful expectation:

> A bad day? The only good one. To me it was like coming into my own. Like the breaking of new ground; the planting of new trees. (p. 72)

In the Bridegroom's words there is for her a new beginning:

> MOTHER: For my head is full of things; of men, and fights.
> BRIDEGROOM: But now the fights are no longer fights.
> (pp. 72-3)

But once more there are darker, more disturbing currents that ruffle the surface of the scene. The Bride's melancholy, in particular, is a constant, jarring note. Her agitation erupts violently and spasmodically, as when the Bridegroom embraces her. She describes to the Servant the dull, nagging heaviness that has settled upon her: 'It's as though I'd been struck on the head.' (p. 72). Her unease has its counterpart in the disquiet of the Wife, anxiously seeking Leonardo, uncertain of his whereabouts, her entrances and exits a broken thread in the pattern of the whole. And as for Leonardo, his presence is discerned from time to time, a restless figure pacing in the background.

In all its aspects the scene is an image of life's totality, for here is all the movement and rhythm of human affairs, their continuity, their state of flux, their joys and enthusiasms, their sense of elation. The wedding celebrations, with all their emphasis on music and song, and embracing too young and old, family and village, is, in a way, the great dance and ritual of life. But life is a composite of many things, of things which have their different sides and facets, and if the general impression and impact of this scene lies in its bubblng gaiety and joyfulness, it is, alternatively, the sombre strains within it that accumulate and darken its conclusion. The happy, animated movements of men and women become suddenly, dramatically, their agitated seeking of Leonardo and the Bride. As the Wife enters and announces their escape, the ending of the Act is transformed into its beginning. The Mother, who seemed to have put behind her the grief and anguish of the past, is confronted by it in another form as her son is now betrayed, and her words capture the sense of a fate that relentlessly pursues her: 'The hour of blood has come again.' (p. 74). But now the screw is turned more tightly, for it is not the Mother alone who is exposed to inevitable suffering, but the Bridegroom, the Father, the Wife, and the Bride and Leonardo too. In the past two families have been locked in conflict – the Félix family and the Mother's – but now there are three, as though for Lorca there is within the human kind a blight which progressively extends its influence. Indeed, the Mother's earlier image of Leonardo as part of an infected family-line returns in her description of the Bride:

> FATHER: That's not true! Not my daughter!
> MOTHER: Yes, your daughter! Spawn of a wicked mother, and he, he too. But now she's my son's wife! (p. 74)

Hers is, of course, a jaundiced and irrational view of things, but it instinctively exposes those fatal, destructive influences that, existing singly in individuals and collectively in men and women grouped together in marriage or society, infect the family of man. Within each individual there are conflicting forces finely balanced or in uneasy tension with each other. And within marriage and society there are tensions which may be harmonized, cancelling out each other, or which, in given circumstances, detonate themselves. In one direction the movement of this play is positive, caught and reflected in the efforts of men and women to shape their lands and families into ordered, harmonious patterns, and to resist and over-come the inner forces that threaten to disrupt their lives. But finally, for all his forward-looking and constructive striving, it is the individual and collective tragedy of men and women that they cannot deny the reality of those powerful and often anarchic elements that are contained within their being. The conclusion of the Act returns to and is dominated by the symbol of the horse on which Leonardo and the Bride escape:

> They've run away! They've run away! She and Leonardo. On the horse. With their arms around each other, they rode off like a shooting star. (p. 74)

Its wild and frenzied movement expresses the unleashed passions of the lovers. But now there are other horses that gallop in pursuit:

> MOTHER [to the son]: Go! After them. [He leaves with two young men.] No. Don't go. Those people kill quickly and well . . . but yes, run, and I'll follow! (p. 74)

The curtain falls upon the pessimistic vision of a world where all the optimism of the wedding celebrations is dispelled by the spectacle of human beings immersed in the savagery of their own destructive instincts – the hunters and the hunted. The circle of riders extends outwards, enclosing Leonardo and the Bride. But the pursuers too are enclosed and isolated in their own rage and violence, and the image of men imprisoned is complete.

The initial setting for the final Act is the humid forest in which Leonardo and the Bride seek to conceal themselves from their pursuers. Hemmed-in and encircled by the trees

and the darkness of night, the lovers are surrounded too by
their pursuers. But the physical imprisonment of the fleeing
couple is merely the consequence of the way in which they are
progressively hounded by their natures, ruled by a passion
that cannot be denied.

> SECOND WOODCUTTER: You have to follow your passion.
> They did right to run away.
> FIRST WOODCUTTER: They were deceiving themselves but
> at the last blood was stronger.
> THIRD WOODCUTTER: Blood!
> FIRST WOODCUTTER: You have to follow the path of your
> blood. (p. 75)

It is repeated a little later:

> SECOND WOODCUTTER: Her body for him; his body for
> her. (p. 76)

The setting of the great wood is the evocative symbol, both of
enclosure and of the forces that in the rural tragedies work as
much through men as Nature, and it is appropriate that
Leonardo and the Bride, Nature's children, should be
cocooned within this womb-like place. And what is true of
them is true now of the Bridegroom too, for he is equally the
instrument of instinct, pursuing the lovers blindly, drawn to
their hiding-place by some mysterious power. Later in the
scene the Bridegroom himself gives eloquent expression to the
force that, greater than himself, works through him:

> Be quiet. I'm sure of meeting them there. Do you see this
> arm? Well, it's not my arm. It's my brother's arm, and my
> father's and that of all the dead ones in my family. And it
> has so much strength that it can pull this tree up by the
> roots, if it wants to. And let's move on, because here I feel
> the clenched teeth of all my people in me so that I can't
> breathe easily. (p. 80)

His words echo his mother's in Act II, Scene Two, when she
speaks of the cry within her that will not be suppressed (p. 66).

The sense of human beings worked upon is immeasurably
heightened in this scene by its prevailing mood and atmos-

phere. From the outset the two violins create an insistent, inescapable melancholy, and the woodcutters intone their persistent, dirge-like chorus into which the audience is increasingly drawn. But the aura of doomed inevitability that descends upon the scene is suggested most effectively by the intervention in the affairs of men and women of the super-human agencies represented here in the figures of the Moon and Death.[23] The forces that in Acts I and II are said to inter-vene in our affairs but whose influence seems merely part of the belief of men and women, suggested but unproven, are seen now to be a reality, a controlling power in the lives of human beings. The Moon's words are full of menace. This figure with a white, inhuman face illuminates the world of human beings with a terrible, merciless and icy light from which no one and nothing can escape. And the Moon has, as its co-conspirator, Death, in the form of an old beggar woman, her features, like those of the moon, lacking a distinguishable human form: [*Her face can barely be seen among the folds.*] (p. 78). They are formidable and frightening adversaries who accentu-ate the smallness and insignificance of their human victims, for it is they who between them control the action, arrange the scenario and mark the spot where human beings are about to meet their end:

> MOON: There they come!
> [*He goes. The stage is left dark.*]
> BEGGAR WOMAN: Quick! Lots of light! Do you hear me?
> They can't get away! (p. 79)

And when the focus moves to the pursuers, the Bridegroom and his companion, they are less individuals than pawns in a game whose moves have already been decided, in which human beings hunt and pursue each other, and in which the Bridegroom and the Youth come to symbolize all men. The Youth comments:

> FIRST YOUTH: This is a hunt.

And the Bridegroom extends the implication of his words: 'A hunt. The greatest hunt there is.' (p. 80).

As the scene concludes, the theme of human helplessness achieves its most intense expression in Leonardo and the

Bride. She has described already the uncontrollable nature of
her physical attraction to Leonardo and she repeats it now in a
form more powerful still, her helplessness equated with the
blade of grass tossed on the wind:

> and I follow you,
> like chaff blown on the breeze. (pp. 83-4)

In the instinctive nature of their passion for each other there is
that pure animal quality devoid of everything to do with
reason, logic and common sense. The Bride expresses the
animal nature of her feelings in a powerful outburst of self-
denigration:

> And I'll sleep at your feet,
> to watch over your dreams.
> Naked, looking over the fields,
> as though I were a bitch.
> Because that's what I am! Oh, I look at you
> and your beauty sears me. (p. 84)

Leonardo, too, blames the irrational, indefinable attraction of
like to like that is part, not of the mind and intellect of men and
women, but of their physical nature:

> Oh, it isn't my fault –
> the fault is the earth's –
> and this fragrance that you exhale
> from your breasts and your braids. (p. 83)

And as the Bride is, despite herself, drawn to him, so he,
regardless of his will, is irresistibly tied to her. It is, significantly, the symbol of the horse that returns to convey the
ultimate surrender of the individual to the predominance of
passion and instinct. Leonardo rides the horse but neither
guides nor controls it. As the stallion's instinct determines its
movements, so Leonardo's instinct for the Bride is greater than
his will:

> Because I tried to forget you
> and put a wall of stone
> between your house and mine

But I was riding a horse
and the horse went straight to your door. (p. 83)

The emphasis of the ending of the scene is upon their
inseparability, for they are fused and linked together in both a
physical and emotional sense, inseparably bound by Nature,
symbolized here in the moonlight that welds into a single form
their intertwining bodies:

Nails of moonlight have fused
my waist and your chains. (p. 85)

As they speak their final words and exit embracing each other,
they assert and yield to the ultimate truth of their passion for
each other:

LEONARDO: [embracing her]:
  Any way you want!
  If they separate us, it will be
  because I am dead.
BRIDE: And I dead too. (p. 86)

But this is no Romantic victory, no inspiring or joyful surrender. It is the pitiful spectacle of human beings worked upon,
fragile vessels broken by forces greater than themselves.
And the ultimate victory is Death's who, as the curtain falls,
dominates physically and symbolically the centre of the stage,
heightening the smallness and insignificance of mankind:

At the second shriek the BEGGAR WOMAN appears and stands
with her back to the audience. She opens her cape and stands in
the centre of the stage like a great bird with immense wings.
(p. 86)

The initial impact of the play's final scene is one of starkness
and simplicity, of timelessness and monumentality. The room
with its white walls, its white floor, and its total lack of shadow
and perspective, is simultaneously the world, the cell that in a
multiplicity of forms is the sphere of our birth, our living and
our dying. Within the room the female figures, darkly dressed
and unwinding the thread of red wool, are starkly symbolic.

L

On the one hand they are village girls engaged in the simple, traditional art of knitting, but throughout the scene, as elsewhere in this and other plays, there is another, symbolic level of meaning whereby the girls become the Fates who unwind the thread of life and control the destinies of human beings. Their initial song has, in one sense, a popular character, for it is one of those songs that throughout the ages has accompanied the tasks of ordinary people, but there are, too, deeper implications that are all to do with life and death:[24]

> FIRST GIRL: Wool, red wool,
>   what would you make?
> SECOND GIRL: Oh, jasmine for dresses,
>   fine wool like glass.
>   At four o'clock born,
>   at ten o'clock dead. (p. 87)

Moreover, the conversation of the girls, shaped into a stylized and poetic form, acquires a fateful, dirge-like tone. As village girls they are curious about and ignorant of the events of the wedding and their outcome, but the first girl responds to her companion's questions to the wool with an ambiguity and a double-meaning that is heavy with the inevitability of fate:

> SECOND GIRL: Wool, red wool,
>   what would you tell?
> FIRST GIRL: The love is silent,
>   crimson the groom,
>   at the still shoreline
>   I saw them laid out. (p. 88)

The brief appearance of the Mother-in-Law and the Wife, themselves ignorant of the outcome of events, restores the level of the action to a realistic plane, but even so the Mother-in-Law's words suggest inevitable grief and suffering, the joy of life transformed into a permanent solitude and bitterness that is the fate of all women. The image of the Wife, alone, ageing, weeping, in a house whose doors are locked and windows barred, is a desolate and soul-destroying echo of all those other moments in the play that suggest the ultimate loneliness of man:

You, back to your house.
Brave and alone in your house.
To grow old and to weep.
But behind closed doors. (p. 89)

Indeed, it is significant that the two women, unaware of
Leonardo's fate, should be immediately replaced by Death
(the Beggar Woman) who informs us of it. In other words, the
human figures are framed here on either side by the Fates and
by Death itself. It suggests the way in which in life itself human
beings are surrounded, enclosed and dwarfed in their smallness and ignorance by forces which control them.

The deaths of Leonardo and the Bridegroom evoke in this
final scene the tragic sense of loss, of waste. The three girls,
First Girl, Second Girl, and Little Girl, assume the role of the
Chorus, setting in motion the elegiac lament that grows in its
intensity as the action draws to its conclusion. Their words
capture the essence of youth and beauty pitifully sullied and
destroyed:

FIRST GIRL: Dirty sand.
SECOND GIRL: Over the golden flower.
LITTLE GIRL: Over the golden flower
               they're bringing the dead from the arroyo.
               Dark the one,
               dark the other.
               What shadowy nightingale flies and
                 weeps
               over the golden flower. (pp. 90-91)

The grieving relatives express their sense of loss in terms of the
beauty of Nature withered and turned to dust. The Mother
cries out: 'But now my son is an armful of shrivelled flowers.'
(p. 91). And Death itself has earlier described the vigour and
vitality of human beings stilled: 'I saw them: they'll be here
soon: two torrents still at last, among the great boulders.'
(p. 90).

The conclusion of the scene is a final statement of the
proximity of man and Nature, of the Lorca universe that in this
play is always to the fore. The Mother's grief comes from deep

within her, from her roots, as though she were part of the soil itself:

> Your tears are only from your eyes, but when I'm alone mine will come – from the soles of my feet, from my roots – burning more than blood. (p. 91)

And when she alludes to the cemetery where her husband and her eldest son lie, and where the Bridegroom will now lie too, she uses instead of the common word one which suggests that the earth is man's natural resting place, and that in death he returns to be comforted and sheltered by it:

> But no; not graveyard, not graveyard; the couch of earth, the bed that shelters them and rocks them in the sky. (p. 91)

She, indeed, the mother from whom the child has been born, shares her grief with Mother Earth which will now contain his body, and her words establish clearly the link between them:[25] 'I want to see no one. The earth and I. My grief and I.' (p. 91).

The final appearance of the Bride expresses the same idea in relation to the attraction of men and women. For her the Bridegroom was a small stream, Leonardo a deep, dark, mysterious river, drawing her to him:

> but the other one was a dark river, choked with brush, that brought near me the undertone of its rushes and its whispered song. (p. 93)

Both of them draw from her a natural response, for both call upon her instincts, her womanliness, her maternal feelings, her longing for love and children. But, of the two, it is the force embodied in Leonardo that is irresistible and that despite herself, draws her to him, working upon her and through her as totally as in the world around them the creatures of Nature are instinctively drawn to each other:

> I didn't want to; remember that! I didn't want to. Your son was my destiny and I have not betrayed him, but the other one's arm dragged me along like the pull of the sea, like the head toss of a mule, and he would have dragged

me always, always, always, – even if I were an old
woman and all your son's sons held me by the hair.
(p. 93)

Our awareness of the helplessness of human beings,
together with our recognition of the pitiful destruction of their
beauty and of all the point and purpose of their lives, dominates the ending of the play. If Leonardo and the Bride are
powerless to control their passion for each other, the Mother,
the Bridegroom, the Father and the Wife are equally helpless
both to alter the course of events and to escape their grief, fear
and despair. On this account we pity them intensely. The
lamentation for youth and beauty uselessly destroyed underlines that pity. The Wife expresses it well:

He was a beautiful horseman,
now he's a heap of snow.
He rode to fairs and mountains
and women's arms.
Now, the night's dark moss
crowns his forehead. (p. 94)

But most pitiful of all is our final realization of the ultimate
isolation of men and women who are locked in the solitary
world of their own inescapable anguish. The Mother rejects
the Bride:

But what does your good name matter to me? What does
your death matter to me? What does anything about
anything matter to me? (p. 93)

The lament which concludes the play, involving the Wife, the
Mother and the Bride, is a common one, for they grieve the
same event, echo each other in their utterances, and they are,
of course, in close proximity to each other on the stage. [26] But in
the last resort they are isolated from each other, their individual anguish as unshareable as it is incommunicable. There
is also a common bond between them to the extent that the fate
of the one is or becomes the fate of another. The Bride and the
Wife, inasmuch as they have lost their husbands by the play's
conclusion, are what the Mother was at its commencement.

And the Wife's child, together with her unborn baby, parallel the Bridegroom in the sense that they have no father. But again the common nature of their fate heightens our awareness of their common isolation, and the final curtain falls on the spectacle of women weeping, a communal and collective weeping – *The* NEIGHBOURS, *kneeling on the floor, sob.* – that is a composite of individual and solitary anguish – the essence of the tragic suffering presented to us in the bleak and pessimistic vision of this play.

It has been said of Chekhov that 'it is very much his method of building a play to keep violent acts and emotional climaxes away from the center of things . . .'[27] Of Lorca's rural tragedies we can justifiably say the opposite, for they reveal the most powerful human passions and the most violent confrontations. Indeed, the trivia of human lives, the ordinary events and the desultory conversations that are the stuff of many dramatists, are almost entirely absent. Instead, Lorca goes to the heart of the matter, stripping away the commonplaces of experience in favour of all that is heightened, intense and concentrated. This is, of course, the material of melodrama, and for many theatregoers, particularly the more phlegmatic North European, it remains the difficulty of appreciating fully Lorca's plays. He is, indeed, very Spanish and very Andalusian, rarely given to understatement. But if his plays are a series of hammer blows, we should not assume that, in terms of stagecraft, they are in any way crude.[28]

Let us consider, firstly, the character and function of the stage settings.[29] There are seven in all, each of them different, and some of Lorca's stage directions are much more detailed than others. They do, however, have one important thing in common, for the play, though dealing with the stuff of real life in a Spanish village, is far from naturalistic, and the sets, far from being cluttered, are spare and simple, as stark and as stripped of detail as the heightened emotional situations to which they form a background. The stage pictures are an integral part of the scene.

Act I, Scene One, conveys, above all else, the obsessive nature of the Mother's grief for her dead husband and her

elder son, and her fear for her one remaining son. The stage
picture that sets the scene and forms the frame for the expression of its powerful emotions is very simple. Lorca has, in the
published text, just one short instruction: [*A room painted yellow.*] (p. 33). He does not specify its tone, but we may imagine
the harsh yellow of the bare kitchen walls forming a background to the black of the Mother's dress.[30] Within this frame
she will be seated as the curtain rises, downstage in all proba-
bility. The combination of colours and the static posture of the
silent figure create a mood of dark, brooding melancholy
before a word is spoken. The words and actions that follow are
anticipated by the setting and harmonize with it at every stage.

The second scene initially suggests the domestic bliss that
exists in the house of Leonardo and his wife but gradually
presents the ominous and disruptive nature of Leonardo's
passion for his former sweetheart. The stage picture is suggested here in detail:

> *A room painted rose with copperware and wreaths of common
> flowers. In the centre of the room is a table with a tablecloth. It is
> morning.*
> [*Leonardo's* MOTHER-IN-LAW *sits in one corner holding a child
> in her arms and rocking it. His* WIFE *is in the other corner
> mending stockings.*] (p. 40)

Every element is important – the predominant rose colour of
the walls, the glow of the copperware, the brightness of the
flowers, of the light of morning, and the tablecloth.[31] We have
not a clash but a harmony of colour very different from Scene
One. The seated figures of the women have a different effect
too, for they blend into the background, creating a sense of
balance and tranquillity. The spectators are lulled by its soothing impact, but, in contrast to Scene One, the ensuing actions,
involving Leonardo's violent conflict with the Wife and
Mother-in-Law, offset the stage picture and are themselves
thrown into greater relief by it.

The stage settings for Act III are interesting in a different
sense. The events of the first two Acts, leading to Leonardo's
abduction of the Bride, are, though heightened, on a human
plane. The sets, portraying the rooms of the various houses or

the landscape outside those houses, are, reduced to the bare, necessary elements, accompaniments to human affairs and emotions. By the final Act the action is transposed to the level of the supernatural, for the awesome figures of Moon and Death control and manipulate the lives of human beings. The sets should be seen now not as stage pictures which accompany and underline the conflicts within and between human beings but as frames which emphasize their smallness and insignificance.

Act III, Scene One, for instance, presents Leonardo and the Bride concealed in the wood, pursued by the Bridegroom and his companions, and then Leonardo and the Bridegroom hounded by the Moon and Death. The stage picture is briefly described, but it suggests the elements necessary to convey to us the vastness and the mystery of the forces that circumscribe human lives:

> *A forest. It is night-time. Great moist tree trunks. A dark atmosphere. Two violins are heard.*
> [THREE WOODCUTTERS *enter.*] (p. 75)

While the earlier sets are precise, even though their starkness gives them a certain symbolic quality, the setting of the great wood is, in accordance with the movement of the play, much more symbolic.[32]

The dialogue, for all its seeming naturalness, is highly stylized. An Act I, Scene One, the exchanges, firstly between the Mother and the son, then between the Mother and the Neighbour, are carefully constructed, full of repetitions of words and phrases that convey to us the obsessive nature of the Mother's grief and fear. The son asks for a knife with which to cut the grapes, the word unleashes her emotions, and in the outburst that follows, 'knife' or 'knives' occurs six times, 'pistols' twice, and 'guns' once. In addition, there are throughout the passage the same repeated patterns of speech:

> If I lived to be a hundred I'd talk of nothing else . . .
> . . . No, I'll never be quiet.

> No. No. Let's not quit this talk.

No . . . If I talk about it it's because . . . Oh, how can I help talking about it . . . (p. 34)

Through the language and its insistent rhythms Lorca reveals to us with power and immediacy the emotions that haunt the Mother throughout the play. The son's lines are few in comparison but they are important in terms of contrast. His adoption of different emotional positions – resignation, aggression, coaxing, cajoling – both fail to stem the tide and throw into greater relief his mother's obsessive concerns.

In the middle section of the scene the Mother's obsessions remain a constant undercurrent. There are two important pauses that accompany her allusions to her son's future wife, for they reveal the thinking processes that underlie her words. Firstly:

Forgive me.
[Pause.]
How long have you known her? (p. 35)

And secondly:

Go on. You're too big now for kisses. Give them to your wife.
[Pause. To herself.]
When she is your wife. (p. 36)

At other points the idea of her being left alone is repeated twice: 'I'll be left alone. Now only you are left me . . .' (p. 35). 'I have no one but you now!' (p. 36). She refers to her dead husband three times. The tempo is slower but the dialogue still reflects the Mother's nagging and insidious worries. Finally, in the scene's concluding moments her questions, repeatedly punctuating the conversation and becoming more insistent, acquire an obsessive character, building to the climactic revelation of the name of the Bride's former sweetheart and the confirmation of the Mother's fears:

You know my son's sweetheart?
And her mother?
How do you remember it?

Who was the boy?

Félix, a slimy mouthful.

[*She spits.*]

It makes me spit – spit so I won't kill! (pp. 37-8)

The Mother appears again on three occasions and the patterns already noted in the dialogue occur again, suggesting the narrow areas of emotional experience in which she moves, the repeat performances which she is always giving. In Act II, Scene Two, in the conversation with the Bride's father after the wedding, the mention of Leonardo's name has the same effect on her as the previous reference to the knife. The Mother uses the word 'blood' six times and, to a lesser extent, 'killing', 'killed', 'knife-wielding' (pp. 66-7). We note, too, precise echoes of Act I, Scene One:

When the talk turns on it, I have to speak. And more so today. Because today I'm left alone in my house. (p. 66)

The repetitions and rhythmic patterns of the dialogue given to the Mother must be seized upon by the actress who wishes to convey to the audience the intensity and permanence of the Mother's obsessive thoughts and feelings.[33]

Lorca's use of poetry can be considered in relation to many scenes. In Act I, Scene Two, for instance, Lorca uses verse to heighten mood and atmosphere in what is a fairly static situation rather than one which, presenting characters in conflict with each other, demands the cut and thrust of prose dialogue. Secondly, the use of poetry here is in no way jarring, for, taking the form of a lullaby, it fits perfectly into the context of the scene. But its effect is magical and beautifully managed. The delicate colour tones of the stage setting and the gentle rocking of the baby are enhanced by the words and rhythms of poetry, especially in the lullaby's refrain:

WIFE [*softly*]: Carnation, sleep and dream,
the horse won't drink from
the stream. (p. 40)

But slowly, in its central section, the lullaby becomes, more than an accompaniment to the sleeping child, a lament for the thirsty, bleeding horse, and, in a marvellously evocative way, the earlier associations with the room and the baby are transformed into the sinister splash of blood and the icy light in the horse's eyes that glints like a knife:

> MOTHER-IN-LAW: . . . His poor hooves were bleeding,
> his long mane was frozen,
> and deep in his eyes
> stuck a silvery dagger.
>
> And his blood was running,
> Oh, more than the water. (pp. 40-41)

The poetry in performance, with due attention to its powerful pictorial and rhythmic qualities, should construct a verbal picture which takes the spectators' attention from the visual picture of the room and only slowly allows them to return to it, but with the verbal picture and all its ominous implications firmly imprinted on their minds. No producer should ignore the different levels on which the lullaby works.[34]

The middle section of the scene, in prose, presents Leonardo in relation to his wife and mother-in-law and the emotional tensions that exist between them. In contrast to the slow tempo of the lullaby and the static postures of the women who intone it, there are now three dramatic climaxes, each more powerful than the previous one, the carefully graded interplay of word, action and movement about the stage to the point where Leonardo storms out. The conclusion of the scene returns to the lullaby in a way which links its implications firmly to the characters themselves. Its impact should be much harsher, coloured by the weeping of the Wife and the Mother-in-Law in such a way as to make the lamentation for the horse a simultaneous lamentation for themselves:

> MOTHER-IN-LAW: Carnation, sleep and dream,
> the horse won't drink from the stream.
> WIFE: [*weeping, and leaning on the table*]:
> My rose, asleep now lie,
> the horse is starting to cry. (p. 46)

By this stage the figures of the women, initially part of the tranquil setting of the room, are a discordant element within it.

In Act II, Scenes One and Two, poetry is used in the form of song in association with the wedding. In the first scene the Servant begins to intone the song that, taken up by others as the scene unfolds, builds slowly into a moving and lyrical celebration of marriage and of the Bride and Bridegroom:

> Awake, O Bride, awaken,
> On your wedding morning waken!
> The world's rivers may all
> Bear along your bridal Crown! (p. 55)

Its effectiveness in the scene lies at first in the fact that its optimism, caught in the imagery and the gently insistent rhythms, is bounded on either side by the conflict of the Bride and Leonardo within themselves and in relation to each other. It is, indeed, swamped by the savagery of their clash. But then the song is taken up again, sung by the guests, the distant chorus coming slowly nearer, growing and assuming a sustained momentum that banishes the earlier tensions of the scene. In addition, the performance of the song, essentially stylized in the distribution of its lines and refrains and through the movements of the singers, raises the action to a more symbolic plane, substituting individual passions with and absorbing them into generic and universal patterns.[35] Here, as in Act I, Scene Two, poetry both heightens the atmosphere of the scene itself and, through its allusive nature, extends its meaning. The song acquires the character of age-old ritual, the Bride and Bridegroom the mythical proportions of archetypal lovers, and the joy of the guests the impulse towards all that is creative and harmonious that is deeply rooted in human nature. As the scene ends, the incantation begins to fade with the departure of the guests for the wedding, and snatches of song are interwoven with a return to the tension between Leonardo and his wife. A magical and harmonious climax has been built only to descend again into the final and more ominous discord of personal relationships. It is a scene in which the performance of the poetry in terms of changing tempo and emphasis and the suggestion of its different levels of meaning is both demanding and vitally important.

In the first two Acts poetry takes the form of songs, but in Act III it is part of the dialogue itself, both between the supernatural figures of the Moon and Death and between Leonardo and the Bride. Indeed, even in the prose dialogue of the Woodcutters that begins Scene One the rhythms of poetry are very prominent and, in performance, must acquire that insistent, inescapable beat that will create the sense of inevitability that pervades the scene:

FIRST WOODCUTTER: By now he must be loving her.
SECOND WOODCUTTER: Her body for him; his body for her.
THIRD WOODCUTTER: They'll find them and they'll kill them
FIRST WOODCUTTER: But by then they'll have mingled their bloods. They'll be like two empty jars, like two dry arroyos. (p. 76)

This poetic prose leads into the poetry itself, into the Moon's anguished, menacing soliloquy:

I want no shadows. My rays
must get in everywhere,
even among the dark trunks I want
the whisper of gleaming lights,
so that this night there will be
sweet blood for my cheeks . . . (p. 78)

In contrast, Death, in the form of an old woman, delivers her lines in an urgent yet sinister whisper:

They won't get past here. The river's whisper
and the whispering tree trunks will muffle the
torn flight of their shrieks. (p. 78)

If the potential of the scene, whose atmosphere lies as much in its poetry as in anything else, is to be realized on the stage, every attention must be given to the delivery of the lines in terms of pitch, rhythm and changing tempo.

The poetry of the concluding section, revealing to us the passion, the guilt and the fear of the Bride and Leonardo, conveys those emotions to us in a form more stark and more

immediate than any prose could do. Lorca's stage direction
suggests the intended effect: [*This whole scene is violent, full of
great sensuality.*] (p. 85). It is a mood which must be caught in
the delivery of lines as simple yet as evocative as these:

LEONARDO: The birds of early morning
           are calling among the trees.
           The night is dying
           on the stone's ridge.
           Let's go to a hidden corner
           where I may love you for ever,
           for to me the people don't matter,
           nor the venom they throw on us. (p. 84)

As a last example there is the final elegy for Leonardo and
the Bridegroom. This is a static scene, the mourners in set
positions. The movement of the scene lies solely in the movement of the lines they speak. Through repeated lines and
rhythms there is created a sustained momentum. Moreover,
there will be an interplay not merely of lines but of voices, of
the Wife, the Bride, the Mother, the Neighbours, which will
vary the tone of the passage and maintain its sense of forward
movement, giving to the whole a ritualistic, chorus-like effect:

MOTHER: Neighbours: with a knife,
         with a little knife,
         on their appointed day, between two and
           three,
         these two men killed each other for love.
         With a knife,
         with a tiny knife,
         that barely fits the hand
         but that slides in clean
         through the astonished flesh
         and stops at the place
         where trembles, enmeshed,
         the dark root of a scream.
BRIDE: And this is a knife,
         a tiny knife
         that barely fits the hand:

fish without scales, without river,
so that on their appointed day, between two
  and three,
with this knife,
two men are left stiff,
with their lips turning yellow.
MOTHER: And it barely fits the hand
but it slides in clean
through the astonished flesh
and stops there, at the place
where trembles enmeshed
the dark root of a scream. (p. 95)

There should be no restraint, no holding back in the speaking
of these lines. Their intense emotion must be transmitted to us
by the whole range of vocal resources that the actors can
command.[36]

The first of these two scenes is the real climax of the play,
and in its effectiveness lighting plays a significant part.[37]
Elsewhere lighting is used to enhance atmosphere, as in Act I,
Scene Two, or to suggest a change of mood, as in Act II, Scene
One, where darkness gives way to dawn, conflict to the
greater optimism of the wedding. In Act III, Scene One, it does
these things to a much greater degree, in accordance with the
greater dramatic nature of the scene, and it also pinpoints the
climactic moments of the scene. It begins in darkness – *A dark
atmosphere* (p. 75) – which, allowing us to see only the shapes of
the trees and the dim forms of the woodcutters, cloaks the
stage in mystery and foreboding. When the Moon appears
there is at first *a shining brightness at the left* and then – *The stage
takes on an intense blue radiance* (p. 77). The blue light, illuminating the whole stage, creates a very eerie effect and a setting in
which the figure of the Moon, with a white face and in the
centre of the stage, is literally spotlighted. Within this cold
light the Moon's soliloquy becomes more chilling. With the
Moon's exit and the appearance of Death the stage reverts to
darkness, an appropriate setting and accompaniment to her
furtive movements and then to the searching of the Bridegroom. Within the darkness the movements of individuals,

the slow movements of the Woodcutters, the passionate words of the Bride and Leonardo, the music of the two distant violins, demand our attention even more, are emphasized more because of the darkness. Finally, as the Bride and Leonardo try to escape, the blue light fills the stage again, dramatically spotlighting their death, giving to the ending of the play that sense of something cold, inhuman, merciless, from which there is no escape. It is an impression enhanced further by the way in which the black shape of Death enters and dominates the downstage area, silhouetted against the light in a wonderfully evocative and dramatic stance: [. . . *She opens her cape and stands in the centre of the stage like a great bird with immense wings* . . .] (p. 86).

CHAPTER V

YERMA

Yerma, the second of the rural tragedies, followed in quick succession after *Blood Wedding*. Lorca gave a reading of the play at the home of Carlos Morla Lynch on 3 December, 1934, and Morla graphically describes the occasion – Lorca seated at a table, his face illuminated by the greenish light of a table-lamp. The reading of the play took more than two hours but the audience was entranced by Lorca's performance, especially by his magical rendering of Act II, Scene One – the village women at the mountain stream – to which he brought an 'unbelievable dynamism'. Morla himself was overwhelmed by the play. It is 'terrible and beautiful', it has a truly rural authenticity, but it also transcends its setting, and the language, 'so unadorned and real, is transformed, as though by magic, into music and poetry'.[1]

The première took place at the Teatro Español in Madrid on 29 December, 1934, performed by Margarita Xirgu and her company and directed by Cipriano Rivas Cherif. Morla again gives us a vivid account of the excitement of the opening night.[2] The theatre was completely sold out, the first-night audience composed of distinguished people. At the same time there were some who envied Lorca's rapid rise to fame, and others who resented the hospitality shown by Margarita Xirgu to an ex-government Minister after his release from gaol. There were early signs of trouble in the auditorium and at one point the performance came to a halt. It then proceeded without interruption, gripping the audience more and more, and, as the final curtain fell, the applause was instantaneous. Lorca, calm and confident, took his bow. Then he presented Margarita Xirgu, exhausted after her performance as Yerma, and allowed the public to pay its homage to her. The play, says Morla Lynch, is a triumph. Everyone is comparing it to *Blood Wedding*. But things, he concludes, are neither 'better' nor 'less good'. They are different and 'equally beautiful'.[3]

Yerma, unlike *Blood Wedding*, did not have its origins in a real-life event. The central theme of the frustrated woman is, on the other hand, one that occurs in Lorca's poetry and in many of his plays. In his first book of poems it is present in the 'Elegy to Doña Juana, the Mad' *(Elegía a Doña Juana la Loca)*:

> Princess who loved and was not loved.
> Red carnation in a deep and desolate valley.
> The tomb that holds you exhales your sadness . . .
>
> Where are your kisses, borne on the wind?
> Where is the sadness of your unfortunate love?
> In the coffin of lead, within your frame of bone,
> Your heart is broken in a thousand pieces.[4]

The poem entitled 'Elegy' is a lament for the spinsters of Lorca's native city:

> In your white hands
> you bear the thread of your illusions,
> dead forever, and in your soul
> a passion hungry for kisses of fire
> and a love of motherhood that dreams far-off
> dreams of cradles in quiet places,
> weaving with your lips the blue of lullaby.

By its conclusion it has become an elegy to all those Andalusian spinsters who dream and wait in vain and whose lives slip by into the long sadness of old-age:

> What depth of sadness you must carry in your soul,
> for in a heart now tired and exhausted you feel
> the passion of a girl newly in love!

In *Songs* the theme can be seen in 'The Unmarried Woman at Mass' *(La soltera en misa)*:

> Lulled by the incense,
> half asleep.

The eyes of a bull gazed upon you.
Your rosary was rain.
In your black dress of silk,
do not move, Virginia.
Give the dark melons of your breasts
to the murmur of the Mass.

In *Gipsy Ballads*, 'The Gipsy Nun' (*La monja gitana*) reveals the subdued instincts and the fantasies of love aroused as the nun embroiders flowers:

She wanted to be weaving
Imaginary flowers.

Across the eyes of the nun
Two loping riders move.
A dull and distant murmur
Loosens her white apparel . . .

O far-extending plain
With twenty suns above!
O streams on tiptoe poised
By glimmering fancy seen![5]

And the theme of frustrated love runs too through 'Ballad of the Black Sorrow' (*Romance de la pena negra*) and Somnambulistic Ballad (*Romance sonámbulo*). In the former Soledad Montoya is asked by the poet:

Whom are you seeking
Alone at this hour?

She replies:

Never mind whom I seek,
What is it to you?
I seek what I seek,
My joy and myself.

Waiting for a love that never comes she speaks finally of the effect upon her of her loneliness and solitude:

Terrible trouble
Turning jet-black

Body and clothing,
Shirts that were linen,
Thighs that were poppies.[6]

In these poems the lyrical expression of the theme of frustration often has the dramatic quality which is such a constant feature of Lorca's poetry as a whole. It is not surprising, then, that the theme should be a central one in the dramatic works themselves. In *The Butterfly's Evil Spell*, the love of Curianito for the beautiful butterfly is one that is unreciprocated and that leads to his emotional and physical death. He cries out in anguish:

Who gave me these eyes I hate?
And these hands that try
to clutch a love I cannot understand
and that will end with my life?
Who has lost me among shadows?
Who bids me suffer because I have no wings?[7] (p. 238)

In *Mariana Pineda* Mariana's love for Pedro is frustrated by events. The death of her hopes is hinted at in the song:

My hope died
by the edge of the water
without anyone seeing it.[8] (p. 781)

Similarly, the younger man, Fernando, loves Mariana in vain, his hopes of her frustrated by her love of Pedro and, finally, by her death. The shoemaker's wife, in the play of the same name, dreams of young and handsome lovers in contrast to her old husband, and her desire for a child is uppermost in her mind: 'Children? Maybe I'll have better-looking ones than all of them . . .' (pp. 66-7). In *When Five Years Have Passed* the Secretary loves the young man but is rejected by him, thrown back on her anguish and despair:

What explanation can I give? There is only one explanation and that is . . . that I love you . . . I can still feel that blood, alive like a red serpent, trembling between my breasts.[9] (p. 965)

In the same play the figure of the Mannequin reflects the

shattered dreams of the Secretary for the young man and of the Bride for the Rugby Player. Later in the play the Girl seeks a lover she will never find:

> My lover waits for me
> at the bottom of the sea. (p. 1019)

And the Secretary, rejected earlier by the Young Man, pursues her vision of a tall and curly-headed lover: 'If my friend were to come – so tall, with his hair curled, but curled in a special way . . .' (p. 1027). In *Blood Wedding*, of course, the Bride's yearning for Leonardo is frustrated and destroyed, and so are the Mother's dreams of the grand-children that her son will give her. Throughout the poems and plays that preceded *Yerma* the theme of the frustrated woman was clearly a central one, and in the plays that followed – *Doña Rosita, the Spinster*, and *The House of Bernarda Alba* – it continued to be so. In *Yerma* itself Lorca focused his attention on sterility as a particular aspect of the theme, but in the depth and futility of her illusions Yerma is one of a long line, 'the long gallery of women consumed in useless waiting, of women who in convents and clean provincial homes hide away the intimate failure of their lives, the perpetual conflict between their virgin imaginations and the passing of life; a gallery too of unsatisfied married women.'[10]

Another major theme in *Yerma* is the theme of honour, for it is partly Yerma's belief in honour that keeps her from adultery and, despite her longing for a child, faithful to an uncaring husband.[11] Moreover, the significance of honour and reputation in the lives of the characters is emphasized throughout. In Act II, Scene One, the women gossip about Yerma and one of them observes: 'Whoever wants a good name, let her earn it.' (p. 116). As Yerma's frustration grows and her absences from home become more frequent, her husband Juan is more and more concerned about the neighbours' talk and its effect upon his name. In Act III, Scene One, Juan encounters her as she returns at dawn:

> I'm not the one who sets it there [a man's name]. You do it by your conduct, and the town's beginning to say so. It's beginning to say it openly. When I come on a group, they all fall silent; when I go to weigh the flour, they all

fall silent, and even at night, in the fields, when I
awaken, it seems to me that the branches of the trees
become silent too. (p. 136)

In Yerma Lorca embodies the concept of honour as virtue and
moral rectitude, in Juan honour as public image, the two facets
of honour which were, of course, so central to the drama of the
Golden Age. In his earlier plays Lorca presented the theme of
honour in different ways. The shoemaker's wife, tormenting
her older husband, scandalizes the villagers by her behaviour,
flouts their narrow concept of honour, and, when her husband
disappears, rejects her numerous suitors, asserting that for
her honour is her virtue and self-respect. It is, in a sense, the
honour of Yerma treated in a lighter and more humorous
way. In *Don Perlimplín* the old man, deceived by his wife, is
presented not as the ruthless defender of his honour, but as
someone who, accepting dishonour and rejecting vengeance,
flouts convention when he sings:[12] 'Don Perlimplín has no
honour! Has no honour!' (p. 128). In a farce the traditional
concept of honour is seen from a humorous and farcical angle.
Blood Wedding, on the other hand, shifts the emphasis to honour as an element of tragic conflict, an ingredient in the clash
between the individual and society. The instinctive attraction
of the Bride and Leonardo towards each other pulls them in
one direction, while their awareness of their social obligations,
of which honour is a part, acts as a restraint upon them. The
Mother of the Bridegroom and the Father of the Bride seek to
arrange for their children an honourable marriage. When the
Bride and Leonardo flee they affront the moral and the social
code, and if in their pursuit the Mother and the Bridegroom are
driven by a terrible thirst for vengeance, in particular against
the Félix family, it is also a vengeance that in the eyes of others
will restore their honour. If the theme of honour in *Blood
Wedding* is not the most important, it is always part of the
conflicting forces in the play which lead to tragedy.

   While Lorca was influenced in many ways by the drama of
the Golden Age, the honour plays affected him profoundly.
The theme of honour, both as inner virtue and as public image,
is an almost unbroken thread in the drama of the seventeenth
century, and when it is not the central theme it is often a

secondary one. In *Peribáñez* and *The Sheep Well*, for example, Lope de Vega presents both aspects of the theme. In the former he contrasts the honour that is rank and privilege with the honour that is virtue in the clash between the Commander, the overlord of the village of Ocana, and the upright and dignified peasant, Peribáñez, while in *The Sheep Well* the Commander, a man of rank and honour, is shown to have no honour in his ruthless tyranny of the villagers under his protection. In *The Knight from Olmedo* the protagonist, Don Alonso, is an honourable man both socially and morally, but his passion for Inés clouds his reason, leads to an illicit affair with her and ultimately to his tragic death. It is a play in which the clash between individual passion and the demands of social convention is powerfully illustrated. But of all the dramatists of the Golden Age it was Calderón who produced the most impressive plays on the theme of honour, notably *The Surgeon of his Honour (El médico de su honra), The Painter of his Dishonour (El pintor de su deshonra)*, and *A Secret Vengeance of a Secret Offence (A secreto agravio secreta venganza)*. In all these plays the requirements of honour as name and reputation dominate the lives of individuals, women and men alike, and women in particular, cruelly exposed to the attentions of marauding males, are the innocent victims of their husbands' fears, doubts, suspicions, and ultimately of their bloody vengeance. They are plays which influenced Lorca greatly, not so much in the details of the plot of *Yerma*, but in the sense that in the society in which Yerma and Juan live the concept of honour is one which still exerts its tyranny. And finally, perhaps, Lorca was influenced by Calderón more than by Lope in the sense that in many of the plays of Calderón there is a single, dominating central character, an axis around which the other characters revolve and to which they are subordinate. Yerma dominates the play as completely as does Segismundo in Calderón's *Life is a Dream*.[13]

The title of the play distinguishes it from and links it to the other rural tragedies.[14] The tragedy of a family or families is here the tragedy of a single woman, focused on her to the point where, in relation to her suffering, the other characters seem

almost insignificant. On the other hand, Yerma is linked by
her name to the soil, to Nature, and the relationship between
men and women and the natural world, which is a dominant
theme of the other rural tragedies, is as much a central issue
here. Indeed, it is precisely in her growing awareness of herself as part of the barren, unproductive processes of Nature,
and in consequence, of her isolation from its beauty and abundance that Yerma's tragedy lies. Her physical sterility becomes
the emotional and spiritual emptiness of despair, the richness
of her spirit pitifully withered. But Yerma, because she towers
above the other characters, is more than the voice of barren
and despairing women. She projects a sense of the terrible
emptiness of life itself, of men and women who are, like
God-forsaken areas of the earth, abandoned, desolate,
'yermo'. If Yerma seems different from the people who surround her, it is she, not they, who by the play's conclusion
conveys its real meaning, the sense of the pain and pointlessness of human life.

The beginning of the play suggests the significance in
Yerma's life of illusion and reality. The shepherd and the child
in white are part of Yerma's dream, the former the symbol of
the man for whom she yearns, the latter the embodiment of
her deepest longing. [15] But if the dream is vivid, it is also
insubstantial, fading quickly, leaving the reality of Yerma's
life: the room, the sewing-basket, the concrete symbols of her
domestic role, and the chiming of the clock that signifies, as in
many of Lorca's plays, the passing of the years, the continuing
reality of her life without a child. Secondly, the dream dissolves into the bursting vitality of Spring as Yerma awakens:
[... *the light changes into the happy brightness of a Spring morning.*
YERMA *awakens.*] (p. 99). There is established, as in many other
plays, a link between the world of Nature and the men and
women who are permanently close to it. As far as Yerma is
concerned, the awakening Spring is the setting and the symbol of her hope of becoming fruitful.

The initial conversation between Yerma and Juan develops
the themes already stated. Yerma embodies the vital impulses
of Nature, declaring beautiful the humble flowers that others
spurn:

The rain just by the force of its falling on the stones softens them and makes weeds grow – weeds which people say aren't good for anything. 'Weeds aren't good for anything', yet I see them plainly enough – moving their yellow flowers in the wind. (p. 100)

She is in word and action the outpouring of a warm and generous nature, her capacity for joy, for love, for life immense. She alludes to the joy of her wedding-night:

I know girls who trembled and cried before getting into bed with their husbands. Did I cry the first time I went to bed with you? Didn't I sing as I turned back the fine linen bedclothes? (p. 100)

As Juan is about to depart, she affirms her faith in love, embracing him: [YERMA *embraces and kisses her husband. She takes the initiative.*] (p. 101). In every sense Yerma, though childless, is a child of Nature, synonymous with its vital and creative spirit, and part of the positive movement of the play.

Juan is Yerma's opposite. Her conversation is impassioned while his is lifeless. Her physical movements, especially her embracing of her husband, emphasize the lack of response in him. And while she is endowed by Nature with a great vitality, so Juan grows thinner and paler as the years go by:

YERMA: You work a lot and your body's not strong enough for it.
JUAN: When men grow thin they get strong as steel.
YERMA: But not you. You were different when we were first married. Now you've got a face as white as though the sun had never shone on it. (p. 99)

There is already a disturbing irony in the fact that Juan works close to Nature but is in every other way divorced from it. As Yerma says, the processes of Nature are reversed in him: 'Twenty-four months we've been married and you only get sadder, thinner, as if you were growing backwards.' (p. 99). The difference between them that becomes the tragic conflict of the play is already clear. [16]

With Juan's departure the theme of dream and reality in Yerma's life is taken up again, reinforcing earlier suggestions.

The stage-direction underlines both aspects of the theme:

> [. . . YERMA *walks toward her sewing. She passes a hand over her belly, lifts her arms in a beautiful sigh, and sits down to sew.*] (p. 101)

The sewing basket and the act of sewing evoke once more the reality of Yerma's life, and her drawing of her hand across her stomach her dream of childbirth. Of the two it is the latter that, paradoxically, becomes for Yerma the true reality, for the act of sewing, symbolic of all her unproductive domestic tasks, is merely an accompaniment to the song that proclaims the creativity of Nature and her longing for a child:[17] 'From where do you come, my love, my baby? . . .' (p. 101). But if for Yerma the dream is the true reality, its insubstantial nature is also the source of her growing isolation from reality itself, and her awareness of it the source of her increasing anguish.

María, interrupting Yerma's song, is the embodiment of Yerma's dream, another strand in the play's positive momentum. She, in contrast to Juan, is testimony to the productive role of Nature in human lives, identifying closely with it. Her thoughts are expressed in terms of the natural world of which she feels herself to be a part. Her child is a bird that stirs within her: 'Have you ever held a live bird pressed in your hand?' (p. 102). Her husband's eyes are like green leaves: 'When he's close to me his eyes tremble like two green leaves.' (p. 103). To the extent that she is one with Nature, María is all that Yerma longs to be. At night, indeed, Yerma herself often walks barefoot, identifying with the soil, so that it will in turn become in all its life-giving magic part of her: 'Many nights I go barefooted to the patio to walk on the ground. I don't know why I do it.' (p. 104). But the links between the women are in many ways less important than the differences. In comparison with Yerma, childless but intuitively knowledgeable, María appears uninformed, and it is Yerma who advises her. And María herself observes: 'But you know more about these things than I do.' (p. 103). 'In addition, María is full of fear at the prospect of the pain of childbirth, while Yerma, dismissing majestically her trivial fears, sees in it only the beauty and virtue of self-sacrifice:

That's a lie. That's what weak, complaining mothers say. What do they have them for? Having a child is no bouquet of roses. We must suffer to see them grow. I sometimes think half our blood must go. But that's good, healthy, beautiful. (p. 104)

If, in the earlier conversation with her husband, Yerma emerged as a woman of exceptional quality, dwarfing his dullness, her encounter with María consolidates our image of her. She becomes a figure of heroic stature, towering over those around her in the splendour of her being. But it is our awareness of her worth that intensifies our sense of life's unfairness and thus the degree of our pity for her.[18] Yerma is more deserving of a child than is María, and deserving too of a husband who approaches her in attitude and feeling. There is already about her that sense of waste that is part of tragedy and which awakens our compassion, but there is too something else that deepens the tragic nature of her plight – her own awareness that, despite her longing to be like other women, she is different from them. Her worth as a woman is already becoming her sense of worthlessness, the richness of her personality transformed into a corrosive, self-destructive force: 'I don't think it's right for me to burn myself out here . . . If I keep on like this, I'll end by turning bad.' (p. 104).

The appearance of Victor accentuates our sense both of Yerma's isolation and life's unfairness. He is, like Juan, a silent man but in every other sense a contrast to him – strong and positive – and Yerma's counterpart.[19] If María increases Yerma's anguish, Victor marks another stage in it, sharpening her awareness of the void in her existence. When he leaves, she rushes to where he stood, drawing into herself the vitality that Victor represents;

> [YERMA, *who has risen thoughtfully, goes to the place where* VICTOR *stood and breathes deeply – like one who breathes mountain air* . . .] (pp. 105-6)

But the place where he stood is a void, as empty of Victor as Yerma's life must always be, and her action draws attention to its futility. Indeed, it is the reality with which she is confronted that once again dominates the closing of the scene. The song sung earlier by Yerma, expressing her longing, is sung again with greater passion: 'When, child, when will you come to me?' (p. 105). Her eyes are fixed on a point in space, on the dream that fills her imagination. But challenging it are those solid, unchanging objects – the sewing-basket – that are the permanent reminders of her reality. The ending of the scene returns to its beginning, its circular structure a pointer to the inevitable nature of Yerma's fate: ['. . . *after that she sits down and takes up the sewing again. She begins to sew*' . . .] (p. 106). The act of sewing is, more than previously, a cruel contrast to Yerma's conception of creativity, and now there is the added irony that she sews the garments for someone else's child. The passionate, dynamic woman becomes the seated figure who sews mechanically and dreams impossible dreams. It is an image that anticipates the passive role which is gradually imposed upon her, the opposite of all that she aspires to.

The setting for Scene Two is Nature itself, the fields where the men work and their women bring them food. The First Old Woman is an older version of María, a more painful embodiment of Yerma's dreams. But equally poignant is the realization in her of all the vigour that Yerma has but which in her will be pitifully wasted. The First Old Woman has enjoyed and enjoys still the rich variety of life:

> I've been a woman with her skirts to the wind. I've run like an arrow to melon cuttings, to parties, to sugar cakes. Many times at dawn I've rushed to the door thinking I heard the music of guitars going along and coming nearer, but it was only the wind.
> [*She laughs.*]
> You'll laugh at me. I've had two husbands, fourteen children – five of them dead – and yet I'm not sad, and I'd like to live much longer. (pp. 107-8)

She symbolizes too, in a positive way, the traditional domestic role of women, for, though complaining, she willingly fetches and carries for her husband. Much more than María, she is the combination of wife and mother, the fulfilment of roles which, for Yerma, are, if they are to be meaningful, interdependent.

For her the unfulfilment of the role of mother accentuates the
meaninglessness of her domestic role, and what are for The
First Old Woman and María positive and even creative things
are for Yerma empty and pointless activities:

> Why am I childless? Must I be left in the prime of my life
> taking care of little birds, or putting up tiny pleated
> curtains at my little windows? (p. 108)

Yerma's encounter with the First Old Woman merely makes
her further aware of her own inadequacy.

While the roles of wife and mother are important, the role of
love is more important still, for it underlies them both, and
here is the source of Yerma's tragedy. Her marriage, like
that of many Spanish women, has been arranged for her, a
marriage of convenience more than love. From the outset she
has seen it less as a joyful, loving union than as the means of
fulfilment of her longing for a child. Love, indeed, has never
been part of her relationship with Juan, for there is between
them no natural feeling or attraction:

> FIRST OLD WOMAN: Don't you tremble when he comes
> near you? Don't you feel something like a dream when
> he brings his lips close to yours? Tell me.
> YERMA: No. I've never noticed it. (p. 109)

But if this is so, the possibility of love that grows within a
marriage has been blighted by Juan's emotionally stunted
nature, the loveless beginnings of the marriage accentuated in
the course of it. Yerma despises Juan for his lack of concern. As
a consequence of and a compensation for the emptiness of her
life, her need for a child becomes more desperate and more
hopeless. And it is not so much that she or Juan are responsible
for the situation as that the situation, initially imposed upon
them, makes demands with which, given their characters and
aims, they cannot cope. They are caught in the vicious circle of
their own incompatibility, brought together by custom and
tradition, and bound by the inflexible demands of honour. For
María and The First Old Woman there is freedom in their love
of their husbands that has its source in the natural attraction of
like to like. For Yerma freedom lies, in contrast, in her instinc-

tive but impossible attraction to Victor while her marriage,
devoid of love and slowly of hope, becomes her prison:

> He took me by the waist and I couldn't say a word to him,
> because I couldn't talk. Another time this same Victor,
> when I was fourteen years old – he was a husky boy –
> took me in his arms to leap a ditch and I started shaking
> so hard my teeth chattered.[20] (p. 109)

The First Old Woman is immediately replaced by two young
women, one of them Yerma's opposite, the other both a
parallel and a contrast to her, and both of them accentuating
her plight. The pattern of Act I is, indeed, a series of encounters whereby the reality of Yerma's fate is progressively
borne in upon her. The First Girl has a child and personifies all
that Yerma longs for. The Second Girl is a parallel to Yerma in
the sense that her marriage too has been arranged. She paints
a vivid picture of the way in which women, in particular, are
burdened by traditional roles and duties. But she is Yerma's
opposite in the sense that for her a child would be not a release
from but an addition to her existing burden: 'Anyway, you
and I, not having any, live more peacefully.' (p. 111). The
childlessness that for her is a source of freedom is a mockery of
Yerma's childlessness even more cruel than the spectacle of all
the women in the play who have given birth.

The conclusion of the Act presents Yerma in relation to
Victor and Juan, and Juan and Victor in relation to each other.
Victor sings off-stage the song in which a woman invites a
shepherd to come and let him comfort her. Yerma transforms
its general character into the poignant reality of their natural
attraction to each other. Moreover, her description of his voice
and its effect upon her, linking Victor to Nature, evokes
dramatically her capacity to respond to him:[21] 'And what a
vibrant voice! It's like a stream of water that fills your mouth.'
(p. 113). We are reminded of The First Old Woman's words:
'Men have got to give us pleasure, girl! They've got to take
down our hair and let us drink water out of their mouths.'
(p. 109). And we are reminded too of all the other allusions to
water in the play that suggest the theme of creativity. Again,
Yerma trembles in Victor's presence in a way which recalls

María's earlier allusion to her husband. And, inasmuch as Yerma seems to hear the crying of a child, she reminds us of María whose child will soon be born. Yerma's encounter with Victor suggests, more than the possibility, the reality of their feeling for each other, their contact with the lives of others and the world of Nature of which they are a part.

Juan's arrival presents, in contrast, the reality that Yerma must accept. To Victor she has observed of Juan: 'It's his character – dry.' (p. 113). It is a view borne out by his dryness to Victor and his curtness with her. All the feeling of the scene with Victor dissolves into the emotional emptiness of this final scene with Juan. His concluding words to her, ironically concerned with the fertility of the fields, emphasize his dryness, the void of his relationship with Yerma, and thus the hopelessness of her dream of a child:

YERMA: All right. Shall I expect you?
JUAN: No. I'll be busy all night with the irrigating. There's very little water; it's mine till sun-up, and I've got to guard it from thieves. You go to bed and sleep. (p. 115)

By the end of Act I we are made aware of the growing gulf between the reality that Yerma seeks and the reality that faces her. And we begin to perceive too how it leads to her tragic isolation from the generality of men and women, from an identification with Nature's creativity, and, worst of all, to a sense of alienation from her real self.

The initial setting of Act II is the mountain stream, the open air, the women's voices intoning the song, their hands washing and pounding the garments, all suggestive of Nature's vitality and of human actions that are lively and vigorous in Nature's setting. But the stream is also a place for gossip, and the women, inasmuch as their conversation centres on the lives and activities of other individuals, serve to announce, albeit briefly, the theme of honour that grows in importance in the play. In a more particular sense, the women inform us of an important change in Yerma's circumstances whereby her existing plight grows worse. Juan's house is occupied now by his spinster sisters. They are like Juan himself, a replica of his sterility. The village-women express Juan's lifelessness and

dryness in the image of the lizard: 'Just stands around blankly
– like a lizard taking the sun.' (p. 118). His sisters are like the
weeds that grow and spread in cemeteries, as though they
feed on lifeless bodies and choke the beautiful flowers that
grow around them: 'They're like those big leaves that quickly
spring up over graves.' (p. 116). Moreover, they grow inwards
instead of outwards, embodying, like Juan, Nature's processes in reverse. Finally, the sterility of their natures is
reflected in their constant polishing and cleaning of the house,
day in, day out, in silence, a parallel to Yerma's meaningless
domestic tasks:[22]

> She and her sisters-in-law, never opening their lips,
> scrub the walls all day, polish the copper, clean the
> windows with steam, and oil the floors. (p. 118)

On the one hand, Juan and his sisters contrast with the liveliness of the village women and Nature's setting, and on the
other we are made aware of Yerma increasingly surrounded by
hostile forces.

The gossip of the women suggests too another growing
pressure imposed upon her – Yerma at the centre of the
villagers' scorn and malice. The Fourth Laundress is particularly harsh, blaming Yerma for her childlessness. The Fifth
Laundress is equally venomous:

> That's the way those mannish creatures are. When they
> could be making lace, or apple cakes, they like to climb
> up on the roof, or go wade barefoot in the river. (p. 117)

It is significant that of the five who discuss her here only one,
the First Laundress, defends her. Yerma, no less than Juan, is
the object of public ridicule and must, because of it, become
increasingly aware of the sense of shame that her childlessness embraces. To the futility of her longing and the stifling
presence of Juan's sisters is added the painful burden of public
recrimination.[23]

The second part of the scene, a hymn to the process of
creation, begins by presenting its opposite in the form of
Juan's two sisters. In their black clothes and silent manner
there is a lifelessness which contrasts with the animation of the

other women and which personifies as well the melancholy of Yerma's life: [*There is whispering. Yerma's* TWO SISTERS-IN-LAW *enter. They are dressed in mourning. In the silence, they start their washing.*] (p. 119). And there is a contrast too with the energy of Nature expressed here in the bursting Spring and the sheep and lambs that are its product and its symbol. They flood the scene with lively movement and dazzling whiteness: 'It's a flood of wool. They sweep everything along. If the green wheat had eyes it'd tremble to see them coming.' (p. 119). The colour of the wool off-sets the black of the sisters' dresses and is a contrast too to the dull, uniform whiteness of the walls of Yerma's house. And there is a further contrast between the sisters, engrossed in the washing of the clothes and oblivious to Nature's wonder, and the other women who, attuned to Nature, seek to absorb into themselves its magic:

> FOURTH LAUNDRESS [*taking a deep breath*]: I like the smell of sheep.
> THIRD LAUNDRESS: You do?
> FOURTH LAUNDRESS: Yes. And why not? The smell of what's ours. Just as I like the smell of the red mud this river carries in the winter. (p. 119)

We are reminded here of Yerma who in Act I sought to draw into herself Victor's essence (pp. 105-6). The parallel links Yerma to the women of the village but points as well to her alienation from them.

The theme of Nature's vitality, typically Lorquian and part of the play's positive dynamic, is expressed throughout the remainder of the scene in the village women's song that acquires, in its unfolding, that insistent, accumulative power that seems itself the pulse of Nature. The opening lines intoned by the Fourth Laundress, echo the beginning of the scene:

> Here in this icy current
> let me wash your lace,
> just like a glowing jasmine
> is your laughing face. (p. 119)

The circular form of the scene evokes the cycle and continuity

N

of Nature. Moreover, between its beginning and conclusion is suggested the way in which in a broader sense Yerma's life is circumscribed by the village women and all the things they symbolize – fertility, normality, tradition.

The song celebrates firstly the joyful relationship of each of the women with her husband.[24] The Fourth Laundress refers to her husband and herself in lines which capture the beauty and the passion of their love and its connection with the flourishing natural world of which they are a part:

> Through night skies he comes,
> my husband, to bed,
> I, like red gillyflowers,
> he, a gillyflower red. (p. 120)

The Second Laundress sings in very sensual terms of her sexual pleasure with her husband:

> Down the hillside he comes
> at lunchtime to me,
> my husband with one rose
> and I give him three. (p. 120)

The First Laundress, on the other hand, introduces the theme of the childless wife:

> Alas for the barren wife!
> Alas for her whose breasts are sand! (p. 119)

The image of sand, of dryness, clashes with all the allusions to softness, delicacy, flowers, air, and water, and the word 'dry' itself recalls Yerma's earlier description of her husband (p. 113). Inasmuch as the village women are here individuals, Yerma as an individual is apart and distinguished from them.

The progression of the song is, however, one in which the separate loves and lives of the women merge, and they express with a common voice the theme of procreation and childbirth. They are, indeed, Woman, six voices that are one, a line or couplet taken up and passed from one individual to another in a chant whose movement and rhythm are as intertwined as are the women in their common identity. The theme of creation is set in motion by the First Laundress:

And flower to flower must be wed
when summer dries the reaper's blood so red. (p. 120)

The Sixth Laundress announces the theme of childbirth:

> [*appearing at the topmost part of the swiftly flowing stream*]:
> So that a child may weld
> white crystals in the dawn. (p. 121)

We may imagine the women kneeling at different levels of the
stream, each of them touched and linked by the water, symbolic of the life-force which links them and which is transmitted to them by their husbands.[25] Their posture, moreover, is
one of worship at the fountain of Nature, for they kneel in
adoration, paying homage to the miracle of birth. The womb,
indeed, is a chalice that contains the miracle of the unborn
child:

FIFTH LAUNDRESS: Joy, joy, joy,
                     of the swollen womb beneath the
                     dress!
SECOND LAUNDRESS: Joy, joy, joy!
                     The waist can miracles possess!
                     (pp. 121-2)

The chorus rises to an ecstatic climax that expresses all the joy
of childbirth. It concludes with a lament and a prayer for the
childless woman. The individual Laundresses become, mov-
ingly, the common voice of women, sharing the anguish of the
barren wife and praying for her subsequent fertility. It is a
powerful and touching ending. In one way Yerma is not alone,
but in another she seems more isolated from other women and
their function in the pattern of creation.

   The second scene, embodying the negative movement of
the play, concentrates on Yerma's growing imprisonment and
isolation. It opens as night begins to fall and ends in complete
darkness. The encroaching darkness of night parallels Yerma's
growing anguish and the closing-in upon her of her circumstances. Now, more than previously, the theme of honour as a
source of her imprisonment is strongly emphasized, for Juan is
especially concerned with Yerma's absence from the house:

'But you've known all along I don't like her to go out alone . . .
My life's in the fields, but my honour's here.' (p. 123). To
Yerma herself he repeats the idea in a form where the idea of
imprisonment is clear: 'I don't like people to be pointing me
out. That's why I want to see this door closed.' (p. 125). The
picture of Yerma enclosed within the house and then within
herself is one of a woman driven inwards, her life circumscribed by honour and those who practise it. In Yerma's words
the sisters of Juan become her gaolers: 'Your sisters guard me
well.' (p. 124). And her existence within the house is a condemnation to a living death: 'Women in their homes. When
those homes aren't tombs.' (p. 124). Secondly, Yerma is more
and more the prisoner of the lack of communication between
herself and Juan and of his inability to understand her: 'You
speak in a way I don't understand.' (p. 124). If he com-
prehends her need at all, he does so superficially, for he seeks
to please and thus appease her by offering her gifts, or to
escape her presence by working in the fields. Instead of growing closer they grow apart, each pursuing an objective – Juan
the cultivation of his fields, Yerma the fertility of her body –
which for the other has no meaning. Instead of a common-
ground there is between them a head-on conflict of priorities
and aims, its essence caught in the image of a rock.[26] Juan
observes of Yerma:

> You brood on this one idea till you're half-crazy – instead
> of thinking about something else – and you persist in
> running your head against a stone. (p. 125)

The rock symbolizes his lack of understanding, and, inasmuch
as the rock is lifeless, his sterility. Yerma, in contrast, yearns
for the things that stand for beauty, feeling, freedom, life and
energy: 'A stone, yes; and it's shameful that it is a stone,
because it ought to be a bucket of flowers and sweet scents.'
(p. 125). And again:

> I want to drink water and there's neither water nor a
> glass. I want to go up the mountain, and I have no feet. I
> want to embroider skirts and I can't find thread. (p. 125)

Enclosure, the closed door, the closed mouth, the lifeless rock;

in contrast, the mountains, the running water, the open air, the lovely flowers: they express two different worlds, each exclusive of the other, and thus the gulf that, progressively separating Juan and Yerma, isolates her from him.

In consequence of this, Yerma becomes the prisoner of her sense of failure and of the despair that springs from it. From an awareness of her as the prisoner of other people and of her circumstances, we are made increasingly conscious of her as the prisoner of herself and of the slow and terrible transformation whereby her sense of herself as part of Nature becomes her sense of alienation from it. The soliloquy that follows Juan's departure reveals the character and the direction of Yerma's conflict. On the one hand, there are suggestions of the way in which she is linked to Nature, for within her breasts there are springs of milk and in her body dynamic and instinctive rhythms:

> These two teeming springs I have
> of warm milk are in the closeness
> of my flesh two rhythms of a horse's gallop. (p. 126)

On the other, they are transformed already from their proper function into sources of pain and sorrow. Her breasts in their uselessness are like doves devoid of sight or whiteness:

> Oh, breasts, blind beneath my clothes!
> Oh, doves with neither eyes nor whiteness! (p. 126)

The blood that courses through her body seeking an outlet in a child becomes, contained within her, a poison:

> Oh, what pain of imprisoned blood
> is nailing wasps at my brain's base! (p. 127)

Her body is, indeed, a source of suffering, her womb a prison from which the beauty of a child will never come:

> Oh, what a field of sorrow!
> Oh, this is a door to beauty closed:
> to beg a son to suffer, and for the wind
> to offer dahlias of a sleeping moon! (p. 126)

The dominant mood is that of Yerma's painful awareness of herself as a travesty of Nature.

The appearance of María with her child poignantly underlines the point. If earlier she was a symbol of Yerma's hopes,
she is now a pointer to her hopelessness. In their conversation
the themes and mood of the earlier soliloquy are expanded,
Yerma's hope to be one with Nature transformed through her
sense of alienation from it into a growing self-disgust. Her
physical sterility becomes an emotional one, and she, like Juan
and his spinster sisters, grows inwards instead of outwards,
the process of Nature in reverse as ironically true of her as it is
of them. It is one of the play's most terrible truths that the
woman who at its outset was her husband's opposite should in
the course of time grow like him, and grow to despise herself.

María and the village-women with their children become for
Yerma the proof of her own futility:

> How can I help complaining when I see you and the other
> women full of flowers from within, and then I see myself
> useless in the midst of so much beauty! (p. 127)

But more than this, there is slowly borne in upon her her
growing conviction of her badness in a beautiful world. Yerma
begins to see herself in terms of Nature's useless and ugly
plants: 'A farm woman who bears no children is useless – like a
handful of thorns.' (p. 127). And worse still is her belief, the
ultimate measure of her despair, that God has abandoned her:
' – and even bad – even though I may be a part of this waste-
land abandoned by the hand of God.' (p. 127). It is logical, in
the light of her growing sense of the pointlessness of her
existence, that the whole of creative Nature should now
assume a mocking character, its richness an accusation of her
abnormality:[27]

> For I'm hurt, hurt and humiliated beyond endurance,
> seeing the wheat ripening, the fountains never ceasing to
> give water, the sheep bearing hundreds of lambs, the
> she-dogs; until it seems that the whole countryside rises
> to show me its tender sleeping young, while I feel two
> hammer-blows here, instead of the mouth of my child.
> (p. 127)

Throughout the scene the allusions to water, the symbol of

life, become in their different forms a cruel mockery of Yerma's plight. To Juan she has expressed her desire for a child in terms of water: 'I want to drink water and there's neither water nor a glass . . .' (p. 125). The unborn child is like the rain contained within a cloud:

> and our wombs guard tender infants,
> just as a cloud is sweet with rain. (p. 127)

But of all the images and symbols that surround her here, the most evocative and heartless reminder of her fate are the pitchers that are present throughout the scene, inanimate, lifeless objects, yet full of the life-giving force of Nature in a way that Yerma can never be. She is linked to them too in the sense that Juan and his sisters slowly draw the water from them as they draw the life from Yerma, leaving them dry and empty: [*The other* SISTER *enters and goes toward the water jars, from one of which she fills a pitcher.*] (p. 125). The only kind of water with which she is now associated is, significantly, the water of her tears:

> MARIA [*she enters with a child in her arms*]: I hurry by whenever I have the child – since you always weep! (p. 127)

All that in Nature is meaningful becomes in Yerma the symbol of her anguish. Moreover, while the world of Nature and Yerma's friends symbolize one thing, everything within the house suggests another. And what for Yerma is more terrify- ing still is the fact that Juan and his sisters, silent, lifeless, uncommunicative creatures, constantly in contact with her, the opposite of all that she aspires to, are more and more the living testimony of what she could become, the terrible image of her future. [28]

The ending of the Act deepens the sense of Yerma's isola- tion. In María's attempt to hurry past her door there is the suggestion of her friends' not wishing to see or embarrass her. Secondly, there is Yerma's conviction that Juan and his sisters are arrayed against her: 'They are three against me.' (p. 128). They are like stones that block her path, preventing her escape: 'They're stones in my path.' (p. 128). Thirdly, there is the fact of Victor's departure, stripping Yerma of the consolation of his presence. And inasmuch as Juan has purchased Victor's flocks, there is the cruel irony that it is he who benefits from Victor's leaving, while Yerma, who needs him, is abandoned to her own despair. When he is gone, her anguish is complete. She leaves the house, a dark, huddled figure covered in a shawl, the whole suggestive of dejection. Around her the darkness, intensifying the mood, is descending rapidly: [*They leave cautiously. The stage is almost in darkness . . .*] (p. 131). It has increased steadily throughout the scene and by its conclusion is complete: [. . . *The stage is quite dark.*] (p. 131). As the scene ends the voices of Juan's sisters call out to Yerma, increasingly imperious, signifying their hold upon her. The sound of the shepherds and the sheep-bells, reminding us of Victor, fade in the darkness, drowned by the sisters' voices, symbolic of the world of Juan and his household from which for Yerma there is now no escape.

The second Act has deepened the pity we feel for Yerma. She dominates the Act, as she did Act I, and displays again the qualities that previously evoked compassion. She is, above all, a good and honourable woman who, despite her plight, refuses to compromise her honour. There is both an irony and an injustice, therefore, in the fact that, though she is innocent, she is constantly suspected by her husband and gossiped about by the village-women in a way which constitutes dishonour. Of the young women of the rural tragedies Yerma is in many ways the least to blame and the most deserving of our pity. But most pitiful of all is the spectacle of hope slowly removed from her to the point where, in a manner which catches the pessimism of our time, she is left only with a total sense of her futility.

The beginning of Act III reveals that Yerma in her desperation has sought the advice of Dolores, the local sorceress, in the matter of her infertility. Throughout the Act, indeed, she seeks in superstitious rite and religious ceremony the remedy that lies with Juan, and in her wandering from place to place there is a suggestion of her gradual movement away from him. The opening exchanges emphasize Yerma's terrible yearning for a child, but now this compulsion has a violent and dangerous dimension, expressed in the image of fire that colours Yerma's thoughts and words. When she considers that she might never have a child, a flame rises within her, as though from the earth itself:

> Sometimes, when I feel certain I'll never, ever . . . a tide of fire sweeps up through me from my feet and everything seems empty . . . (p. 133)

She is a woman consumed by her sense of failure, the warmth of her nature transformed into the fire of a desperate and obsessive passion. Moreover, the passion that consumes her already has for Juan ominous implications:

> When he covers me, he's doing his duty, but I feel a waist cold as a corpse's, and I, who've always hated passionate women, would like to be at that instant a mountain of fire. (p. 133)

The extent of Yerma's transformation may be gauged by the way in which the symbol of the mountain that elsewhere is synonymous with freedom, air, and space, is now the volcano that will soon erupt. And fire that is a source of energy and creativity in Nature now has purely destructive connotations.

There is a second, crucial point in the fact that Yerma's hopes are shown to lie where there are none. She knows that her only hope of a child lies with Juan but she knows too that he does not want a child. And though she has no love for him, her sense of honour closes the door on any other possible relationship. She expresses perfectly a situation whose essence is its hopelessness:

> YERMA: . . . The trouble is, he doesn't want children!
> FIRST OLD WOMAN: Don't say that!
> YERMA: I can tell that in his glance, and, since he doesn't want them, he doesn't give them to me. I don't love him; I don't love him, and yet he's my only salvation. By honour and by blood. My only salvation. (p. 134)

This, together with the desperation and the growing violence that are part of it, makes Yerma not only the helpless victim of her circumstances but also, more pitifully, of herself, of a warm and compassionate nature grossly transformed.

Daybreak is for Yerma no longer a symbol of her hope but a further remorseless stage in the prolongation of her hopelessness, the new day another instance of Nature's mockery. It marks, indeed, the appearance of Juan and throughout the confrontation that now develops consolidates in two particular ways her helplessness. Firstly, Juan expounds at length the theme of honour and his own concern with Yerma's conduct. Her absences give food for gossip to the villagers and cause embarrassment to Juan:

> When I come on a group, they all fall silent; when I go to weigh the flour, they all fall silent, and even at night, in the fields, when I awaken, it seems to me that the branches of the trees become silent too. (p. 136)

Against his accusations Yerma advances an honest and impassioned self-defence:

> I won't let you say another word. Not one word more. You and your people imagine you're the only ones who look out for honour, and you don't realize my people have never had anything to conceal . . . Do what you want with me, since I'm your wife, but take care not to set a man's name in my breast. (pp. 135-6)

But whatever her innocence, she cannot escape the villagers' opinion of her and, in consequence, Juan's increasing tyranny. There is, moreover, a terrible irony not merely in her innocence but in the fact that she is driven by her circumstances to a form of behaviour that arouses Juan's suspicions and provides the people of the village with further food for gossip.

The second aspect of her hopeless situation is Juan's lack of sympathy. He cannot comprehend what Yerma seeks from him:

> Because one would have to be made of iron to put up with a woman who wants to stick her fingers into your heart and who goes out of her house at night. In search of what? Tell me! (p. 135)

But his coldness reaches a point where he shuts her out completely. She attempts, in a moment of desperation, to make him aware of her need for him:

YERMA [*bursting out, embracing her husband*]: I'm looking for you. I'm looking for you. It's you I look for day and night without finding a shade where to draw breath. It's your blood and help I want. (p. 136)

It is a gesture that echoes an earlier episode (Act I, Scene One, p. 101) but in a form much more intense. Juan's previous lack of warmth is now his cold, complete rejection of her. And the extent of Yerma's failure to penetrate her husband's lack of understanding is caught in the image of the stone that, applied earlier to Juan, (p. 125), now appears once again:

YERMA [*loudly*]: When I went out looking for my flowers, I ran into a wall. Ay-y-y! Ay-y-y! It's against that wall I'll break my head. (p. 136)

The gradual breaking of day as the scene concludes emphasizes further Yerma's darkness. The depths of her despair are expressed in the image of the pit: '. . . now that I'm entering the darkest part of the pit . . .' (p. 137). She is, moreover, cast adrift in a life which has no meaning or direction, the image of the moon suggesting Yerma's emotional and spiritual death:

YERMA: Look how I'm left alone! As if the moon searched for herself in the sky. Look at me! (p. 136)

Even honour, which for Juan is everything, is now for Yerma meaningless, for if she has no life she has no honour. As the curtain falls, it falls on the terrible spectacle of a once defiant woman drained of her defiance and of her dignity and meaning as a woman. In Act II she has resisted Juan, presenting him with a picture of the woman she will never allow herself to be:

I didn't come to these four walls to resign myself. When a cloth binds my head so my mouth won't drop open, and my hands are tied tight in my coffin – then, then I'll resign myself! (p. 125)

She is now that very woman, and in her final words there is a transformation of her earlier assertiveness: 'It's written, and I'm not going to raise my arms against the sea. That's it! Let my mouth be struck dumb! [*She leaves*]. (p. 137).

The final scene is the culmination of Yerma's degradation as a woman and of her desolation as an individual. The mountain-setting, reminiscent of all the earlier allusions to openness, air, freedom and Nature's vitality in general, is a mockery of all the women who journey there to pray at the shrine for their own fertility. On the one hand they are degraded by their childlessness, the victims of the scorn and mockery of others. On the other they are degraded by the men who prey upon them in increasing numbers, seeing in their desperation the means of their own indiscriminate sexual satisfaction. As for Yerma, the despair of all the women is incarnate in her. For a month the woman who earlier in the play has matched the vitality of Nature has been seated in her chair, a lifeless parody of all that she has been before: 'She's been a month without getting up from her chair.' (p. 139). She is, deprived of hope, almost the corpse that previously (p. 125) she has vowed she will never be.

The prayer of the barren women expresses both their hopes and their sense of hopelessness. The allusions to flowers, to fire, and to God the Creator form the optimistic thread that grows in its intensity through the prayer, while the references to withering, abandonment and darkness are a constant counterpoint:

CHORUS OF WOMEN: Lord, make blossom the rose,
leave not my rose in shadow.
YERMA: Upon my barren flesh
one rose of all the wonder. (p. 140)

The aspirations of the women and of Yerma in particular are linked, as elsewhere in the play, to the processes of Nature, but it is in the central section of the scene, where the ritual of the prayer becomes the pagan sensuality of a fertility rite, that the theme of creativity assumes its most intense, rhapsodic and incandescent form. There is about the whole a sense of magic. On the right three girls appear, above them another seven. The magic numbers set the scene and it is then intensified by the appearance of the two masked figures, symbolic of Man and Woman, figures of great beauty, as though of the earth itself:

[. . . *two traditional* MASKS *appear. One is Male and the other Female. They carry large masks. They are not in any fashion grotesque, but of great beauty and with a feeling of pure earth* . . .] (p. 141)

In the dance and the chant that follow there is an uninhibited sensuality that suggests the magic of love and passion. The story of the song is the story of the woman who waits and is made fertile. As she is enacted by the masked figure, she is, of course, all the women who wait, the incarnation of all their deepest dreams and desires expressed in a form both moving and dramatic. The actors dramatize a myth that is timeless and universal, expressing the deepest feelings and relationships of human beings in relation to each other and to the world around them. The song, accompanied by a rhythmic clapping and the wild movements of dancing figures, is a truly climactic celebration of the Lorca theme of erotic love.

The conclusion of this scene is, appropriately, a prelude to the final and fatal confrontation of Yerma with Juan and the expression of all her violent frustration. Moreover, the hope of fertility embodied in the ritual scene is something that for Yerma is finally stripped away, her sense of desolation ruthlessly exposed. If Yerma comes to the shrine with little hope, the First Old Woman's revelation dashes what little hope she has:[29]

The fault is your husband's. Do you hear? He can cut off my hands if it isn't. Neither his father, nor his grandfather, nor his great-grandfather behaved like men of good blood. (p. 144)

Her sense of honour forbids that she take another man and she rejects the First Old Woman's suggestion of her son. Caught in the twin predicament of childlessness and her husband's impotence, honour closes the door on her and her course is set. It is the moment in the play when Yerma finally accepts what, despite herself, she has struggled to keep at bay – the reality of a future without a child, the reality of a future that for her is meaningless:

Barren, yes, I know it! Barren! Ever since I married, I've

been avoiding that word, and this is the first time I've heard it, the first time it's been said to my face. The first time I see it's the truth. (p. 145)

The climax of the play, given Yerma's sense of degradation and of the pointlessness of her existence, is entirely convincing. Juan, in seeking to persuade her of the joy of life without a child, chooses the worst moment to do so. It illustrates again their alienation from each other. For Juan Yerma is an object of sexual attraction, a woman to gratify his physical desires:

YERMA: What are you looking for?
JUAN: You. In the moonlight you're beautiful.
YERMA: You want me as you sometimes want a
    pigeon to eat. (p. 147)

For her his advances are a mockery of everything she seeks, the attempted embrace an insult that degrades her no less than the pursuit of all the other lustful men who avail themselves of barren and desperate women. Juan's words, denying his interest in a child, stifling her hope, fall like blows upon her ears, and his arms and lips, seeking her for pleasure, are a final, unbearable affront. It is appropriate that, as Juan has suffocated Yerma's aspirations, depriving her of space and room to breathe and grow, she should in the end suffocate him physically, choking out of him the very breath of which, metaphorically, she has been deprived.[30] There is a terrible and tragic irony in the fact that Juan's attempted embrace of Yerma becomes her deadly embrace of him, her hands locked around his throat. She ravages him, indeed, as he has ravaged her. But whatever the poetic justice of the act, it is less, far less, than the enormous pity that Yerma generates. The killing of Juan is the final assurance – her own assurance – of her childlessness:

Barren, barren, but sure. Now I really know it for sure. And alone . . . Now I'll sleep without startling myself awake, anxious to see if I feel in my blood another new blood. My body dry for ever. (p. 147)

If there is in it a consolation, it lies only in the removal of doubt and hope. The emphasis of the ending of the Act is not on

Yerma's peace of mind but on her utter loneliness, her isolation both from other women and within herself:

> Don't come near me, because I've killed my son.
> I myself have killed my son!
> [*A group that remains in the background, gathers.*
> *The chorus of the pilgrimage is heard.*] (p. 147)

She stands alone, at the front of the stage, separated from the others. The sound of the distant fertility rite underlines the fact that Yerma is herself forever distanced from that possibility. But if she seems an isolated figure, different from the others, it is her anguish and her sense of the emptiness of life which is the predominant, haunting and desolate image which we are left to ponder on. In the figure of one woman there is concentrated with enormous power that pessimistic Lorca vision of the world that, expressed in the other rural tragedies in the larger unit of the family, is something that touches on us all.

Francisco García Lorca has observed that Lorca sought in *Yerma* a greater simplicity and sobriety, believing that his theatre 'would benefit by a more austere technique.'[31] It is certainly true that in the play he has pared away the symbolic and supernatural elements that in *Blood Wedding* are so theatrically brilliant and that, in addition, there is a greater concentration both on fewer people and on their inner lives. The play's sub-title, *Tragic Poem in Three Acts and Six Scenes (Poema Trágico en Tres Actos y Seis Cuadros)*, suggests a greater emphasis on the expression of the deepest feelings of its characters, notably Yerma's, and it is therefore no coincidence that, of the three rural tragedies, it is *Yerma* which has often been described as the most poetic and the least realistic. Francisco García Lorca makes the point: 'Of the trilogy . . . *Yerma* is the play which has the smallest number of elements directly inspired by reality.'[32] In a recent book Mildred Adams, referring to the poetic qualities of the play, suggests that, played realistically, it achieved only reasonable success, and that only in the famous production of Victor García in 1972 did it achieve international acclaim:

Victor García, the producer, abolished all literal details of scene and stage furniture, and put in their place a dirt-coloured trampolin on which characters moved as though walking on thick sand. The setting was of no colour; its lifelessness became the symbolic background against which the tragic drama took on added strength and meaning. By mechanical means, in the Romería scene, this device was raised to become a mural back-ground for the hanging vision of Yerma's inflamed dream. The performance brilliantly justified Federico's confidence in the powers of imagination when making use of surrealist means. In literal productions, *Yerma* had been poetic but not convincing. Here, with an avant-garde setting and interpretation, decades after its author had felt the first force of that theory, *Yerma* came into its own.[33]

The point is one which brings us to a consideration of the character and purpose of Lorca's stage-settings.

Yerma, like *Blood Wedding*, was written with the traditional, picture-frame stage in mind, but Lorca's stage-directions are more stark and stripped of detail than those of the earlier play.[34] The setting of Act I, Scene One, is a room in Yerma's house, but there is no description of the room, its colour or its furniture. One concrete object only is emphasized, both at the beginning and the conclusion of the scene: *When the curtain rises* YERMA *is asleep with an embroidery frame at her feet . . .* (p. 99). This single object is sufficient to suggest Yerma's domestic role, for it is present throughout the scene, the more effective for being a solitary, isolated object. In contrast to it, as the curtain rises, is Yerma's dream of fertility and maternity that quickly fades. In the two things, the one transitory, the other constant, the elements of illusion and reality in Yerma's life are quickly juxtaposed. The stage-setting, pared down to its barest, simplest elements, is essentially symbolic.

For Act II, Scene Two, the description of the setting is also very brief: [YERMA's *house. It is twilight.* JUAN *is seated. The* TWO SISTERS-IN-LAW *are standing.*] (p. 123). In the course of the scene two details are important. Firstly, Yerma enters with

two pitchers full of water and sets them down. They remain
throughout the scene, like the embroidery frame in Act I,
Scene One, an ironic, mocking contrast to the dry, infertile
Yerma, her husband and his withered sisters. Secondly, the
doorway is significant, especially in relation to the two sisters.
From time to time they are framed in the doorway: [*The* TWO
SISTERS *appear at the door.*] (p. 126). Later, it is one of them: [*The*
SECOND SISTER *appears and goes slowly toward the door, where she
remains fixed, illuminated by the last light of evening.*] (p. 130).
Finally, as the curtain falls, they both move to the door, calling
our for Yerma:

> [. . . *They look at each other and go toward the door.*]
> SECOND SISTER-IN-LAW [*louder*]: Yerma!
> FIRST SISTER-IN-LAW [*going to the door, and in an imperious
> voice*]: Yerma!

Of all the physical features of the room only the doorway, the
access to the outside world, is important, and, in conjunction
with it, the extent to which Yerma's freedom of movement is
more and more restricted. Only those aspects of the setting
need be emphasized which are relevant to the emotional and
psychological patterns of the characters' developing experience.

Act I, Scene Two, is an example of an outdoor scene. The
opening stage-direction reads: [*A field.* YERMA *enters carrying a
basket. The* FIRST OLD WOMAN *enters.*] (p. 107). Lorca specifies no
further details, nor in the dialogue is there any specific reference to the setting. But the suggestion, not in any fussy,
naturalistic way, but in a simple, symbolic manner, of openness and brightness is crucial, for the setting is a frame that
contrasts more and more as the scene unfolds with Yerma's
growing awareness of her own infertility and with the poison-
ous darkness of her thoughts.

The dialogue of *Yerma* is highly concentrated, revealing the
characters as individuals and in relation to each other. In Act I,
Scene One, there is established immediately the contrast and
the clash between Juan and Yerma that becomes the tragic
conflict of the play. Juan's words are few, abrupt, suggestive of
his dry and uncommunicative nature. Yerma, in contrast,

o

expresses herself with passion, seeking to communicate, to penetrate the defensive wall which he has built between them:

> YERMA: But not you, you were different when we were first married. Now you've got a face as white as though the sun had never shone on it. I'd like to see you go to the river and swim or climb up on the roof when the rain beats down on our house. Twenty-four months we've been married and you only get sadder, thinner, as if you were growing backwards.
>
> JUAN: Are you finished?
>
> YERMA [rising]: Don't take it wrong. If I were sick I'd like you to take care of me. 'My wife's sick. I'm going to butcher this lamb and cook her a good meat dish.' 'My wife's sick. I'm going to save this chicken-fat to relieve her chest; I'm going to take her this sheepskin to protect her feet from the snow.' That's the way I am. That's why I take care of you.
>
> JUAN: I'm grateful. (p. 99-100)

The powerful flow of Yerma's words, met by Juan's stony coldness, captures the essence of their relationship. When Juan next appears, at the conclusion of Act I, the situation is identical. In Act I he has appeared only twice and briefly, but every phrase he utters reveals his attitude to Yerma.

In Acts II and III Juan appears on four occasions, twice in Act II, Scene Two, once in Act III, Scene One, and once in the final scene. Three of these occasions present his growing conflict with Yerma, each a more violent clash than the previous one. Juan seems a more expressive, more passionate man. But his words revolve unceasingly around the things that matter to him most – his fields and his honour. His dialogue, repeating the same thing endlessly in different ways, reveals both starkly and economically the obsessions that haunt him ceaselessly.[35]

While Juan's concerns are revealed almost entirely in relation to Yerma, she is revealed in relation to all the other characters. Even so, every passage of dialogue, however different from the previous one, exposes Yerma's obsessions and her growing anguish. In the first encounter with María there is not a line of dialogue that is not related to Yerma's desire for a child and her anguish that she does not have one. She is revealed in a whole variety of moods before the fact of María's pregnancy – surprise, curiosity, wonder, envy, compassion (p. 102-5). She seems a much more integrated personality than Juan, but in the fixed nature of her obsession she is exactly like him, and she inevitably returns to the subject of her own despair:

> If I keep on like this, I'll end by turning bad . . . Every woman has blood for four or five children, and when she doesn't have them it turns to poison . . . as it will in me. (p. 104)

As the play unfolds, the patterned structure of the dialogue becomes more prominent, and, secondly, there is a greater and more terrible weight about it that suggests despair. The second encounter with María, in Act II, Scene Two, reveals that now there is only pain and a sense of Yerma's uselessness, expressed in repetitions and in images of ugliness that themselves become a kind of repetition in the play:

> How can I help complaining when I see you and the other women full of flowers from within, and then see myself useless in the midst of so much beauty! . . . A farm woman who bears no children is useless – like a handful of thorns – and even bad – even though I may be a part of this wasteland abandoned by the hand of God . . . Because I'm tired. Because I'm tired of having them [hands], and not being able to use them on something of my own. For I'm hurt, hurt and humiliated beyond endurance . . . (p. 127)

The dialogue is carefully shaped throughout, concentrating on the central themes and issues, and stripped of anything extraneous to them.

Poetry in the play takes, almost without exception, the form of songs. There are seven examples, five of them involving Yerma, and, as is the general case in Lorca's drama, the poetry underlines a particularly emotional and dramatic moment.[36] In Act I, Scene One, Yerma has failed to move Juan, she is alone, and she sings a song that expresses all the sadness of her unfulfilled dream of a child. The song is itself a drama, which, enacted between an imaginary child and Yerma, conveys the immediacy of her deep and unsatisfied longing. The child, answering Yerma's questions, assumes the living form that she would give it. Yet, though it seems so real, its need and hers so great, they look at each other from far away, the gulf between them unbridgeable:

> What want you, boy, from so far away?
>
> When, boy, when will you come to me? (p. 101)

The song suggests a physical isolation so vivid and stark that Yerma's emotional solitude seems almost tangible.

In Act I, Scene Two, there is another moment when Yerma is alone. Her conversation with the First Old Woman and the two girls has increased her sense of isolation. Suddenly she hears Victor singing a traditional shepherd song. For Victor it has no meaning but for Yerma it has every meaning, and when she takes it up she becomes herself the shepherdess singing to her lover, her own feelings matching its words at every point:

> Why, shepherd, sleep alone?
> On my wool-quilt deep
> you'd finer sleep.

It is a beautifully managed, theatrically magical moment in which what is meaningless for Victor becomes expressive of all Yerma's love for him.[37]

In Act II, Scene Two, following a bitter confrontation with her husband, Yerma is again alone. She feels more isolated still, for Juan's two sisters have come to live with him. The poetry which expresses her deepening despair is an echo of her first song in Act I, Scene One, but its mood is altogether darker. It is linked to the earlier song by the allusion to the child still hoped for:

> But you must come, sweet love, my baby,
> because water gives salt, the earth fruit,
> and our wombs guard tender infants,
> just as a cloud is sweet with rain. (p. 127)

But now the predominant images of the passage are of pain, of beauty that withers and life whose purpose is destroyed:

> Oh, what a field of sorrow!
>
> Oh, breasts, blind beneath my clothes!
> Oh, doves with neither eyes nor whiteness!
> Oh, what pain of imprisoned blood
> is nailing wasps at my brain's base! (p. 126-7)

Here in evocative images and strong rhythms, is the expression of a deepening anguish. Each of the moments in the play signalled by song or poetry becomes a sign-post marking another stage in Yerma's painful and solitary journey.[38]

The song of the LAUNDRESSES in Act II, Scene One, is altogether different. Like the wedding songs of *Blood Wedding* it is a celebration of love, marriage and childbirth and of men and women as part of Nature's vital and creative processes. Its tone, in contrast to Yerma's increasingly melancholy lines, is vibrant, its rhythms full of spring, its imagery replete with life and colour:

> SECOND LAUNDRESS: Down the hillside he comes
> at lunchtime to me,
> my husband with one rose
> and I give him three.
>
> FOURTH LAUNDRESS: Through night skies he comes,
> my husband, to bed.
> I like red gillyflowers,
> he a gillyflower red. (p. 120)

As the women in turn joyfully intone the song, it becomes more vigorous still, its lines shorter and more emphatic until the final verse, repeating the first and sung by all the women, completes a circle that is suggestive of the cycle of birth and love celebrated in the song itself.[39] It has a parallel in Act III, Scene Two, in the prayer for the barren women. Poetry and song, as in *Blood Wedding*, highlight individual dramatic moments, and through their allusive, incantatory power, extend and broaden the range of reference.

Movement in the play often accompanies or reinforces dialogue. In Act I, Scene One, Yerma's attempt to communicate with Juan in words leads to her powerful and even desperate embrace of him, as though her action is finally more expressive than her words: [YERMA *embraces and kisses her husband. She takes the initiative.*] (p. 101). Her failure to move him, sharpening her sadness, is reflected in the much more passive, seated posture which then accompanies her singing of her song, her despair conveyed to us as much by her physical position as by the words she sings. Throughout the subsequent exchanges with María, Yerma's movements – rising, holding María, looking at her, pressing her hands against María's stomach – underline her fluctuating moods and, like her words, reveal the nature of her preoccupations. There are also repeated movements in the play which are significant. In Act III, Scene One, Yerma embraces Juan as she did earlier in the play: YERMA [*bursting out, embracing her husband.*] (p. 136). The embrace is now more desperate, and the parallel with the earlier incident makes the point. Similarly, as Yerma holds María in Act I, Scene One, so she holds the First Old Woman in Act I, Scene Two, demanding from her what she wants to know. In this particular sense, repeated movements, like repetitions in the dialogue itself, draw attention to Yerma's increasingly anguished state of mind.[40]

There are many expressive movements in the play, unaccompanied by dialogue. As the curtain rises on Act I, Scene One, the slow, tiptoe, silent movement of the shepherd and the child across the stage has all the unreality of dream: [*A* SHEPHERD *enters on tiptoe, looking fixedly at* YERMA . . .] (p. 99). Later in the scene, before she sings of her hope for a child, Yerma's movements, unaccompanied by words, express all her deepest aspirations: [JUAN *leaves.* YERMA *walks toward her sewing. She passes a hand over her belly, lifts her arms in a beautiful sigh, and sits down to sew.*] (p. 101). Again, at the end of the scene Yerma moves to the point where Victor has been standing and finally back to her sewing. In some respects it is a movement which recalls the earlier one (p. 101), but because Victor has in the meantime come and gone, it pinpoints more precisely Yerma's thoughts:

[YERMA, *who has risen thoughtfully, goes to the place where* VICTOR *stood, and breathes deeply – like one who breathes mountain air. Then she goes to the other side of the room as if looking for something, and after that sits down and takes up the sewing again. She begins to sew. Her eyes remain fixed on one point.*] (p.106)

As a final example we may consider the slow, silent movements of Juan's two sisters about the house, notably in Act II, Scene Two: [*The* FIRST SISTER*enters slowly and walks towards some shelves.*] (p.125). And again: [*The other* SISTER *leaves with a platter in almost a processional manner . . .*] (p.126). The way in which they move suggests their lifelessness and the manner in which they haunt Yerma more and more.

There is one particularly striking moment in the play where the absence of movement highlights the emotion of the scene. At the end of Act I Yerma and Victor are alone and Yerma imagines that she hears the crying of the child for which she longs. The stage-direction reads: [*. . . The silence is accentuated and without the slightest gesture, a struggle between the two begins.*] (p.114). The thoughts, the words, the feelings, especially of Yerma, are the most important aspect of the scene, and the lack of movement calls attention to them, focusing on the inner drama of two individuals locked in a purely emotional conflict with each other. The resolution of the conflict is suggested by only the slightest movement: [*She looks at him fixedly.* VICTOR *also looks at her, then slowly shifts his gaze as if afraid . . .*] (p.114).

In contrast to the movement or lack of it that highlights the speech and feelings of individuals, there are those much more ritualistic moments in the play where the collective, stylized, often balletic movements of groups of people broaden the meaning and implications of the action. In Act II Scene One, the Laundresses' celebration of love and procreation is accompanied by their increasingly vigorous pounding of the clothes they wash in the stream: [*They move the clothes in rhythm and beat them.*] (p.122). The rhythmic, pulsating movement is a primitive beat that accompanies their singing, but it suggests too the rhythm of life, even of the physical act of love. Similarly, in Act III, Scene Two, the appearance of the symbolic

figures of the Male and Female is preceded and accompanied
by balletic movements and rhythmic clapping that give to the
scene the character and atmosphere of a fertility rite:

> [GIRLS *running with long garlands in their hands appear from*
> *the left. On the right, three others, looking backward . . .*
> *Higher up appear the* SEVEN GIRLS *who wave the garlands*
> *towards the left . . .*] (p. 141)

We may imagine how the various figures move in the scene,
their stylized movements in relation to each other giving to the
whole that simple yet haunting quality of a drama that has
been acted out from time immemorial.

    Lighting is another important part of the play's closely-
woven texture. Broadly speaking, Yerma's movement into the
blackness of despair is reflected physically in the lighting of the
stage. At the outset light fills the stage and suggests both
Yerma's dream and her optimism: [. . . *The stage is in the*
strange light of a dream . . .] (p. 99). Act II, Scene Two, begins in
a twilight symbolic of Yerma's fading hope: . . . *It is twilight . . .*
(p. 123). By the end of the scene it has grown completely dark,
Victor has gone away and Yerma is left alone with an uncaring
husband and his two withered sisters: [*The bells and horns of the*
shepherds are heard. The stage is quite dark.] (p. 131). Act III, Scene
One, takes place in darkness. Day is about to break but Yerma
has spent the night in the darkness of her own despair, seeking the help of the sorceress, Dolores. When she leaves her she
encounters Juan, his anger, his implacable concern with honour, and her darkness grows and deepens. Act III, Scene Two,
commences as night begins to fall: [. . . YERMA *enters with* SIX
WOMEN *who are going to the chapel . . . Night begins to fall.*]
(p. 139). The women are full of hope but their hopes are set,
suggestively, in the growing darkness of night: [. . . *The back of*
the stage fills with people who shout and comment on the dance. It has
grown quite dark.] (p. 141). It is a darkness that does not lift
again.

    Light, in contrast, suggests in a number of scenes the fresh-
ness, vigour and vitality of Nature. In the very first scene the
light that suggests Yerma's dream fades and becomes instead
the brightness of a Spring morning, symbolic of bursting life:

[. . . *When the* SHEPHERD *leaves, the light changes into the happy brightness of a spring morning* . . .] (p. 99). In the second scene it is morning, for the women are taking food to their husbands at mid-day. The setting of the field where Yerma's conversation with the First Old Woman and the two girls takes place is itself an image of Nature's abundance that off-sets Yerma's infertility. The sunlight, flooding the scene, is an ironic contrast to Yerma's darkening thoughts. Finally, Act II, Scene One, is a scene that is full of light, reflecting on the one hand the vitality and optimism of the women washing the clothes and, through them, the fertility of Nature, on the other contrasting with Juan's two sisters whose dark clothes and lifeless movements represent that despairing world that is increasingly Yerma's.

The settings, dialogue, poetry, movement and lighting of *Yerma* reveal quite clearly the closely-textured nature of the play. Francisco García Lorca has said:

> A confluence of traditional Spanish theatre tendencies, plastic and musical, is brought about in this play. This is achieved in a purer classic conception, toward which the poet turned his eyes in search for simplicity and sobriety. (p. 26)

Yerma, inasmuch as it does not have those supernatural figures that distinguish Act III of *Blood Wedding*, lacks the brilliant and startling theatricality of that play. But there can be no doubt that in the greater concentration of all its elements on the single, central figure of Yerma herself, the play has an equally searing dramatic power.

CHAPTER VI

DOÑA ROSITA THE SPINSTER
(DOÑA ROSITA LA SOLTERA)

Doña Rosita the Spinster was conceived in Lorca's imagination
in 1924, the same year as *Mariana Pineda*, and there is a clear
link between the plays, though *Doña Rosita* was not completed
until June 1935. Carlos Morla Lynch describes a private reading of the play by Lorca when, after lunch, he suddenly
decided to acquaint a few of his friends with the new play.[1] For
Morla the title of the play was itself evocative, both of love and
of the sadness of love. The action of the play has none of the
violence or passion of *Blood Wedding* or *Yerma*, but it presents,
on the other hand, a very human situation and has all the bitter
sweetness of life itself. The comic episodes are amusing but
contain an element of sadness. The ending, unlike the ending
of the two preceding plays, is open, but its open-endedness is
also its effectiveness, for it suggests, beyond what we actually
see, a continuing and deepening sadness that is all the greater
for our having to imagine it. And for Morla the mood and the
structure of the play, moving in a straight line and towards an
unavoidable conclusion, are perfect, making it, in his opinion,
one of Lorca's best works.

Doña Rosita received its première on 13 December, 1935, at
the Teatro Principal Palace in Barcelona, the cast headed by
Margarita Xirgu as Rosita and directed by Cipriano Rivas
Cherif. Antonio Espina, reviewing the performance in *El Sol*,
observed that 'it is not simply another good play amongst the
few that exist in the modern Spanish theatre . . . It is an
extraordinary play by a writer who combines his great talent as
a poet with his equally outstanding gifts as a dramatist'.[2] And
María Luz Morales, writing in *La Vanguardia*, concluded that
Lorca 'affirms with this play, and in a very positive way, his

vocation and his direction as a dramatist . . . *Doña Rosita* . . . broadens limitlessly the possibilities for this poetic dramatist. It is a work of fine literary quality, its essence – I repeat – theatrical, and it can compare with the best works of theatre in Europe at the present time.'[3]

As far as the sources of the play are concerned, Lorca was quite specific:

> I conceived my latest play, *Doña Rosita la soltera*, in 1924. My friend Moreno Villa told me one day: 'I am going to tell you the beautiful story of the life of a flower – the mutable rose – from a seventeenth-century book on roses.' Then he began: 'Once upon a time there was a rose . . .' And by the time he had finished the marvellous story of the rose, I had already written my play. It came to me finished, unique, impossible to change.[4]

Moreno Villa has himself confirmed the story, and it is clear that, as in the case of *Blood Wedding* and *The House of Bernarda Alba*, an idea implanted in Lorca's imagination grew and took shape over many years. Francisco García Lorca has observed:

> This play haunted the poet's imagination for many years and was the longest in maturing among all that he wrote. Its conception was such a task to him that I know that when he saw it finished it was a load off his shoulders . . . I believe that with *Doña Rosita*, written with great care, he overcame the private failure of *Mariana Pineda*.[5]

Alfredo de la Guardia, quoting a conversation with Margarita Xirgu, suggests another possible source for the play.[6] According to the actress, it was Lorca's habit to rummage in the cupboards and chests of the family house near Granada, and on one occasion he had unearthed an old book on the cultivation of flowers which contained a chapter on the rose. Subsequently his mother would have told him something about the history of the book and in so doing would have evoked for Lorca the sense of a period, and perhaps of particular individuals, now gone. This, given Lorca's obsession with passing time, would have been enough to implant in his mind the idea for a play on the subject. A later conversation with

Moreno Villa, involving the mutable rose itself, would have
given a more concrete and specific form to the idea that Lorca's
imagination was already working on.

If the immediate source of the play is to be found in either,
or both, of the circumstances described above, the themes of
frustration and passing time had, as we have already seen, a
central importance in the whole of Lorca's work. In considering the sources of the theme of frustration in *Yerma*,
the importance of Lorca's early 'Elegy', a lament for the
waiting, dreaming spinsters of Granada, has already been
emphasized. There are many other poems which express
the theme – the 'Elegy to Doña Juana, the Mad', 'The Unmarried Woman at Mass', 'The Gipsy Nun', 'Ballad of the
Black Sorrow' – but in the 'Elegy' in particular Lorca seems
almost to rehearse the circumstances of Rosita in the play:

> But the shadows deepen around your eyes
> and your black hair is turning silver;
> your breasts slacken giving off their perfume,
> and your fine back begins to bend.

> The great sadness that haunts your eyes
> tells us of your failed and broken life,
> the monotony of your poor circumstances
> as you watch the people passing from your window,
> and listen to the rain falling on the bitterness
> that dwells in the old provincial street,
> while in the distance can be heard the sound,
> unclear and confused, of the tolling bells.[7] (pp. 130-31)

It is a situation virtually echoed by Rosita in the play's final
Act, for when she appears there she has aged a great deal, and
later she observes to the Aunt: '. . . I also know that my back
will bend more each day . . .' (p. 187). In addition, as the
removal men carry furniture from the house, the tolling of a
bell is heard, and at the end of the Act, as the Aunt, Rosita and
the Housekeeper finally leave the family home of many years,
the rain, symbolic of the sadness and desolation of their lives,
begins to fall. The line between the poem and the play is
straight and clear.

In Lorca's plays, from the final anguished cry of Curianito in *The Butterfly's Evil Spell* to the unfulfilled yearning of the women in *The House of Bernarda Alba*, the theme of frustration occupies a central place too, but Rosita is anticipated most, perhaps, by the various female figures of *When Five Years Have Passed* and, of course, by the tragic figure of Yerma. In the former the Secretary, rejected like Rosita, feels only the pain of broken dreams, the Girl searches for the lover she will never find, and in the Mannequin, dressed in the wedding gown that will never be worn, are personified all the women who waste their lives in waiting:

> . . . This silk yearns,
> thread by thread, strand by strand,
> for a mouth that is warm.
> And my petticoats wonder
> where are the warm hands
> that grip my waist. (p. 1011)

Yerma, even though her frustration is of a different kind, is unquestionably the most eloquent and moving personification of the theme in the whole of Lorca's drama. Through the course of the play she moves, as does Rosita, from hope and optimism to a growing sense of isolation and inner emptiness, alienated from the beauty of the world around her. But whereas Yerma's tragedy is conveyed with a searing, relentless power, Rosita's experience is presented in a form more muted and restrained. She is, indeed, Yerma in another key.

We have seen in the discussion of *The Public* and of *When Five Years Have Passed* that the theme of passing time is another obsession in both the poems and the plays. Ruined buildings, broken arches, the weeds and grass that spread between stones are the images of passing time that brings decay. In the plays, in particular, Mariana's love for Pedro is, at least in part, defeated by passing time. In *The Public* the beauty of Juliet and her capacity for love have been overtaken by death, time's accomplice, the same remorseless process that 'Gently pushes the empty houses, brings about the fall of columns' (p. 91). In *When Five Years Have Passed* many of the characters are, in effect, particular stages in the life of the individual –

childhood, youth, adulthood, old age. They are different vantage points in time but all equal in relation to its passing. The Second Friend, attempting to cling to the beauty and innocence of childhood, feels the march of time within him:

> But my face is mine and they are stealing it away from me. I was young and I used to sing, and now there is a man, a gentleman [*To the Old Man*] like you, who is inside me with two or three masks ready. (p. 985)

The Old Man himself alludes to it: 'Our clothes wear out, anchors rust, and we move on . . .' (p. 985). In the nightmarish vision in the middle of Act I the Dead Boy and the Dead Cat, recalling the simple pleasures of life, struggle in vain to keep at bay the darkness, the terrible void that finally engulfs them: 'Don't bury me. Wait a few minutes . . .' (p. 979). But there is no waiting, and their fate is the fate of all the other characters, of the Young Man, the Old Man, the Bride, the Secretary, the Girl, their dreams, their existence destroyed by time and by death. At the end of the play the Young Man dies alone, listening to the echo of his own voice. At the end of *The Public* snowflakes fall on a stage where the Director dies alone, accompanied by death. At the end of *Doña Rosita* the white curtains flutter, like falling petals, and the stage is empty, providing a perspective on Rosita's future. They are endings that are variations on a theme, all of them suggestive of the emptiness that lies at the end of our passage through time, and in this respect Rosita will be no different.

The beginning of Act I has a predominantly comic note stemming from the Uncle's fussiness and the affection lavished on his plants, and in contrast, from the Housekeeper's practical concerns and lack of sentiment about her master's flowers:

> But here . . . roses to the right, basil to the left, anemones, sage, petunias, and those new fashionable flowers, the chrysanthemums, tousle-headed like gypsy girls. How I long to see planted in this garden a pear tree, a cherry tree, or a persimmon! (p. 135-36)

She is capable, too, of shocking her mistress by the earthy nature of her observations:

The mouth is useful when we eat,
The legs are useful when we dance,
And women have a thing quite neat . . . (p. 136)

But if all this is superbly comic, the comedy has serious undertones, for the opening sequence announces, in relation to
the flowers, one of the play's main themes: beauty and its
vulnerability. The Uncle refers to the trampled seeds: 'Yesterday I found the dahlia tubers trampled underfoot.' (p. 135).
The Housekeeper's scandalous remark underlines the further
point that the beautiful woman, indeed, any woman, has
sexual needs that seek fulfilment.

The appearance of Rosita, immediately following these
observations, makes their relevance to her clear. She is,
indeed, dressed in pink, in name and in appearance the
human form of her uncle's flowers: [. . . *She is dressed in rose, in
the style of 1900* . . .] (p. 136). She is in a hurry, looking for her
hat, and when she leaves the Housekeeper's comment introduces another important theme, the theme of passing time, in
relation to Rosita:

> She wants everything in such a hurry. She wishes that
> today were the day after tomorrow. She starts flying and
> slips through our hands . . . (p. 136)

We are reminded of the Friend in *When Five Years Have Passed* as
he rushes from one experience to another, seeking to defeat
the relentless march of time. And when the focus of the conversation moves from Rosita to the rose which the Uncle has
found crushed, the fate of the flower and the woman is
inseparable in the meaning of the lines:

> It's all very well for the tubers to be trampled, but it's
> simply unbearable for the rosebush I most cherish to
> have its leaves broken . . . (p. 137)

Furthermore, when in a passage of great beauty the Uncle
reads from his book the description of the *rosa mutabile* whose
beauty fades as day passes into night, the words recall the
Housekeeper's earlier reference to Rosita who 'slips through
our hands' (p. 136) and they acquire an even more poignant
meaning:

She opens in the morning
red as blood.

At noon, full-blown,
she is hard as coral.

When the birds begin
to sing among the branches,
and the afternoon faints
on the violets of the sea,
she turns pale, with the pallor
of the cheek of salt.
And when night is blown
on a soft metallic horn,
while the stars advance,
while the winds retreat,
on the very edge of darkness
her petals begin to rain. (p. 138)

Indeed, as Rosita's first appearance followed the House-keeper's comment on the sexual needs of women, so she appears now once more, and the structure of the Act is seen to be one in which the rose and Rosita alternate as the focus of attention while the link between them is continuously under-lined.

The mood of the play's beginning is largely comic, the Uncle and the Housekeeper amusing in their clashes. There is too laughter in this household, for between its inhabitants there exists, despite their arguments, both tolerance and under-standing. The Housekeeper's superstitious nature makes them laugh (p. 139), Rosita exits *laughingly* (p. 139). On the other hand, all the allusions to trampled seeds, the crushed rose, and the passing of time form a dark and ominous pattern which, underlying and interwoven with the laughter, sug-gests, together with the gaiety of life, the sorrow that will inevitably come, the bitterness of life that constantly accom-panies its sweetness. It returns again now as Rosita leaves and the aunt is left alone sewing. The laughter of the house becomes its silence, and in that silence the clicking of the bobbins, the distant voice of the pedlar, and the Aunt's count-

ing aloud of the stitches seem to emphasize, like the regular
tick of a clock, the quiet but relentless march of time:

> [*The stage is silent and only the clicking of the bobbins is heard.*]

> AUNT [*talking to herself*]: . . . The next time he comes . . .
> thirty-seven, thirty-eight . . . (p. 140)

The appearance of the Nephew, Rosita's betrothed, and his
announcement of his departure for South America change the
mood completely. Gaiety and laughter become the Nephew's
disappointment and the Aunt's anger with him. And there
begins to take place in Rosita's life and in the life of the
household as a whole that process of inevitable change that
blights the rose as day passes into night. Rosita, like many of
Lorca's characters, and through no fault of her own, is the
victim of circumstances she cannot change: of her feelings for
the Nephew, of the consequences of his departure, of the
anguish of waiting and the ravages of time that lie ahead. The
Aunt's bitter words echo the loneliness and isolation of the
women in *Blood Wedding* – the Mother, the Bride, Leonardo's
Wife – and anticipate the useless waiting of the daughters of
Bernarda Alba:

> . . . because my child will be left alone within these four
> walls and you will go free across the ocean, across those
> rivers, through those citron groves, and my little girl
> here, one day just like another . . . (p. 142)

We begin to feel a deep compassion for Rosita. But the
Nephew is a prisoner too, torn between his feelings for the girl
and his duty to his father who has summoned him home. And
beyond both individuals the other members of the household
are deeply affected by the changed nature of their lives. The
housekeeper's raucous laughter, the measure of the play's
initial mood, is now her sobbing: [*The* HOUSEKEEPER *weeps with
great sobs.*] (p. 142). The Aunt's life has suddenly been em-
bittered: 'I'm the one who must force you to take the boat. But
you will embitter my life.' (p. 141). We are made aware of the
way in which not merely Rosita's life but all their lives are
changed, and of the way in which this household is the symbol

P

of other households and other families whose happiness, as vulnerable as the rose itself, is suddenly destroyed.

Rosita's arrival with her friends, laughing, unaware of what has happened, brightens the mood as we hear the off-stage laughter. But for us that brightness is already darkened by our awareness, borne in upon us by the play's events so far, that the joy of life has another side, and, even as the girls appear, their gaiety becomes their sighs, evocative of the bitter-sweetness of the play in general:[8]

> FIRST MANOLA [*entering and closing her parasol*]: Ay!
> SECOND MANOLA [*likewise*]: Ay, what coolness.
> THIRD MANOLA [*likewise*]: Ay!
> ROSITA [*likewise*]: For whom are the sighs
> of my three lovely Manolas? (p. 143)

The increasing sadness of the play is caught now in Rosita's song which describes the Manolas of Granada who walk to the Alhambra in search of love. On the one hand, the girls are extremely beautiful, in the fullness of their youth and of their hope:

> Which lovers will expect them?
> Under which myrtle will they rest?
> Whose hands will steal the perfume
> from their two round flowers? (p. 145)

But even the beauty of the Alhambra is touched by melancholy and a sense of suffering:

> Ay, how dark is the Alhambra!
> Where will the Manolas go
> while the fountain and the rose
> suffer in the shade? (p. 145)

As the poem ends, night is seen to fall and the hopes of the girls are unfulfilled.

This lovely poem expresses, of course, a universal sadness and the girls are symbolic of all young women who search in vain for love. Indeed, they become Rosita's friends as the latter transfer the situation of the poem to themselves:

THIRD MANOLA: White frost laces trim
               our bridal clothes.

They are themselves the girls of the poem walking to the Alhambra:

FIRST MANOLA: We go up to the Alhambra,
               in threes and fours, alone. (p. 146)

But they, in turn, are Rosita too, and the play, through the allusive and suggestive character of poetry, opens out on a sorrow that is general, a disappointment that is universal and of which Rosita is a part. But since she is a part of a greater sadness, she in turn becomes, more than a particular lonely woman, a figure who possesses the sad grandeur of other women like her concentrated in herself. She becomes that woman as the news of her cousin's leaving is broken to her and the Housekeeper's earlier weeping is now her own.

    The final scene of the Act, the farewell scene between Rosita and her cousin, is marked by its romantic sentimentality. The piano plays softly in the distance, providing a romantic accompaniment for the lovers, while they are poised in typically romantic attitudes:

    [. . . *A very distant piano plays a Czerny étude. Pause. The* NEPHEW *enters and on reaching the centre of the room stops because* ROSITA *enters. The two stand regarding each other face to face. The* NEPHEW *advances. He takes her by the waist. She leans her head on his shoulder.*] (p. 147)

The dialogue itself is full of romantic images and sentiments. Rosita describes the awakening of her love:

    While dozing one night
    on my jasmine balcony
    I saw two cherubs descend
    to an enamoured rose . . . (p. 148)

And the Nephew affirms his undying love for her:

    I must return, my cousin,
    to take you by my side
    in burnished golden ship

with sails of happiness;
light and shade, night and day,
I'll think only of loving you. (p. 149)

The scene underlines the idealism, the ardour and the faithful promises of love. We are transported by the lyricism of the poetry, by lines which themselves have the rhythm and the flow of the piano accompaniment. But in its closing lines the romantic dream fades quickly as Rosita reads aloud the poem about the fading rose. The reality of passing time and beauty devastated dashes all the self-deluding sentiment of the lovers' farewell. It is an appropriate ending to the Act that the lines read previously by the Uncle should now be spoken by Rosita herself, for as the curtain falls the identification of Rosita and the rose is complete:

And when night is blown
on a soft metallic horn,
while the stars advance,
while the winds retreat,
on the very edge of darkness
her petals begin to rain. (p. 151)

When Act II begins fifteen years have passed. El Señor X, a suitor of Rosita, is a symbol of the present, a champion of progress and technology, exemplified in the motor-car:

My friend, Mr Longoria, of Madrid, has just bought an automobile with which he can hurl himself along at the fantastic speed of eighteen miles per hour; and the Shah of Persia, who certainly is a most pleasant man, has also bought a Panhard Levasson motor car of twenty-four horsepower. (p. 152)

Between Mr X and Rosita's uncle, disconcerted by and out of step with this new age of largely material concerns, there is a world of difference:

UNCLE: And I say: where are they going in such a great hurry? (p. 152)

The beginning of the Act, contrasting past and present, clearly suggests the theme of passing time and change. It does so

largely in a comic way, for Lorca caricatures in Mr X the
fanatical devotion of modern man to scientific progress. Even
his present to Rosita is an affirmation of his faith:

> Deliver to her for me this pendant. It is a mother-of-pearl
> Eiffel Tower over two doves which carry in the bills the
> wheel of industry. (p. 153)

But while it is comic, there is an underlying sadness in the fact
that in the modern world the Uncle and all he represents, the
whole romantic world of Act I and of which Rosita is a part,
have been overtaken and left behind by passing time. When
Mr X has left and the conversation of the Housekeeper and the
Aunt turns to Rosita, we see that she is living in the past in the
sense that she clings to a vision of the Nephew, and of herself
as his bride, that she has fashioned in the world of her imagination since the day of his departure:

> HOUSEKEEPER: . . . she doesn't realize how the time
> passes. She will have silver hair and still be sewing satin
> bands on the ruffles of her honeymoon nightgown
> (p. 155)

Between the self-deluding dream and reality there is, the
Housekeeper suggests, a distance that, sadly, Rosita is unaware of:

> Yesterday she had me with her all day at the gate to
> the circus because she insisted one of the puppeteers
> resembled her cousin.
> AUNT: And did he resemble him really?
> HOUSEKEEPER: He was as beautiful as a young priest
> when he comes to sing his first mass. But your nephew
> just wishes he had that waist, that white throat, that
> moustache. They didn't look at all alike. In your family
> there aren't any good-looking men. (p. 155)

Rosita's tragedy lies both in the fact that she clings to a dream
and that with every passing day the nature of that dream
grows more remote from the reality that inspired it. The
Housekeeper, the practical woman of the play, expresses all
the futility of Rosita's hopes:

> Sometimes I'd like to throw a shoe at her head. Because
> from so much looking at the sky she's going to get eyes
> like a cow's. (p. 155)

But the sadness awakened by Rosita's plight is also a sadness
occasioned by the household as a whole as it is overtaken by
the passing years. The gift bought by the Housekeeper for
Rosita, a sentimental, romantic piece with fountains, roses
and bowers, contrasts with Mr X's more modern taste and
is another example of the growing gulf between past and
present:

> In the middle of the velvet there's a fountain made out of
> real shells. Over the fountain there is a wire arbour with
> green roses. The water in the basin is a group of blue
> sequins and the stream of water is the thermometer itself.
> The puddles around are painted in oil and upon them a
> nightingale drinks, all embroidered in golden thread . . .
> (p. 156)

Furthermore, in the clash between the Aunt and the Housekeeper, there is, as the Uncle perceptively observes, an almost
desperate attempt to keep alive, or rather to give new life to,
the ordinary issues and concerns whose edge is slowly blunted
by passing time:

> There comes a moment in which people who have lived
> together many years make a pretext for ill humour and
> anxiety out of the smallest things, in order to put inten-
> sity and worry into what's definitely dead. When we
> were twenty years old we didn't have any such conversa-
> tions. (p. 158)

The comedy of the beginning of the Act fades as we are made
progressively aware of the changes in the lives of all these
individuals.

   Rosita's first appearance in the Act suggests, maintaining
the association with the rose, that time has passed since the
conclusion of Act I, for the style of her dress has changed:
[ROSITA appears. She comes dressed in rose. The styles have changed
from the leg-o'-mutton sleeves of 1900 . . .] (p. 158). She, on the

other hand, waits still as she has waited for fifteen years, steeped in memories of the past as time passes her by, seeking to deny and defeat its passing but constantly reminded of it.[9] Around her physical reality is slowly transformed:

> It's just that in the streets I become aware of how time has passed and I don't want to be disillusioned. They've built another new house in the small plaza. I don't want to find out how time goes. (p. 160)

People too are a reminder of its passing: 'If it were not for seeing people, I could believe that it's just a week since he left . . .' (p. 160). As the Act unfolds there is an increasing sadness about Rosita, for everything in the course of it accentuates her growing isolation from reality. She is, in this particular sense, another Yerma, less anguished and tormented, but in her own right deserving of pity and compassion.

The arrival of the Mother with her three spinster daughters restores the play to a comic level, for they, like Mr X, are caricatures, their dress, their manner, their remarks a source of amusement:[10]

> [. . . The three awful GIRLS and their MOTHER enter. The three SPINSTERS wear immense hats trimmed with bad feathers, most exaggerated dresses, gloves to the elbow with bracelets over them, and fans hanging from large chains. The MOTHER wears a faded black dress with a hat of old purple ribbons.] (p. 160)

The Mother, complaining about her health and striving to preserve appearances, is a querulous, pretentious woman, the incongruity between her real and desired state as much a source of humour in her as it is a source of pathos in Rosita:

> And what anguish I've gone through, madam, so that these daughters could continue wearing hats. How many tears, how many pains for a ribbon or a cluster of curls. Those feathers and those wires have cost me many a.sleepless night! (p. 162)

The daughters, vulgar, over-dressed, pretentious creatures, echo each other, parrot fashion:

> MOTHER: I don't lack refinement – what I lack is money.
> FIRST SPINSTER: Mamma!
> SECOND SPINSTER: Mamma!
> THIRD SPINSTER: Mamma! (p. 162)

But if they introduce a comic note which, following the melancholy presentation of Rosita, underlines once more the bitter-
sweetness of the play, they also serve to sustain the ever-
present theme of passing time. The Mother, for example, is
steeped, like Rosita, in the past, and her words, even though
we are amused by them, draw attention to her altered circumstances:

> But you know very well that since I lost my poor husband
> I have performed real miracles in order to manage on the
> pension we have left. I still seem to hear the father of
> these girls when, generous and gentlemanly as he was,
> he would say to me: 'Henrietta, spend, spend, spend, for
> I am earning seventy duros now!' But those times are
> gone . . . (p. 162)

And if she complains about the poverty that has overtaken
her, she complains too about the change of attitude in servants
in contrast to what they used to be:

> I have a girl who cleans the flat in the afternoons; she
> used to earn what they have always earned: one peseta a
> month and leftovers, which is enough in these times.
> Well, the other day she flew off the handle saying she
> wanted five pesetas . . . (p. 164)

The arrival of the Mother and her daughters is followed by
the arrival of another group, the Misses Ayola. They too are
dressed in a way which calls attention to the time in which the
action of the Act is set: [. . . *They are richly dressed in the greatly
exaggerated style of the period.*] (p. 164). But, more than this, their
youthfulness and gaiety, evident in all they say and do, off-
sets Rosita and is an uncomfortable reminder to her of her
sadness and her lost youth. Throughout the scene the Ayola
sisters are high-spirited and full of laughter: [*They laugh.
Pause. The* AYOLAS *begin an uncontrollable laughter that communi-*

cates itself to ROSITA, *who tries to stop them . . .*] (p. 164). Their youthful spirits are constantly provoked by the affectation of the Mother and her pretentious daughters: [*The* AYOLAS, *who have been containing their laughter, burst out now in great peals . . .*] (p. 165). Rosita, in contrast, cannot laugh: [. . . ROSITA, *turning her back to the* SPINSTERS, *also laughs, but controls herself.*] (p. 165). Moreover, one of the girls was only six years old when the Nephew was courting Rosita:

> When I was six years old I used to come here and Rosita's sweetheart got me used to drinking. Don't you remember, Rosita? (p. 166)

For her everything is an increasingly painful memory, and her fading looks are accompanied by an ever-decreasing capacity for joy.

As the Act draws to its conclusion, the three spinster daughters and Rosita sing a song in which the slow rhythm and the haunting melancholy of Rosita's lines, echoing the earlier poem on the rose, isolate her from the others. On the other hand, the sudden arrival of the Nephew's letter, suggesting marriage by proxy, transforms the mood, and, as the room is filled with laughter once again, Rosita is part of it, joining in the final dance. But it is a gaiety which does not lose its melancholy. In the first place, nothing has really changed, for the Nephew's promises at the conclusion of Act I have merely become his letter. Secondly, the Uncle has cut the last rose, presents it to Rosita, and its colour is already fading; or will have faded in a little while:

> White like the dove,
> like the laughter of the sea;
> white with the cold whiteness
> of a cheek of salt. (p. 173)

Rosita holds the rose, symbolic of love and hope, and the words of the song sung by the girls has a particular relevance to her:

> Because I caught a glimpse
> Of you beside the sea,
> Your languor sweet perceived

> Was reason for my sighs;
> And that most subtle sweetness
> Which was my fatal dream,
> Within this moonlight pale,
> In shipwreck here you saw. (p. 173)

It is the song of a young man to the woman who has awakened his love for her, but in the allusions to pale moonlight and shipwreck there are suggestions of hopes and dreams destroyed. As the rose has three phases, so the second Act concludes the second phase, and there remains only the third when 'her petals begin to rain' (p. 138). The laughter and dancing that conclude Act II are seen to be a temporary respite that precedes the death of Rosita's hope.

The final Act begins in silence punctuated only by the chiming of the clock:[11] [*A small living room with green shutters opening on the garden. The stage is silent. A clock strikes six in the evening . . .*] (p. 174). In this silence the Housekeeper crosses the stage with a box and a suitcase, and then the clock strikes six again. In addition, the Housekeeper is visibly older. Before a word is spoken, everything calls attention to the theme of passing time and change.

The opening conversation between the Aunt and the Housekeeper emphasizes, above all, the emptiness of their lives and announces the sense of desolation that is the keynote of the Act. For the Aunt, in particular, the house has come to signify the emptiness of her own existence after her husband's death, and her words suggest individuals searching for themselves in a vast and empty wilderness:

> Since my husband died the house is so empty that it seems twice as large, and we even have to search to find each other. Some nights, when I cough in my room I hear an echo as if I were in a church . . . (p. 174)

Furthermore, the Housekeeper contrasts the raised voices and the quarrels of the past, that were a sign of life, with the silence that now exists:

> . . . But we've grown mute. Before, we used to shout –

How about this? How about that? How about the
custards? Aren't you going to iron any more? . . . (p. 175)

The sense of emptiness experienced by the Aunt is experienced now by Rosita too, the death of the Uncle paralleled by
her desertion by the Nephew, for he is now married. Her
waiting is over, but the passing of hope is accompanied by a
terrible grief and a useless longing which has no end:

> HOUSEKEEPER: . . . but the dead are dead. They're dead –
> so let's cry. The door closes, and we keep on living! But
> this about my Rosita is the worst. It's to love someone
> and not be able to find him; it's to cry and not to know
> for whom one weeps; it's to sigh for someone that one
> knows doesn't deserve those sighs. It is an open wound
> that gives off without ceasing a little thread of blood and
> there is no one, no one in the whole world, to bring the
> cotton wool, the bandages, or the precious piece of ice.
> (p. 177)

When Rosita appears for the first time, it is evident that her
beauty, as well as her spirit, has been ravaged by the passing of
the years: [ROSITA *appears. She wears a dress of light rose colour in
the style of 1910. She wears long curls. She has aged much.*] (p. 176).
From the beginning of the Act the sense of individuals trapped
in a growing loneliness and isolation as time moves on is very
strong.

Don Martín, the old schoolteacher who appears now, is
another character who exemplifies the theme of passing time.
He has about him an air of great sadness, and if the Aunt
alludes to the emptiness of her existence, Don Martín speaks
of his own uselessness:

> Same old life. I've just come from lecturing to my class in
> Rhetoric. A real Hell! It was a wonderful lecture: 'Con-
> cept and Definition of Harmony.' But the children
> weren't interested at all – and what children! For me,
> since they see I am disabled, they have a little respect . . .
> (p. 178)

Furthermore, his description of the inconsiderate behaviour of

the pupils towards their teachers, and of the lack of concern of
their wealthy parents, adds to the impression of the characters
of the play as victims both of changing times and of the heartlessness of other people. As the Aunt sadly observes: 'Oh,
Don Martín! What a world this is!' (p. 179).

In some respects Don Martín is, of course, a comic figure.
His red hair and his crutch are physical details which have all
the boldness of caricature. His recitation of the lines from what
was clearly a very bad play of his, contrasted with his genuine
cultural taste, has a great comic incongruity:

> A mother unexcelled! Now turn your gaze
> to her who lies in abject trance undone;
> receive you these refulgent jewels of mine
> and the horrid death rattle of my combat! (p. 179)

But if he is to some extent a comic figure, he is also a figure of
great pathos, for his deepest hopes of being a poet and a
dramatist have never been fulfilled:

> I dreamt always of being a poet. I was born with a talent,
> a natural flower, and I wrote a play that was never pro-
> duced. (p. 179)

Like the Aunt he is a relic of the past, his respect for cultural
values and even his way of speaking out-dated in the modern
world. As the Housekeeper observes: 'It's just that there's no
more taste. With such a precious manner of speaking as you
have!' (p. 181). And like the Aunt he is a lonely individual, for
he has never married, and his loneliness increases with the
years. At this particular point his allusion to his play, a symbol
of the past, is juxtaposed with the reality of the present in the
form of the removal men who begin to take away the furniture,
and this, in turn, is accompanied by the tolling of the bells
outside, evocative of passing time and change: [. . . *Two strokes
of a bell are heard while the two* MEN *cross out with the divan.*]
(p. 180). And more importantly, of course, Don Martín, denied
love and confronted only by the passing years, is the image of
what Rosita will become.

The concluding scenes are full of a sense of desolation. The
Housekeeper's condemnation of the rich has its humour but

this does not obscure her real sense of outrage. The Aunt, whose love for her husband has been so great, cannot conceal her bitterness towards him: 'I would like your uncle to see us. Foolish old man! . . . The extravagant thing! The weakling!' (p. 184). And then, of course, there is Rosita. In a very moving passage she reveals the nature and extent of her own particular desolation. She is the victim and the prisoner of many things. In the first place she was the prisoner of her illusion, and now that hope has been extinguished she is equally the prisoner of her hopelessness and disillusionment:

> . . . and now that these things no longer exist, I continue going around and around in a cold place, looking for a way out that I shall never find . . . and I can't even cry out, but go on, with a mouth full of poison . . . (p. 185)

Beyond this she is the victim, like Yerma, of the mockery of others that comes with spinsterhood: '. . . and I found myself pointed out with a finger that made my engaged girl's modesty ridiculous . . .' (p. 185). Thirdly, she is the prisoner of her own awareness of passing time. But, worst of all, she is the prisoner of lingering hope, tortured by it even though she knows that there is no hope: 'And yet, hope pursues me, encircles me, bites me; like a dying wolf tightening his grip for the last time.' (p. 186). Rosita emerges here as a truly tragic figure, not merely in the sense that she is beset by life but in her recognition and acceptance of her destiny: 'I am as I am. And I can't make myself change. Now the only thing left for me is my dignity.' (p. 186). There is, indeed, an immense dignity in her courageous acceptance of the future:

> . . . I also know that my back will bend more each day . . . I know you are remembering your sister, the old maid . . . the old maid like me. She was bitter and hated children and every one who put on a new dress . . . but I won't be like that. (p. 187)

Even so, the ending of the play seems to undermine this moving and inspiring vision of human dignity, for it is an ending that is bleak and full of a sense of emptiness. As the family leaves the house that has been their home for many years, it grows dark, the wind rises, and the rain begins to fall. Rosita, dressed in white, becomes the rose in its final wither- ing, and she almost faints, just as the rose wilts. Her closing lines, the final lines of the poem, have a symbolic counterpart in the rain that falls on the family as they move to another house. And as they leave and the stage is left empty, the white curtains fluttering in the wind, like the white petals falling from the dying rose, provide the final perspective on Rosita's future. [12]

As far as its presentation on the stage is concerned, *Doña Rosita the Spinster* is, to all appearances, the most 'realistic' of all Lorca's plays, for here the simple, stylized settings of plays like *Blood Wedding* and *Yerma* become, in a manner reminiscent of Chekhov, the representation of real rooms in all their detail. The photographs of the Barcelona première of 1935 depict, for example, the three settings of the play – three rooms in Rosita's house – complete with chairs, sofa, sideboard, table, pictures, wallpapered walls, curtains, and French windows. Lorca's stage-directions in the published version of the play are them- selves very brief and convey no sense of detail: [*A room leading to a greenhouse* (p. 135). *A room of* DOÑA ROSITA's *house. The garden in the background.* (p. 152). *A small living room with green shutters opening on the garden . . .*] (p. 174). On the other hand, his indications for the costumes of the characters are detailed and precise, and their aim in every case is to emphasize the sense of period of each Act and thus the sense of passing time that is central to the play in general. It is clear, therefore, that the set for each Act should be seen not as a piece of realism but as something stylized, its purpose not simply to present on stage an accurate picture of the time in question but, in select- ing and highlighting particular characteristics of that time, to capture its essence. The frame for the action of each Act becomes, indeed, a period photograph whose stylization marks it off from each of the other Acts, and Lorca uses the sets, as he does the costumes, to reinforce the idea of time's relentless march. The family photograph is also, of course, something meaningful for all of us, whatever its evocations. In using the device in relation to the settings for his play, Lorca

discovered a way both of evoking the theme of passing time
and of establishing between the characters and the spectators a
feeling of greater intimacy as a consequence of which the
experiences presented on the stage are made more meaningful.

The costumes of the characters, as has been suggested,
serve to underline the sense of passing time. When Rosita
appears at the beginning of each Act, the pink of her costume –
its only constant feature and a symbol of her beauty – is seen to
be subject to changing fashion, suggestive of the way in which
her youth and beauty are themselves exposed to change. In a
purely visual manner the nature of Rosita's tragedy is immediately borne in upon us: [ROSITA *appears. She wears a dress of light
rose colour in the style of 1910. She wears long curls. She has aged
much.*] (p. 176). Similarly, the stylized dresses of the three
Spinsters and the two Ayola sisters in Act Two are intended to
evoke the time in which the action of the Act takes place: [*The*
AYOLA GIRLS *enter and greet* ROSITA *gaily. They are richly dressed in
the greatly exaggerated style of the period.*] (p. 164). The mother of
the three Spinsters is, in contrast, the embodiment of a bygone
age: [. . . *The* MOTHER *wears a faded black dress with a hat of old
purple ribbons.*] (p. 160). In this respect she has a parallel in the
Uncle, the Aunt, the Housekeeper and Don Martín, for they
are all figures who are left behind by passing time and the
point is made by their presence in settings and in relation to
other characters where in visual terms they are incongruous.
In addition, costume plays its part in creating the bitter-sweet,
laughter-and-tears mood that is so distinctive in the play. In
the second Act especially, the three Spinsters have the bold,
caricatured character of figures of farce:

> [. . . *The three* SPINSTERS *wear immense hats trimmed with bad
> feathers, most exaggerated dresses, gloves to the elbow with
> bracelets over them, and fans hanging from large chains* . . .]
> (p. 160)

Their appearance, in conjunction with their manner, introduces into the sad and worsening situation of Rosita a note of
the absurdly and ridiculously comic. But, though the mood is
in one way lightened, it is also darkened, for in the juxta-

position of Rosita the spinster with the three awful, pretentious, empty-headed spinsters who are her counterpart
and yet her opposite, there is a kind of mockery of Rosita's real
anguish, a laughter that is cruelly out of place in her increasingly tragic world. It is an element that is caught too in the
sadly comic figure of Don Martín in the final Act and in the
contrast in Act Two between the Uncle, rooted in the past, and
Mr X, the symbol of material progress. In the visual contrasts
of figures on the stage Lorca suggests the conflicting and
changing moods that lie at the very heart of the play.

The dialogue, like the sets, has all the appearance of a
greater realism, for while the rooms of Rosita's house have an
authenticity far removed from the spare and simple settings of
the rural tragedies, so the conversation of the characters often
centres, to a greater extent than in the other plays, on the
ordinary, day-to-day concerns of their existence. In Act One,
for instance, the Uncle talks about his flowers, and the Aunt
and the Housekeeper about domestic matters. In Act Two the
conversation of Rosita, the three Spinsters and the Ayola
sisters centres on largely frivolous topics. And in Act Three
Don Martín gossips with the Aunt and the Housekeeper about
his present way of life in contrast to his past. They are, in
content and in style, the desultory, commonplace conversations of everyday life, sometimes amusing, sometimes sad. On
the other hand, they are conversations which, almost without
our being aware of it, touch upon the play's main themes: the
themes of fading beauty and passing time, of frustration, and
of the past overtaken by the present. The apparent naturalness
of the dialogue conceals an artfulness which is as great here as
in any of the major plays of Lorca. In the third Act, of course,
Doña Rosita takes on a more tragic colouring and the dialogue,
particularly of Rosita herself, is much more like that of the
rural tragedies – impassioned, full of repeated patterns and
insistent rhythms that convey with power and immediacy the
feelings and obsessions of the character:

> . . . And today one friend gets married, and another and
> another, and tomorrow, she has a son and he grows up
> and comes to show me his examination marks, and they

build new houses and make new songs and I stay the same, with the same trembling, the same; I, just as before, cutting the same carnations, looking at the same clouds . . . (p. 185)

It is as though, in the final Act, the ordinariness of life, reflected in the earlier dialogue, has been stripped away to reveal the real tragedy that lies beneath it.

If for much of the play the dialogue has the flatness of life itself, it is a flatness that is punctuated at given moments by passages of poetry that are marvellously evocative and full of feeling. In Act One the poem of the rose (p. 138), describing its beauty and its dying, is both a beautiful and a moving piece, its visual appeal one with its emotional impact. But if it is effective in itself, its effectiveness is doubled through its resonances and implications for Rosita, herself the rose in her beauty and her dress. Similarly, later in Act One Rosita recites the beautiful poem about the girls of Granada who look for love and do not find it (pp. 144-6). It is a poem full of hope yet full of sadness too, its wondering the wondering of all young women who hope for love, its melancholy a reflection of all their fears:

> Where will the Manolas go
> while the fountain and the rose
> suffer in the shade?
> Which lovers will expect them?
> Under which myrtle will they rest? (p. 145)

But its effectiveness, as in the poem on the rose, lies particularly in the relevance of a universal situation to Rosita herself, a transition made when she and the three Manolas substitute the first person for the third:

THIRD MANOLA: White frost laces trim
                 our bridal clothes.

SECOND MANOLA: Through darkened streets
FIRST MANOLA: We go up to the Alhambra,
                 in threes and fours, alone. (p. 146)

The poetry of the play, shifting from the universal to the

Q

particular, acquires in the process an altogether sharper poignancy that is all to do with our recognition of the relevance to an individual we feel for of an experience whose sadness we are all aware of. In this play, more than in the others, there is a difference between the prose dialogue, especially of the first two Acts, and the poetic passages that gives to the latter a particular intensity, like shafts of sunlight through grey clouds. If in the writing of *Yerma* Lorca aimed at a greater sobriety, which involved a much more sparing use of poetry, he seems in *Doña Rosita* to have returned to the lyricism which is such a constant feature of *Blood Wedding*, though it is employed now less extensively.

The movements of the characters on the stage are, often, of course, a further pointer to their changing moods and emotions. At the beginning of Act One, for instance, Rosita's hurried entrance and exit underline her eager and careless enjoyment of life: ROSITA [*enters rapidly . . .*] [ROSITA *takes it (the hat) and goes running out.*] (p. 136). Just afterwards she enters again in search of her parasol and, after a quick search and a few light-hearted exchanges, leaves (pp. 138-9). It is a sequence whose liveliness is followed by one in which the Aunt sits motionless and only the clicking of the bobbins can be heard (p. 140), an episode that anticipates already the final solitude that all the characters will experience. Indeed, by the end of Act I Rosita, weeping and seated on the 'vis-à-vis', has been transformed from the lively, animated woman of the play's beginning into a passive figure, someone already overcome by life's misfortunes. In Act Two the action largely centres on the three Spinsters and the Ayola sisters and for most of the time they are seated as they gossip. Their minds are on nothing in particular. In contrast, Rosita's mind is on the awaited letter from her cousin and her movement reflects her agitation. Before the other girls arrive, we see how her actions betray her thoughts:

> [. . . *She crosses the stage quickly with a pair of scissors in her hand. In the centre she pauses.*]
> ROSITA: Has the postman come? (p. 158)

During the frivolous chatter of the girls, she is preoccupied:

[*walking around the stage as if arranging things*] (p. 165). In the third Act the postures and movements of the characters in the house that is slowly emptied of its furniture suggest the sense of emptiness that has overtaken them. At the beginning of the Act the Aunt sits in the silent room, an image of despair: [. . . The AUNT *appears and sits on a low chair in the centre of the stage...*] (p. 174). There is now a slowness and laboriousness about her movements which reflect her physical and emotional weariness: [*The* AUNT *sits down slowly* . . .] (p. 183). She is echoed too in the figure of Don Martín: [*The* HOUSEKEEPER *helps* DON MARTÍN *to rise.*] (p. 182). Later in the Act Rosita kneels in front of the Aunt who is seated (p. 185). Finally, Rosita, the Aunt and the Housekeeper slowly leave the house, the two older women supporting Rosita (p. 191). Throughout the Act there is a lack of animation in the physical movements of the characters which reinforces its presentation of their growing sense of hopelessness.

As far as the lighting of the stage is concerned, the action of the first two Acts takes place in a normal light that matches the realistic nature of the settings. Only in the last Act, when the play's mood has become more tragic, is lighting used to underline and emphasize its darkening mood. It is already evening when the curtain rises and towards the end of the Act, as the family prepares to leave the house finally, the light begins to fade: [. . . *Evening is falling.*] (p. 189). The ending of the play takes place in a half-light: [*The stage is in the sweet half-light of evening.*] (p. 191). Against it Rosita's dress is all the more effective: [ROSITA *appears. She is pale, dressed in white* . . .] (p. 191). Through the lighting she is transformed into the rose which 'when the night arrives/her petals begin to rain'. Though Lorca uses lighting sparingly in the play, he uses it in this final scene to create an atmosphere that is as vivid as it is anguished.

CHAPTER VII

THE HOUSE
OF BERNARDA ALBA
(LA CASA DE BERNARDA ALBA)

The House of Bernarda Alba, the last of the rural tragedies, was completed on 19 June, 1936, shortly before Lorca's death. Carlos Morla Lynch describes a private reading of the play on 24 June, 1936, at the home of the Count of Yebes.[1] Before a small gathering Lorca read the play in the simple yet elegant drawing room, creating through the marvellously evocative power of his voice both the differences between the characters and the mood and atmosphere that dominate the play. For Morla himself it was a dark and powerful work, more expressive of the harshness of Castile than of the passionate spirit of Andalusia. In terms of technique, Lorca had 'exiled the poet that dwells within him' and that had inspired much of *Blood Wedding* and *Yerma* in order to focus more closely on the stark, unadorned reality of his theme. He had informed his audience that the play was intended to be 'a photographic documentary', an opinion justified in Morla's view by its powerfully realistic flavour. As Lorca finished the reading and folded the manuscript, he seemed to Morla a dramatist who had scaled further heights and grown in stature.

The first performance of *The House of Bernarda Alba* took place not in Spain, ravaged by the Civil War and its aftermath, but in South America. It opened on 8 March, 1945, at the Teatro Avenida in Buenos Aires and was performed by Margarita Xirgu and her company. Its success, like that of the earlier plays, was immediate, and a few days after the first performance a bronze plaque in memory of Lorca was unveiled in the foyer of the theatre. In subsequent years *The House of Bernarda*

Alba was to be presented in most of the major cities of the world and has been regarded by many as Lorca's best play. In Spain itself the first performance took place on 10 January, 1964, at the Teatro Goya in Madrid, twenty-eight years after the play's composition. It was presented by the company of Maritza Caballero, directed by Juan Antonio Bardem, and the part of Bernarda was taken by Candida Losada.

The play, like *Blood Wedding*, had a realistic source. In a conversation with Morla Lynch in 1936, Lorca had described a personal experience in Granada:

> . . . There is, not very far from Granada, a small village where my parents owned a small property: Valderrubio. In the house immediately next to ours lived 'Doña Bernarda', a very old widow who kept over her unmarried daughters an inexorable and tyrannical watch. They were prisoners deprived of all free will, so I never spoke with them; but I saw them pass like shadows, always silent and always dressed in black . . . at the edge of the patio there was a joint well, now dry, and I used to go down into it to observe that strange family whose enigmatic way of life intrigued me. And I was able to watch them. It was a silent and cold hell beneath the African sun, a tomb for the living under the harsh rule of a dark gaoler. And so – he concludes – there was born *The House of Bernarda Alba*, its enclosed women Andalusian, though, as you say, they do have, perhaps, something of that harsh colouring more in keeping with the women of Castile.[2]

It is certainly the kind of experience likely to leave a deep impression on the mind of a young and imaginative boy. In addition, it has been said that the character Pepe el Romano was modelled on Pepe de la Romilla, the lover of one of the daughters.[3] If *Blood Wedding* had, as one of its sources, a newspaper report, it had none of the personal involvement of the episode that inspired *The House of Bernarda Alba*.

On the other hand, as in the case of the newspaper story, the memory of a childhood experience was for Lorca merely a point of departure for the further working-out of those obsessive themes that distinguish all his work. *The House of Bernarda Alba* fuses in particular the themes of passion and frustration evoked so powerfully elsewhere. In the figure of Adela, for example, we hear again echoes that reverberate from Lorca's earlier creative work. In *Book of Poems* 'Summer Madrigal' *(Madrigal de verano)* celebrates the theme of sensuous love:

> Join your red lips to mine,
> Oh! Estrella, gipsy one.
> Beneath the golden mid-day sun
> I will bite the apple.[4] (p. 137)

In *Songs* the poem 'In Malaga' *(En Málaga)* describes Leonarda's sensuous charms:

> Lovely Leonarda,
> Pontifical flesh in white dress,
>
> . . . Oscillating
> – shell and lotus –
> move your buttocks
> of Ceres in marble rhetoric. (p. 329)

In *Gipsy Ballads* 'The Unfaithful Married Woman' and, even more so, 'Thamar and Amnon' portray with great power the sensuality of physical love:

> Leave me in peace, my brother.
> Your kisses on my shoulders are
> wasps and breezes
> in double swarm of flutes.
> Thamar, in your firm breasts
> there are two fishes that call to me,
> and in your fingertips
> the sound of a rose enclosed. (p. 394)

In the drama itself it is the same theme that, at different times and with varying intensity, is expressed by Mariana Pineda, by the young and impassioned Cocoliche of *The Billy-Club Puppets*, by the sensual Belisa of *The Love of Don Perlimplín*, by the Mannequin in *When Five Years Have Passed*, and, above all, by the Bride and Leonardo in *Blood Wedding*:

LEONARDO: The birds of early morning
               are calling among the trees.

               Let's go to a hidden corner
               where I may love you for ever,
               for to me the people don't matter,
               nor the venom they throw on us.
[*He embraces her strongly.*]
BRIDE: And I'll sleep at your feet,
               to watch over your dreams.
               Naked, looking over the fields,
               as though I were a bitch.
               Because that's what I am! Oh, I look at you
               and your beauty sears me.[5] (p.84)

When, at the end of Act III, Adela reveals to Martirio the nature of her passion for Pepe el Romano, she is one of a long line:

> I can't stand this horrible house after the taste of his mouth. I'll be what he wants me to be. Everybody in the village against me, burning me with their fiery fingers; pursued by those who claim they're decent, and I'll wear, before them all, the crown of thorns that belongs to the mistress of a married man. (p.198)

The theme of frustration, as the discussion of *Yerma* has shown, also has a long lineage in Lorca's earlier work, extending in the poems from the early 'Elegy', the lament for the spinsters of Granada, to the lonely, waiting Soledad Montoya of the *Gipsy Ballads*, and in the plays from the dreaming Curianito of *The Butterfly's Evil Spell*, through Mariana Pineda, her love frustrated by circumstance, the Secretary and the Bride of *When Five Years Have Passed*, longing for a love that never comes, to the anguished, despairing figure of Yerma herself. But most touching and eloquent of all, the culmination of the expression of the theme of frustration, of fading hope and broken illusions, is, of course, *Doña Rosita the Spinster*. For all its comic elements, for all its evocation of a gay and elegant Granada, there is revealed to us in the course of the play's unfolding Rosita's growing sense of desolation. In Act II Rosita observes to her mother:

> It's just that in the streets I become aware of how time has passed and I don't want to be disillusioned. They've built another new house in the small plaza. I don't want to find out how time goes. (p. 160)

By the end of the play she is a woman who waits in vain for the lover who will never come, and the laughter that filled the house has turned to silence. It is a short step from *Doña Rosita* to the spinsters of Bernarda's household and the desolation that fills their lives.

A third theme, also central to the earlier plays, is the theme of honour. In some of them, notably *The Shoemaker's Prodigious Wife* and *The Love of Don Perlimplín*, honour is treated humorously, even farcically, the traditional concept of honour as public reputation mocked and ridiculed. In *Blood Wedding* and *Yerma*, on the other hand, honour is part of the tragic conflict of the characters. *The House of Bernarda Alba* has honour in its sense of name, reputation and public image at the very centre of its tragic conflict. From the beginning Bernarda reveals her concern with the good opinion of her neighbours. In relation to her demented mother, she tells the servant:

> BERNARDA: Go with her and be careful she doesn't get near the well.
> SERVANT: You don't need to be afraid she'll jump in.
> BERNARDA: It's not that – but the neighbours can see her there from their windows. (p. 158)

In Act II she silences her daughters: 'What scandal is this in my house in the heat's heavy silence? The neighbours must have their ears glued to the walls.' (p. 179). And in Act III she commands that no one should know of Adela's shame: 'My daughter died a virgin. Take her to another room and dress her as though she were a virgin. No one will say anything about this!' (p. 201). A concern with honour, blinding Bernarda to the reality of her daughters' needs yet simultaneously sharpening those needs in the process of denying them, is, much more than in the other plays, the spring of tragedy.

While Lorca was influenced in general by the famous honour plays of the Golden Age, and especially by the honour plays of Calderón, *The House of Bernarda Alba* seems to reveal the particular influence of *The Surgeon of His Honour*.[6] Calderón's play has as its protagonist Don Gutierre Solís, a man obsessed with his reputation and haunted by fear of any breath of scandal. His wife Mencía, young and beautiful, terrified that the finger of suspicion point at her, wastes away her life in her husband's country house with its dark and gloomy rooms, its closed doors, its barred windows and its walled garden. She is, despite her protests, ruthlessly pursued by Prince Enrique, a former suitor, suspected by Gutierre of having an affair with him, and, in order to avoid a public scandal, murdered in private at her husband's instigation. Her 'offence' will be buried with her and no one will learn of Gutierre's dishonour.

Gutierre, in his fanatical concern with honour, is very like Bernarda. Throughout the play he reveals that obsession with his public image that rules Bernarda too. For fear of a future scandal he had earlier abandoned Leonor, the woman he wished to marry:

> Although I listened to her explanations and did not entirely believe she had offended me, fear was sufficient to deter me from the marriage.[7] (Act I, 922-26)

Faced with doubts about his wife's integrity, honour becomes at once his main concern: [*Aside*] 'Alas, honour! We have much to talk about in private.' (Act II, 381-82). Gutierre is increasingly, as the play unfolds, that dehumanized human being, that puppet of honour that Bernarda becomes too, their better qualities sacrificed in honour's name. As Bernarda surrenders a daughter to honour's heartless requisites, Gutierre offers up the wife he loves. Mencía, like Bernarda's daughters, is the prisoner of a terrible, unbending code. Like Adela she has spirit and protests against her plight, but like Martirio and Magdalena she is resigned to it, cowed by her hopeless circumstances: 'Heavens, have pity on me! I must live in silence, for I die in silence!' (Act I, 153-54). Through its settings and its images *The Surgeon of His Honour* evokes, moreover, that terrible sense of enclosure that is the very essence of *The House of Bernarda Alba*. Mencía's bedroom becomes her prison as she awaits her death: 'But, alas, the door is locked: no one hears me in the house. Great is my affliction, great my anguish. The grille of the window forms its bars . . .' (Act III, 451-54). The rooms and the garden of Gutierre's house, full of dark and menacing shadows, are the physical equivalents of the doubts and fears that imprison its inhabitants. And slowly, through its three Acts, the play advances, like Lorca's, into a physical darkness that accompanies the movement of its characters towards their tragic fate. There are, of course, many differences between these plays, but the points of contact, and especially the image of a world and its inhabitants ruled and broken by honour, are more than suggestive.

Another possible source is Benito Pérez Galdós's novel, *Doña Perfecta*, one of the best known novels of the nineteenth century.[8] Published in 1876, the novel describes in broad and powerful strokes the clash between Doña Perfecta, a wealthy landowner in the small Castilian Town of Orbajosa, and Pepe Rey, a young engineer from the city who plans to marry her daughter. Doña Perfecta embodies the narrow-mindedness, intolerance and fanaticism of the closed world of a small provincial town that clings to its traditions. She and many of the notables of the town see in Pepe Rey and the liberal, progressive ideas for which he is a spokesman a threat to their power and way of life. Opposed to him on a general level, she is opposed to him too on the particular issue of his marriage to her daughter. From Rosario, whom she loves, Doña Perfecta demands complete and unswerving obedience, regardless of her feelings. For the young girl, on the other hand, her love of Pepe proves stronger than her duty to her mother and she arranges to elope with him. Discovering the plan Doña Perfecta has Pepe murdered. He is shot by a Carlist partisan, and Rosario, her mind unhinged by grief, is placed in a lunatic asylum.

Between Doña Perfecta and Bernarda there is a clear similarity, for both are intolerant, inflexible and tyrannical women. If honour is not the central theme of Galdós's novel, it is nevertheless part of the set of beliefs that comprises Doña Perfecta's narrow-mindedness. The presentation of the stagnant, oppressive, inward-looking world of Orbajosa is not unlike the claustrophobia of Bernarda's house, and the portrayal of Doña Perfecta and Bernarda in bold and clear outline is very similar. The clash between Rosario and her mother reminds us of Adela's resistance to Bernarda. In both the novel and the play there is a final shooting incident, and if Pepe el Romano is a different type from Pepe Rey, their names are curiously alike. It is interesting to note, too, that *Doña Perfecta* was one of the novels which Galdós later turned into a play. Whether or not Lorca knew the play is a matter of conjecture, but in any case he would clearly have responded to the dramatic character of the novel itself.[9]

The House of Bernarda Alba, like the other rural tragedies, is strongly reminiscent of Greek tragedy. The women dressed in black and starkly outlined against white walls, the forceful expression of powerful emotion, the sense of human lives ruled by greater forces – there is much here that captures the mood and spirit of the old Greek plays. In the Greek drama there was often great emphasis on the female characters. It has been said of Sophocles's *Electra* that it is 'a tragedy of women rather than of men'.[10] Similarly, Euripides's *Medea* illustrates the general point that 'this dramatist was more interested in his women characters than in his men'.[11] In thinking of the passionate characters of Electra, Medea, Phaedra and others like them, it is not difficult to see the ancestry of the Mother in *Blood Wedding*, of Yerma, and of Bernarda Alba herself. There is, indeed, in the very title of the play that evocation of a household, a family line that in the Greek plays is so often doomed, its individual members the playthings of the gods. Furthermore, in terms of Aristotle's recipe for tragedy, the tragic 'error' in Bernarda is her pride and obsessive concern with honour, and in Adela an over-passionate defiance of her mother's will.[12] The Greek 'reversal of intention' lies, clearly, in Bernarda's seeking to avert dishonour and cause for scandal yet, through her methods, bringing it about. There is, too, a sense of pity and terror in the play. We are appalled by Bernarda's savagery, by the realization that honour has made a monster of her. We feel pity for her inasmuch as she is manipu-

lated by her beliefs, and pity too for her daughters' fate and the
waste of Adela's life. Throughout the play there is that pitiable
sense of the characters' lives shaped by forces greater than
themselves. And finally, La Poncia, the old servant, fulfils the
function of the Chorus, for she comments on the action and, in
expressing her fears for its outcome, creates in part its tragic
tone. If *The House of Bernarda Alba* owes nothing specific to
Greek tragedy in terms of plot, its debt in terms of tragic mood
and impact is clearly substantial.

The House of Bernarda Alba is a play in which the sense of
imprisonment is almost unrelieved.[13] The theme has its
immediate focus in the house which is a prison and where
Bernarda tyrannically rules her mother, her daughters and her
servants. But the house is simultaneously the symbol of a
condition that exists beyond it, for if Bernarda's household are
her prisoners, she is in turn the prisoner of others – of the
world beyond the house, of the villagers, of their gossip, their
envy and their malice, and of all the values that they stand for:
honour, custom, tradition, all inflexibly revered. It is, indeed,
a world where men and women are the prisoners of each
other, of prying eyes and whispering tongues. But they are too
the prisoners of Nature, for we are made aware throughout the
play of the continuous and burning heat by which these people are oppressed, day in, day out through the long Spanish
summer. In addition, their lives are set in a landscape where
the river-beds are dry and the sense of desolation is intense.
Furthermore, the tyranny of Nature exists within them too in
the force of instinct and passion whose rule is as total and
complete as it is in the animals that in this play are always close
to human lives. The blind and inevitable processes that work
in Nature work too through men and women, and if from time
to time there is a suggestion of a different world where men are
free, it is both fleeting and far-removed from the claustrophobic world of the household of Bernarda which, increasingly dominating our imagination, becomes an image of
humanity at large.

The curtain rises on a room in Bernarda's house that is
white, empty and silent. From the outset the idea of enclosure

is powerfully suggested, for the room with its thick walls, its oppressive silence, and its depressing and inescapable uniformity of colour is the physical symbol of the constraints that in many other ways imprison the people of the play. And the room is also at once particular and general, for while it is part of Bernarda's house, its form and colour evoke too other rooms and houses beyond the house, the totality of the village where Bernarda lives, and other villages like it.[14] Indeed, the tolling of the bells links room and village, extending outwards the sense of unbearable monotony and suggesting the existence beyond the house of that general claustrophobia of which Bernarda's house is but a part. The silence of the room is also part of a larger silence in which dishonourable secrets are suppressed and stifled. Its emptiness evokes the lives of people that are void and meaningless. And the blankness of its walls suggests the sterility of a world in which, as in the case of the pictures that seem strangely out of place, all that is creative is overwhelmed.[15] Without a word being spoken, the mood of the play is quickly established and the nature of its theme clearly defined.

The conversation of the servants, La Poncia and the First Servant, introduces immediately two of the play's important themes: firstly, Bernarda's tyranny; and secondly, associated with her tyranny, her concern with the appearance of things. In alluding to Bernarda's domination of the household, La Poncia employs, significantly, the image of the circle: 'Tyrant over everyone around her.' (p. 152). It suggests the closed world over which Bernarda rules, enhancing the impression created by the physical nature of the setting. But if Bernarda tyrannizes the circle of her family, it is clear that she in turn is tyrannized by the larger circle of the village in the sense that her concern with honour and public image rules her life.[16] It is this obsession which is conveyed already in the servants' frenzied cleaning of household objects:

> PONCIA [*shouting*]: . . . Clean everything up good. If Bernarda doesn't find things shining, she'll pull out the few hairs I have left. (pp. 151-2)

And in the servant's failure to remove the stain, Bernarda's failure to escape the tyranny of honour is anticipated:

> PONCIA [*at the cupboard.*]: The glass has some specks.
> SERVANT: Neither soap nor rag will take them off. (p. 153)

The scene points too to the link between Bernarda's tyranny and her fate, the vicious circle that the domination of the circle of her household eventually becomes. La Poncia and the First Servant, who bitterly complain about Bernarda's treatment of them, curse her, and steal her food behind her back, embody the resistance to her that will be embodied later in her daughters, especially in Adela and Martirio. They may, indeed, be her prisoners, subjected to her will, but in an equally important sense she is their prisoner, for to preserve her honour she is dependent on them. And if to avert the world's tyranny – dishonour – she must herself become a tyrant, she creates within the members of her household the opposition that will bring about her downfall. The idea of the vicious circle, of the remorseless process of cause and effect in which Bernarda will herself be caught, is made apparent to us indirectly in the First Servant's treatment of the beggar woman and her child.[17] Seeking a release for her own frustration, the First Servant sends her packing, dominates the woman as she herself is dominated by Bernarda, and displays towards her that heartlessness and lack of charity that she has suffered at Bernarda's hands. In the sense that tyranny breeds tyranny and example sets example, there are already processes at work whereby individuals shape the inescapable consequences, the circular patterns, of their own acts.

The conclusion of the episode introduces the theme of passion and natural instinct. La Poncia has already shown us that the servants have none of Bernarda's prudery:

> SERVANT: Watch out – you'll strain your windpipe!
> PONCIA: I'd rather strain something else!
> [*Goes out laughing.*] (p. 153)

But it is the First Servant's unrestrained lament for Bernarda's dead husband that is the most effective statement of the theme:

> So take what's coming to you, Antonio María Benavides

– stiff in your broadcloth suit and your high boots – take what's coming to you! You'll never again lift my skirts behind the corral door! (p. 154)

In the figure of Don Antonio who sought release in the embraces of the servant from the prison of Bernarda's stifling prudery, we have a powerful example of the force of passion that anticipates the course of action to be adopted later by his daughters. Moreover, in the common behaviour of different generations – father, daughter – and different social hierarchies – servant, master – the idea of the unchanging patterns and processes of human nature and, by extension, of human beings as part of a greater whole is already suggested.

The first appearance of Bernarda underscores the theme of honour. Her stifling of the First Servant's grief – 'Silence!' (p. 154) – of Magdalena's weeping, and of the girl's protest, is an extinction of spontaneous feeling, and from the private impassioned level of the First Servant's lamentation for lost love the action is strikingly transposed to the level of public image. Here the arrival of the mourners and the exchanges between them and Bernarda constitute all the ritual and formality of grief, its public utterance and expression. From time to time the private feelings, hatreds and resentments of the women are glimpsed in their asides, but they merge finally into the intonation with which the episode concludes:

> BERNARDA [*She rises and chants*]: Requiem aeternam dona eis domine.
> ALL [*Standing and chanting in the Gregorian fashion*]: Et lux perpetua luceat eis. (p. 156)

In its echoing of the tolling bells and its reminder of the public service, the conclusion of this scene achieves two things. Firstly, it establishes the significance in the lives of Bernarda and others like her of tradition and convention. And secondly, inasmuch as the structure of the scene is circular, its conclusion echoing the beginning of the play, it becomes a symbol of the way in which the lives of these individuals are wholly circumscribed by their concern with ritual.

The departure of the mourners leads into the presentation of Bernarda in relation to her daughters, her mother, and finally

˙her servants. Here, in contrast to the earlier scene, is Bernarda's private side, revealed in a number of situations. All of
them anticipate subsequent events, and all of them, displaying
her harshness and inflexibility, stem from her obsession with
appearance and seemliness. Firstly, she rejects the gaiety
symbolized in the fan offered by Adela and asserts instead the
importance of tradition:

> ADELA: Take this one. [*She gives her a round fan with green
> and red flowers*]
> BERNARDA [*throwing the fan on the floor*]: Is that the fan to
> give to a widow? Give me a black one and learn to
> respect your father's memory. (p. 157)

Secondly, to escape the malice and the gossip of the villagers,
she conceals her half-crazed mother from the public view.
Thirdly, to impress the need for seemliness on Angustias, she
strikes her savagely. And lastly, to silence the insinuation of La
Poncia, she reminds the servant of her station. In each and
every case Bernarda dominates these individuals and subjects
them to her will. But the particular imprisonment which she
exemplifies has once more a much more general significance.
There is the house itself, its doors and windows closed against
the world:

> BERNARDA: . . . For the eight years of mourning, not a
> breath of air will get in this house from the street. We'll
> act as if we'd sealed up doors and windows with bricks.
> (p. 157)

The weight of tradition is equally inescapable: 'That's what
happened in my father's house – and in my grandfather's
house.' (p. 157). The women are imprisoned in their black and
lifeless mourning weeds, in their monotonous routine of sewing, and in their own despair. María Josefa is contained within
her room, gagged while the service is in progress, and, when
she is released, confined to the limits of the patio. The darkness of the room has a parallel in the colour of the women's
clothes and in Bernarda's fan. And most striking, perhaps, is
the image that concludes the sequence, of Antonio María
Benevides, his life ended, his face covered with a handkerchief. Between this still and silent figure, whose life is over,

María Josefa secured in her room, her life drawing to a close, and the daughters who are already ageing through their mother's ruthless domination of them, there is a link that extends beyond the members of this particular family. They are all in their different ways the signs and symbols of an imprisonment that, though it is related to Bernarda's tyranny, seems part of a larger metaphor that is all to do with imprisoned humanity at large.

The scene expresses too, in conjunction with this theme, the theme of freedom. María Josefa clings to a dream of love and romance that anticipates the illusions of her grandaughters, especially Adela.[18] Between the brightness of María Josefa's jewellery and the colours of Adela's fan there is a clear parallel: 'She took her rings and the amethyst earrings out of the box, put them on, and told me she wants to get married.' (p. 158). Secondly, La Poncia's story of Paca la Roseta expounds the theme of uninhibited passion. The dominant images are of liberty, power and creativity. There is the description of the girl: 'They say her breasts were exposed . . . Paca la Roseta with her hair loose . . .' (p. 160). The galloping horse on which her lover bears her away has, beyond its sexual symbolism, a wonderful sense of power and freedom.[19] In the way in which the man holds the girl astride the horse there is a great sensuality. The setting for their love-making is the olive grove, an image of fertility, and when they return at dawn, Paca is adorned with flowers, suggestive of all that is creative. In the accumulation of its details the episode presents a world distinct from that presented by the house and its inhabitants and the village with its dry river-bed. But while it is distinct from Bernarda's world, it is also overshadowed by it, contained as effectively by it as La Poncia's pleasure in relating Paca's story is contained and shackled by her ultimate narrow-mindedness, in which she is no different from Bernarda. The dream of passion, for all its uninhibited attraction, cannot escape the reality of tradition, convention and honour, and, inasmuch as Adela is anticipated in the figure of Paca la Roseta, and in María Josefa too, her fate is already presented to us. It is not without significance that the conclusion of the scene should return to the theme of Bernarda's harshness and

R

the cleaning of the house, for both are aspects of the inflexible nature of honour that lies at the heart of the closed world of the play. As Bernarda dominates La Poncia and orders her to clean the patio, we are reminded yet again of the emphasis of the play's first scene. The circular structure of the action is here, as elsewhere, an effective and vivid reminder of the closed world in which the characters are contained and from which there is no escape.

The presentation of Bernarda in relation to her household becomes now an episode which presents her daughters in relation to each other. Martirio, as her name suggests, is, at twenty four, a kind of martyr, the prisoner of her physical ugliness and, through it, of her fear of men and her general disillusionment.[20] Life is for her a mechanical, oppressive process which she is powerless to change: 'I do things without any faith, but like clockwork.' (p. 161). And again: '. . . But history repeats itself. I can see that everything is a terrible repetition.' (p. 162). Magdalena, at thirty the second oldest of the girls, is, even more than Martirio, the victim of despair. For her there are no illusions and the only happiness is in the past. As for the present, she views her own significance with cynicism, Adela's optimism with sympathetic understanding, and Angustias's arranged marriage with uncompromising realism. Older than the others with the exception of Angustias, she is the prisoner of her fading hopes for a different way of life. Amelia, younger than Magdalena, older than Martirio, is less prominent than either, but is the prisoner of her fear of her mother. The three of them, forming a chronological progression, are stages in a journey whose end is represented in the terrible figure of their mad grandmother, María Josefa.

Adela stands at the other end of the spectrum, at twenty the youngest of the sisters both in years and attitude, and throughout the scene her youthful optimism separates her from the others. Magdalena's acceptance of her fate draws from Adela a spirited opposition to it:

> I will not get used to it! I can't be locked up. I don't want my skin to look like yours. I don't want my skin's whiteness lost in these rooms. Tomorrow I'm going to put on

my green dress and go walking in the streets. I want to go
out! (p. 165)

The green of her dress symbolizes her hopes and, echoing
earlier allusions to the green of the flowers that decc~ate her
fan and of the olive grove that witnesses the love-making of
Paca la Roseta, is a contrast in all its freshness and viuality to
the dull, monotonous mourning garments of the other
women.[21] The whiteness of her skin is free so far from the
sallowness and lines that for the other sisters are increasingly
the outward signs of their inner torment. In its lustre 't is a
contrast too to the dull and uniform whiteness of the room, an
image of life contrasted with sterility. All that in the other
sisters crystalizes their subjection to their fate is in Adela
the determination to escape it. Her words draw together
the separate strands of the theme of liberty and freedom
represented elsewhere in the illusions of María Josefa and the
conduct of Paca la Roseta. In their idealism and resolve Adela's
words are intensely moving, but it is the figure of Magdalena
which is more significant here. Echoing her mother, she stops
Adela in her tracks, dispels illusion, and supported by
Martirio and Amelia, reminds Adela of the reality in which
they are all contained:

AMELIA: What happens to one will happen to all of us.
(p. 166)

The conclusion of the Act asserts the nature of this inescapable reality. The theme of freedom is embodied here in Angustias and María Josefa. Her inheritance from her step-father
allows Angustias to escape through marriage to Pepe el
Romano:

ANGUSTIAS: Let me go out, Mother! (p. 167)

María Josefa, Angustias in an older form, seeks escape in the
only way open to her – in the world of illusion: 'I want to get
away from here! Bernarda! To get married by the shore of the
sea – by the shore of the sea!' (p. 168). The older woman takes
up the cry of the younger. They are linked to each other by it
and linked too by the violence perpetrated on them by Bernarda, for she violently wipes the make-up from Angustias's
face and has her mother dragged to her room. But both are

linked in turn to Adela, for their cry was hers: 'I want to go out!' (p. 165). And Adela's dreams and youthfulness have their parallel in María Josefa's jewellery and in the flowers in her hair and at her breast (p. 167). In Bernarda's treatment of Angustias and María Josefa, the fate of Adela is projected once again. If the idea of escape runs through the scene and becomes a kind of chorus – 'I want to go out!' (p. 165),'Let me go out, Mother!' (p. 167), 'Let me go out, Bernarda!' (p. 168) – it is Bernarda's command – 'Lock her up!' (p. 168) – which answers it and echoes through the ending of the Act. It suggests the sense of curtailment that is its dominant mood, the sense of closing-in that has become so powerful. Moreover, the final curtain – QUICK CURTAIN (p. 168) – cuts short, stifles María Josefa's cry for freedom in a way that is vividly symbolic.

The second Act is set again in a room in Bernarda's house. In conjunction with the continuous sewing of the women, it develops and deepens the sense of unending sameness, the monotony and the mechanical nature of their lives. But if they are daughters subjected to a mother's tyranny, they are constrained by other forces too. The theme of Nature's harshness, particularized in the suffocating heat, acquires an insistent force, elaborating further the suggestion of Act I:

THIRD WOMAN: The sun comes down like lead. (p. 155)

Amelia, Martirio, Magdalena and La Poncia evoke the heat that oppresses them, that is inescapable, and that seems to rise from the earth itself:

AMELIA [To PONCIA]: Open the patio door and see if we can get a bit of a breeze [Poncia opens the door]
MARTIRIO: Last night I couldn't sleep because of the heat.
AMELIA: Neither could I.
MAGDALENA: I got up for a bit of air. There was a black storm-cloud and a few drops even fell.
PONCIA: It was one in the morning and the earth seemed to give off fire. I got up too. Angustias was still at the window with Pepe. (pp. 169-70)

The girls begin to assume a much more general significance as

part of a suffering humanity, of the greater family of man beset
by a hostile universe. Moreover, in La Poncia's allusion to
Angustias and Pepe, the heat of the night is linked to the heat
of passion, Nature's external assault matched by its internal
oppression in the demands and needs of individual instincts
and desires.[22] The daughters of Bernarda are individuals, but,
as the play unfolds, they and the events in which they are
involved are part of a larger metaphor.

Their conversation centres for a while on the subject of men
and women, prompted by the imminent marriage of Angustias. They are again individuals, curious, inexperienced,
interested, full of guilt. Thus Amelia: 'These things embarrass
me!' (p. 170). And Angustias: 'My heart was almost coming out
of my mouth. It was the first time I'd ever been alone at night
with a man.' (p. 171). Once more they reflect the particular
level of the play, Bernarda's daughters imprisoned by their
inexperience and their mother's domination. But, in a general
sense, as La Poncia's words suggest, they are also the prisoners of men at large, and of tradition, linked in their subjection
to other women:

> You aren't married but it's good for you to know, any-
> way, that two weeks after the wedding a man gives up
> the bed for the table, then the table for the tavern, and the
> woman who doesn't like it can just rot, weeping in a
> corner. (p. 171)

From this general level the focus of the scene narrows once
more to the clash between Adela and Martirio, from the spectacle of all Bernarda's daughters as the oppressed victims of
their circumstances to the particular conflict of the relentless
and inevitable force of passion exemplified in two of them. In
Adela the dream of freedom achieves a new intensity, but so
does Martirio's sense of hopelessness. Their feelings are
thrown into sharp relief, the sisters' opposition to each other
heightened by their close proximity, Adela's longing to escape
intensified by her constant observation of Martirio's ugliness
and despair, Martirio's bitterness accentuated by her envy of
Adela's beauty – and both of them made still more desperate
by their knowledge of Angustias's imminent marriage. Ber-

narda's tyranny becomes inevitably her daughters' tyranny of each other and passion's tyranny of each of them. In the growing hostility of Adela and Martirio the power of passion to set individuals against each other presents one aspect of the theme, while the other is our awareness of their increasing isolation. Adela reiterates more vigorously her dream of liberty, sweeping aside La Poncia's common-sense advice no less unceremoniously than her strength of feeling will seek to deny and overcome all other obstacles:

> Save your advice. It's already too late. For I'd leap not over you, just a servant, but over my mother to put out this fire I feel in my legs and my mouth. What can you possibly say about me? That I lock myself in my room and will not open the door? That I don't sleep? I'm smarter than you! See if you can catch the hare with your hands. (p. 174)

But the refusal to be constrained is, ironically, its own constraint, for the passions that are the inevitable consequences of events become themselves the source of further consequences whose effects are equally inevitable. Adela voices unconsciously the sense of no escape that slowly descends upon the play:[23] 'No one can stop what has to happen.' (p. 174). And the conclusion of the episode, closing another circle, shows how the structure of the play underlines continually its predominant ideas. Adela's defiant posture yields to the resignation of her sisters, Martirio's in particular: 'But I love nice underwear . . . It's one of the few tastes I've left.' (p. 175)

La Poncia, alluding to other women who can laugh despite their harsh and tedious lives tied to their children, merely focuses attention on the humourless and sterile nature of Bernarda's household. And her final reference to the house as a convent: 'No, fate has sent me to this nunnery' (p. 175) closes the scene, evoking again its opening and fixing more firmly in our minds the image of imprisonment and inescapability.

The appearance of the harvesters announces in an expressive and dramatic form the theme of physical and emotional freedom. Here is a world that is filled with bursting energy, vitality and beauty, symbolic of the creative processes of man and Nature. La Poncia paints a verbal picture of the young men's strength and looks: 'Like weathered trees! . . . a boy with green eyes – tight knit as a sheaf of wheat.' (p. 176). Martirio depicts them bathed in sunlight as they reap: 'They reap through flames.' (p. 176). Their song is of love, their sexual life an integral part of their lives and work:

> The reapers have set out
> Looking for ripe wheat;
> They'll carry off the hearts
> Of any girls they meet. (p. 176)

The setting for their activities is the open air, the expanse of fields. In the accumulation of all its detail the scene encapsulates the dream of freedom coveted by Adela in particular. Indeed, there is about it a certain dream-like quality, a golden light, an air of idealization that separates it from the reality of Bernarda's household. But its effectiveness lies precisely in the extent to which it touches on that household. In one direction there are suggestive links between the scene and earlier incidents in the play. Associated with the harvesters is a woman dressed in sequins who plays the accordion and dances, and who is taken to and enjoyed by the men in the olive-grove: ' . . . a woman who dresses in sequins and dances, with an accordion . . .' (p. 176). The allusions connect her with Paca la Roseta and María Josefa. The green of the young man's eyes echoes the other greens: of the olive-grove, of Adela's dress and the flowers that decorate the fan. And in the red of the roses mentioned in the song: 'The reaper asks you for roses/ With which to deck his crown' (p. 177) there is a parallel with the red flowers on the fan that alternate with green. But in other, more important ways the daughters of Bernarda are isolated from the harvesters and the world they symbolize. The sound of the bells that, at the scene's commencement, announces the return of the harvesters to their work is heard only faintly in the house: [*Tiny bells are heard distantly as through several thicknesses of wall.*] (p. 175). Here, in effect, is a world distanced from Bernarda's. In reply to Magdalena's question: 'Where are they from this year?' (p. 176) La Poncia replies significantly: 'From far, far away.' Throughout the scene, moreover, the sunlight that bathes the harvesters in a golden glow enters the house weakly, barely lightening its shadows, while the energy and animation of the men has its opposite within the house in the seated and silent group of women: [*Tambourines and carrañacas are heard. Pause. They all listen in the silence cut by the sun.*] (p. 176). The song of the harvesters proclaims:

> Throw wide your doors and windows,
> You girls who live in the town . . . (p. 177)

Adela, Angustias and Magdalena, in contrast, observe them from a window that is barely open, the symbol of the fear that inhibits and contains them. And as the men depart and their song fades and recedes, the point is reinforced that it passes by Bernarda's household in a sense that is more than physical. If there are links between these two opposing worlds, they are tenuous, the stuff that dreams are made of, as fleeting as the song that is silenced. The reality is expressed instead in the figure of Martirio, seated, despairing, the image of all her sisters in her suffering: [. . . *Martirio is left sitting on the low chair with her head between her hands.*] (p. 177).

The theme of oppression is consistently unfolded now, exemplified in almost every detail. Martirio alludes to the heat of summer, hoping for relief with winter's coming: 'I was wishing it were November, the rainy days, the frost – anything except this unending summertime.' (p. 177). Amelia denies her such a consolation, evoking instead a picture of Nature's inescapable harshness:[24] 'It'll pass and come again.' (p. 177). And if Martirio is oppressed without by Nature, she is also increasingly oppressed within by her growing jealousy and envy of Angustias and Adela which drive her now to steal the picture of Pepe el Romano. And this, in turn, brings upon her Bernarda's wrath and a reassertion of the importance of honour, linked significantly in Bernarda's outburst to the oppression of the heat of summer: 'What scandal is this in my house in the heat's heavy silence? The neighbours must have their ears glued to the walls.' (p. 179). Moreover, if the sisters are oppressed in all these ways, they also progressively oppress each other, Adela's accusations levelled at Martirio, Martirio's insinuations directed at Adela, and their mutual resentment turned towards Angustias. And if Bernarda strikes Martirio here, as previously she has struck Angustias, her daughters now strike out at her and at each other in other ways that are as desperate as they are insidious. As the scene concludes, Bernarda reasserts her domination, and the image of the girls' imprisonment is further underlined:

> But I'm not old yet – I have five chains for you, and this house my father built, so not even the weeds will know of my desolation. Out of here! (p. 181)

The truth that evades her is that she is equally a prisoner, firstly of honour, then of the consequences of its imposition upon her children. She appears to control and dominate her household only to be controlled and dominated by it, her successive victories won at an ever-increasing cost in a process whose closed and circular movement is again apparent. For as Bernarda sits disconsolately (p. 181) she calls to mind the anguished posture of Martirio earlier in the Act. The daughter's fate is her mother's too, and the sense of human beings subjected to a common suffering, mirrored in each other, is reinforced.

The remainder of the Act strengthens the impression of the oneness and the unchanging nature of things. Bernarda's attempted domination of La Poncia is another form of her domination of her daughters. And La Poncia's resistance to her mistress is, on a craftier and lower level, a duplication of the resistance of the daughters to their mother. Bernarda displays towards the servant the brutality illustrated elsewhere in the play, wounding her with a heartless reference to her origins and her mother: '. . . you know where you came from!' (p. 182) '. . . The whore house was for a certain woman, already dead . . .' (p. 183). La Poncia, in turn, seeking an outlet for the accumulated bitterness of many years, strikes at Bernarda, sowing in her mind the seeds of doubt and suspicion about the family honour. Bernarda, striving to manipulate her servant, is instead manipulated, her own insinuations turned against her. But in their hostility towards each other they are reminders and reflections of other people and incidents: of the First Servant's cruel domination of the beggar woman and her child; of the mourners' cutting asides directed at Bernarda; of the general hostility of the villagers towards her; of the contained bitterness of La Poncia and the First Servant who steal her food and snipe at her behind her back; of sisters who increasingly wound and destroy each other. In short, this is a world in which individuals seem continually besieged and in which human beings prey upon each other; where mothers are the victims of their children, children the victims of their mothers, servants the prey of their mistresses, and all of them the prey of others in the widening circle of man's inhumanity to man.

The conclusion of the Act, focusing on honour, clinches the argument. The girl who has murdered her illegitimate child is hounded by the villagers, and in every sense her helplessness is emphasized. She is a prisoner of male passion, exposed to it and to its consequences. She is the prisoner of her own dishonour, as powerless to escape it as she is to evade the wrath of her accusers as they drag her through the streets and the encroaching menace of the men returning from the fields: 'They're dragging her through the streets – and down the paths and across the olive groves the men are coming, shouting so the fields shake.' (p. 185). It is a powerful picture of individual helplessness, but its particular effectiveness lies in its implications, in the way the picture opens out to substitute its central character and her accusers with other individuals. Adela, pregnant and clutching at her stomach is already the village-girl. As Bernarda screams at the latter: 'Kill her! Kill her!' (p. 186) her anger reverberates in Adela's ears. But for Bernarda the disgrace of someone else will become her own. In the way in which one episode repeats or anticipates another and roles are interchanged, the play conveys the sense in which its characters are, less than the architects of their destinies, the playthings, the puppets, of forces greater than themselves which are also an inescapable part of human nature and experience whose processes continue endlessly. [25]

This sense of human helplessness is increasingly the source of our compassion for the characters, for Bernarda's daughters and for Bernarda too. We feel a compassion for their plight, for the imposition upon young women with hopes and dreams of a way of life which stifles them no less effectively than it destroys their youth and beauty. To this extent Magdalena's sense of resignation and disillusionment is moving in itself. But there is an even greater sympathy for those who, younger than Magdalena, seek to escape her fate, and therefore a keener sense of pity in their failure to do so. In Adela and, to a lesser extent, Martirio, the way of life to which they are subjected heightens their determination to resist it and draws from each of them a powerful reaction to their circumstances. They express that love of life and freedom, those passions and enthusiasms that are common to us all, but these are the things which, given the circumstances in which they find themselves, create increasingly the clash between their natural instincts and the forces that oppose them – honour, tradition, convention – and produce finally the tragic suffering which is the outcome of that clash. Pity, and terror too, lie in the spectacle of human aspiration which, though worthy, carries with it the seed of its own destruction and achieves the opposite of what it seeks. And all that is true of the daughters is true of Bernarda too.[26] She strives to preserve the name and honour of the family, but in so doing unleashes within the family those forces that, unchecked, will bring about dishonour. And to check them is itself a process that carries with it terrible repercussions. Bernarda, no less than her daughters, is caught more and more in the vicious circle of events that are both of her making and of others too. And then there is the pity that is born of a sense of waste, focused in particular in Adela. She has all the qualities that make life precious: youth, beauty, spirit and resolve, and she has them to a degree that compels her to try to live a life which is the measure of her natural attributes. Yet the circumstances of her life are a permanent denial of her dreams, a brutal reality that mocks her and that, forcing her to a desperate assertion of herself, lays her waste, ravages and deflowers her in forms more terrible than Bernarda can imagine and ultimately leaves her broken body for our contemplation.

The circular structure of the play is again suggested as the curtain rises on Act III – [*When the curtain rises, there is a great silence . . .*] (p. 187). It is a silence that repeats the silence of the

beginning of Act I, which accompanies Bernarda's first
appearance: 'Silence!' (p. 154), and which ends the play: 'Silence, silence, I said. Silence!' (p. 201). But Bernarda's domination of her family is again only one example of a sense of
oppression by other things. The women are enclosed within
the confines of the house, but the house is itself enveloped in a
silence that extends outwards, and now, for the first time, in
the darkness of night. Moreover, Bernarda's opening conversation with Prudencia, a neighbour, evokes the sense of an
enclosure that is again particular and general. Prudencia
speaks of the effects of honour upon her family. Her husband
has quarrelled with his brothers over his inheritance and
avoids being seen in public. Their daughter has committed an
offence that her father will not forgive. The individual members of the family are linked both by the rigour and tyranny of
honour and by their suffering, which in the mother is particularly anguished. She is afflicted too by increasing blindness:
'I'm losing my sight' (p. 187), and the oppression of honour's
darkness is seen to have a parallel in Nature. But the fate of
Prudencia and her family is a particular one that has, like other
incidents in the play, much wider implications.[27] The darkness that descends upon her physically and metaphorically is
echoed both in the darkness of night that envelops Bernarda's
house and in the increasing hatreds of its individual members.
Moreover, if Prudencia cannot escape the processes of Nature
that take the form of blindness, neither can Bernarda's daughters escape the reality of passion, the demands of their own
natures and of other human beings. It is something whose
irresistible force and power is expressed here in the reference
to the stallion that, scenting the mares, kicks against the stable
door: 'The stallión. He's locked in the stall and he kicks against
the wall . . .' (p. 188). The allusion evokes the sense of women
as the object of male passion that has a blind and instinctive
force, a primitive urge that must be fulfilled. It captures perfectly the essence of human beings as the instruments of
Nature's inevitable and unending processes. Even when the
conversation turns to the wedding of Angustias, references to
ordinary things continually have deeper implications that
have the effect of suggesting impulses that, beyond the

experience and comprehension of the characters, shape their lives. Prudencia observes, for example, that when she was young the pearls in a ring signified tears. Angustias argues that things have changed, but Adela contradicts her: 'I don't think so. Things go on meaning the same. Engagement rings should be diamonds.' (p. 189). Her words suggest, beyond their obvious meaning, those eternal, ritualistic patterns of human life that are now revealed everywhere in the play. When Bernarda remarks that life is what the individual makes it, Martirio asserts instead the influence of a greater than human power: 'Or as God disposes.' (p. 189). And the closing of the scene, with its emphasis on the tolling of the bells –[*Bells are heard very distantly.*] (p. 189) – which summon Prudencia to confession and which are echoed in the words of the girls – ALL FIVE DAUGHTERS [*at the same time.*]: God go with you! (p. 189) – underlines the point, broadening the sense of ritual from the particular observation of religious rites and practices to the general sense of life as an unending, self-repeating ritual.

The theme of individuals imprisoned is sustained throughout the conversation between Bernarda and her daughters that now precedes their retirement for the night. Bernarda, speaking with Angustias of Pepe, repeats the idea of woman's inferiority:

> You shouldn't ask him. And when you're married, even less. Speak if he speaks, and look at him when he looks at you. That way you'll get along. (p. 190)

And Angustias's allusion to the bars of the window that separate her from Pepe, suggests too the gulf of understanding and sympathy that separates men from women, and of which women, in particular, are the prisoners:

> Many nights I watch Pepe very closely through the window bars and he seems to fade away – as though he were hidden in a cloud of dust like those raised by the flocks. (p. 191)

But as the scene draws to its conclusion, it is the impression of individuals dwarfed and intimidated before the mystery and enormity of Nature that is conveyed to us particularly powerfully. Amelia reacts fearfully to the darkness of night that encloses them as totally now as did the heat previously: 'What a dark night!' (p. 191). Adela describes the white horse in the yard, an apparition in the intense blackness: 'The stallion was in the middle of the corral. White! Twice as large. Filling all the darkness.' (p. 191). For her it is a source of wonder, for Amelia a source of fear: 'It's true. It was frightening. Like a ghost.' (p. 191). Adela's description of the star-filled sky suggests its vastness: 'The sky has stars as big as fists.' (p. 191). In their different ways, wondering or fearful, Adela and Amelia seem small and insignificant in relation to the enormity of the world, both of them the prisoners of the ordinariness, of the small-ness of their lives, of their lack of vision and imagination that Nature's vastness here accentuates. Martirio observes: 'What goes on over the roof doesn't mean a thing to me. I have my hands full with what happens under it.' (p. 191). And Bernarda agrees with her: 'And it's better not to think about it.' (p. 192). If at the beginning of the play Bernarda's domination of her family suggests and symbolizes the power of the individual, and her daughters' resistance to her reflects the significance of their personalities, they are all by now dwarfed by the complexity of things, placed in a world whose mystery they can neither control nor comprehend.

The conversation of mother and daughters is followed, as elsewhere in the play, by the conversation of mistress and servant, of Bernarda and La Poncia, and again the clash between them is a repetition of the many other clashes in the play. La Poncia torments Bernarda with her silence no less effectively than Bernarda has tormented her with insults and accusations. Throwing aside their social differences, they are instead two human beings who nakedly confront each other with a bristling hostility, locked in a primitive battle for domination and survival. Indeed, Bernarda uses an image that captures the essence of their conflict and simultaneously broadens the nature of their struggle: 'Because there's nothing for them to sink their teeth in.' (p. 193). Her words depict the way in which the characters of the play increasingly stalk each other, their instinct for survival sharpened more and more. Bernarda's domination of her daughters, and of her servants too, heightens in each of them a sense of self-preservation that is basic and instinctive. They are, indeed, caged animals for whom, in the case of Adela and Martirio, the need to be free sets them both at Bernarda's and each other's throat. But the world outside the house is equally a primitive and savage place where human beings prey upon each other: the female hounded by the male, neighbours who spy upon each other, families split and divided within themselves, young women persecuted for their errors. It is a world in which, both inside and outside the house, men and women are ruled by basic and instinctive passions, and where, despite the prevalence of a concern with honour and the seemliness of things, human relationships are conducted with unmitigated savagery. La Poncia, after Bernarda's departure, becomes in her conversation with the First Servant the equivalent of the Chorus in Greek tragedy, explaining to us the nature and the outcome of events. The power of human passion is relentless and inevitable and cannot be contained. Confronted by it, all human intervention is in vain: 'I can do nothing. I tried to head things off, but now they frighten me too much.' (p. 193). Adela's passion for Pepe el Romano cannot be denied: 'Adela is set no matter what comes . . .' (p. 194). Neither can Martirio's bitterness and envy: 'She's a pool of poison. She sees El Romano is not for her, and she'd sink the world if it were in her hand to do so.' (p. 194). But neither is to blame and the First Servant's condemnation of them is countered by La Poncia: 'They're women without men, that's all. And in such matters even blood is forgotten.' (p. 194). Human nature is as much an inescapable fact of life as the clash which is its inevitable consequence. Significantly, the world of human beings and their passions is linked here to the world of animals, for the dogs are heard outside barking at the arrival of someone: 'The dogs are barking.' (p. 194). The world of humans and animals alike is ruled by the same undeniable impulses. It is a link that is sustained with the appearance of Adela. She seeks to quench her thirst and cannot sleep: 'I want a drink of water . . . I got thirsty and woke up.' (p. 195). But her need for water, which is so strong, has a parallel in her need for Pepe el Romano which will not let her rest. And the conclusion of the scene establishes again the link between the human and the animal world as Adela's agitation is reflected in the barking of the dogs outside:

SERVANT: The dogs are going mad. (p. 195)

The appearance of María Josefa here is both dramatic and symbolic, for we see personified in her in a final and crucial form the themes of the play and the situation of its characters. She exemplifies once more the dream of freedom that in Adela and Martirio in particular has become so strong, and she captures too the essence of that dream that throughout the play has been expressed in many different ways. Her reference to the fields and to the open doors of houses recalls the harvesters and all the associations of that earlier scene: 'Won't you come with me as far as the fields? I don't like fields. I like houses, but open houses . . .' (p. 196). In addition, the theme of fertility embodied in the figure of Paca la Roseta and her lovers, and the concept of the creative and continuous processes of Nature acquire here a powerful form:

> This baby will have white hair, and I'll have *this* baby, and another, and this *one* other; and with all of us with snow-white hair we'll be like the waves – one, then another, and another. Then we'll sit down and all of us will have white heads, and we'll be seafoam. (p. 196)

The allusions to whiteness echo, moreover, the whiteness of Adela's skin referred to earlier, and now the whiteness of her nightdress. María Josefa's words have the visionary, dream-like quality that marked the harvesters' appearance, but what matters now is that they present that vision to Martirio at a crucial moment in the play.[29]

On the one hand, María Josefa symbolizes the hope to which Martirio clings, while on the other she is the terrible reality that Martirio must accept. Side by side with the presentation of a golden and idyllic future runs a dark and despairing image of the present of which María Josefa is herself the symbol. Her lullaby expresses the nature of the present. Bernarda, her daughter, has a leopard's face, and Magdalena, her grand-daughter, a hyena's:

> Bernarda, old leopard-face,
> And Magdalena, hyena-face. (p. 196)

In other words the cruelty of human beings who, from one generation to another, are as savage and as primitive as animals, is part of the reality of life. The lullaby, sung by María Josefa to the lamb which she holds in her arms, is a comment on her own child's viciousness, and, by extension, of the viciousness of human beings towards each other. She is, indeed, the living testimony both of Bernarda's treatment of her and of the future that awaits Martirio. And it is the awareness of this terrible and terrifying nightmare that, bearing down upon Martirio and making her dream more desperate and necessary, drives her to her final confrontation with Adela.

The scene that ensues is for both of them an assertion of their natural feelings, a sweeping aside of all the constraints to which they have previously submitted. Martirio's raised voice shatters the silence which for Bernarda is an essential part of seemliness and shatters too the suggested image of silent suffering. Within her twisted body and the accumulated bitterness of a spirit accustomed to disappointment, there exists the need and desire to be loved and all the capacity for feeling of any normal woman. For the first time Martirio achieves release in the revelation of her love for Pepe el Romano: 'Yes! Let me say it without hiding my head. Yes! My breast's bitter, bursting like a pomegranate. I love him!' (p. 198). Adela, in conjunction with her, asserts her right to love and to be loved in accordance with her feelings:

> I've had strength enough to push myself forward – the spirit and looks you lack. I've seen death under this roof, and gone out to look for what was mine, what belonged to me. (p. 197)

Between her and Pepe there is a natural affinity, a correspondence of beauty, youth and passion that cannot be denied and that in the arranged marriage to Angustias is made a mockery:

S

'He came for the money, but his eyes were always on me.' (p. 197). Both women, in the assertion of their true and unadulterated passions, achieve here a dignity, an honesty that are as immense as they are moving.

In other ways, however, the autonomy of passion becomes for both of them a new captivity. In the first place they are the prisoners of their feelings, unable to escape them. Secondly, they are the prisoners of each other, for Adela can no more evade the reality of Martirio's love for Pepe than can Martirio Adela's enjoyment of him. In the surrender to passion there is a surrender to the more powerful instinctive forces. Adela expresses her feelings of total helplessness: 'There's no way out here. Whoever has to drown – let her drown.' (p. 198). Martirio bears witness to a force within her whose power is irresistible: 'I have a heart full of a force so evil that, without my wanting to be, I'm drowned by it.' (p. 199). And Adela's words capture the sense of human beings at the mercy of a hostile, frightening universe: 'God must have meant to leave me alone in the midst of darkness . . .' (p. 199). But if passion and instinct are an inescapable and destructive fact, Adela and Martirio encounter in their striving to express and realize themselves forces which, equally instinctive, are equally inescapable: the fears that formulate themselves in the social forms of honour, convention and tradition. Adela depicts the forces of tradition arrayed against her: 'Everybody in the village against me, burning me with their fiery fingers; pursued by those who claim they're decent . . .' (p. 198). They are personified in particular in Bernarda, and although Adela breaks the rod that is the symbol of Bernarda's inflexible sense of honour, it is she who in the end is broken by it. But she is broken too by Bernarda's malice, her suicide induced by her mother's and Martirio's lie of Pepe's death. Adela's lifeless body hanging from the rope becomes in its total stillness and inertia eloquent testimony to the helplessness of human beings before the destructive forces that within and without assail them. But if for her there is in death a kind of escape, for Bernarda there is none. The demands of honour, whose advocate she has been, impose themselves remorselessly upon her, and she is caught finally in the vicious circle of her own making, her triumph obtained at a terrible expense. In the ending of the play, which echoes its beginning, there is a sense of a total closing-in. The bells that tolled for the husband and father toll now for his daughter, her sisters will mourn her too, and a silence will descend upon the house which will not be broken. As the final curtain falls slowly, it symbolically immures the grieving women in their house, establishing the final image of enclosure. They will emerge from it only when the bells toll for them. But they are essentially no different from the rest of us, and their anguish is ours too. The pessimistic vision that marks the conclusion of the play is a vision of human life in which suffering and death are the only certainties and in which we are all condemned to live in our dark and miserable cells.

For all the claims that, of the rural tragedies, it bears the closest approximation to reality, *The House of Bernarda Alba* testifies to Lorca's increasing mastery of dramatic art. Francisco García Lorca has observed of the play:

> *The House of Bernarda Alba*, of these plays, is the one which has the most direct inspiration in reality . . . And in spite of this basic reality, I would say that this is his most artful play and the one which is most disciplined in technique . . .[30]

If in *Yerma* Lorca abandoned the sheer theatricality of the final Act of *Blood Wedding*, in *The House of Bernarda Alba* he eliminated the poetic elements, notably the use of verse at given moments, which distinguish both the earlier works. In the sense that the setting of the play and the exchanges of its characters seem closer to the texture and the possibilities of real life, it is true that, like *Doña Rosita*, it marks a new direction in Lorca's theatre.[31] On the other hand, its dramatic impact is as powerful as either of the earlier tragedies. Lorca achieves here, with greater economy and concentration, the effect previously accomplished by recourse to a whole variety of elements. Far from being a triumph of realism, *The House of Bernarda Alba* is a triumph of Lorca's dramatic craftsmanship.[32]

A consideration of the stage-setting reveals both points of

contact with and differences from the other plays. The seven sets of *Blood Wedding* and the five of *Yerma* are here reduced to three. There, moreover, the various settings are different from each other while here they are essentially the same, each a variation on the preceding one. There is thus a greater concentration, but within this tighter framework, the sets have, as in the other plays, that stark, simplified, symbolic character whereby, encapsulating in a single visual image all that is in the play, they suggest as well something that exists beyond it. Here, more than previously, Lorca simplifies and refines his materials and creates an image that, in its clarity and boldness, bridges the gulf between art and life.[33]

The setting for Act I is a detailed one, but, in its emphasis on particular elements, it is far from naturalistic:

> *A very white room in* BERNARDA ALBA'S *house. The walls are white. There are arched doorways with jute curtains tied back with tassels and ruffles. Wicker chairs. On the walls, pictures of unlikely landscapes full of nymphs or legendary kings.*
> [*It is summer. A great brooding silence fills the stage. It is empty when the curtain rises. Bells can be heard tolling outside.*] (p. 151)

In visual terms the almost unbroken whiteness of the walls suggests an unrelieved monotony. The arched doorways, their form echoing and repeating each other, underline the idea of sameness.[34] The jute curtains and wicker chairs are indicative of a lack of anything soothing or comfortable in this room. And the pictures on the walls, *of unlikely landscapes full of nymphs or legendary kings*, evoke a world of magic and fantasy far removed from the oppressive dullness that surrounds them.[35] The visual impact is then heightened by non-visual elements: the total, brooding silence; the sense of emptiness; the distant, melancholy tolling of the bells. Even before the characters appear, we are presented in the stage-setting with an image of their cloistered, monotonous and meaningless existence. Much more than in *Blood Wedding* or *Yerma* where the characters are on the stage as the curtain rises, the stage-setting has an added meaning and impact in relation to the play in general.

For Act II the setting is a different one, the stage-directions less detailed, but in every sense it sustains and deepens the earlier impression:

> *A white room in* BERNARDA's *house. The doors on the left lead to the bedrooms.*
> [BERNARDA'S DAUGHTERS *are seated on low chairs, sewing.* MAGDALENA *is embroidering.* PONCIA *is with them.*] (p. 169)

Here the black of the women's dresses stands out against the whiteness of the walls, sharpening, as in a photograph in black and white, that sense of the colourlessness of their existence.[36] Secondly, the arrangement and disposition of the figures – seated, immobile – echoing the lifelessness of the room which they inhabit, intensifies the sense of the endless monotony that they endure. We are reminded of the seated figure of the Mother in *Blood Wedding*, burdened and oppressed by sorrow. Once more it is the significance of the setting as a simple, stark and telling image that is so striking. The daughters of Bernarda within the room are individuals who evoke, in turn, other human beings in the world at large who are the prisoners of their dreary and oppressed existence.

The setting for Act III is another variation on what has gone before:[37]

> *Four white walls, lightly washed in blue, of the interior patio of* BERNARDA ALBA's *house. The doorways, illumined by the lights inside the rooms, give a tenuous glow to the stage.*
> [*At the centre there is a table with a shaded oil-lamp about which* BERNARDA *and her* DAUGHTERS *are eating.* LA PONCIA *serves them.* PRUDENCIA *sits apart. When the curtain rises, there is a great silence interrupted only by the noise of plates and silverware.*] (p. 187)

While the scene has moved from the inside to the patio of Bernarda's house, suggesting a greater sense of space, the sense of enclosure is still predominant, the walls of the rooms repeated now in form and colour in the walls of the patio.[38] As in the second Act the figures – apart from La Poncia – are seated, and if they are not sewing they are engaged in what, in effect, is merely another of their dreary, mechanical activities.

As the curtain rises, the silence that marked the beginning of Act I is emphasized once more, punctuated now not by the tolling of bells but by the intermittent clatter of plates and silverware. We are reminded, through the stage-settings, that in this play nothing really changes. And yet, within this static framework there is a kind of change, for the characters are that much nearer their tragic fate. It is hinted at in the only change that differentiates the beginning of Act III from the beginning of the other Acts – the blue tint that colours the white walls. Here is that cold blue light of the moon that, as in the final Act of *Blood Wedding*, is a premonition of death.[39]

The dialogue of the play, almost entirely in prose, has a deceptive appearance of realism. It is, in fact, carefully con- trived, firstly to reveal in bold, economical strokes the essence of each character, and secondly, by doing so, to heighten the differences and thus the developing clash between them. The dialogue, indeed, is as stripped of needless clutter as are the sets themselves. We can say of Bernarda herself that, although throughout the play she uses her stick to reinforce her words, her words are themselves like blows, assaulting in swift, sharp flurries the ears of those around her. In Act I the Third Woman observes that Bernarda has a 'tongue like a knife!' (p. 155) and it is invariably true of her that, whether ordering and question- ing others or defending herself against them, Bernarda's manner is sharp, forceful and decisive. Her dialogue is, characteristically, full of imperatives, from the moment of her first appearance:

> BERNARDA. [*to the* SERVANT]: Silence!
> SERVANT [*weeping*]: Bernarda!
> BERNARDA: Less shrieking and more work. You should have had all this cleaner for the wake. Get out. This isn't your place. (p. 154)

And a few lines later to Magdalena:

> [*They sit down. Pause. Loudly.*]
> Magdalena, don't cry. If you want to cry, get under your bed. Do you hear me? (p. 155)

In Act II, learning of the portrait stolen from Angustias, Ber-

narda confronts the other daughters, her tirade against them a
mixture of rapid-fire questions and imperatives:

> BERNARDA [*fiercely*]: Who? Who?
> ANGUSTIAS: They have!
> BERNARDA: Which of you?
> [*Silence.*]
> Answer me!
> [*Silence. To* PONCIA.]
> Search their rooms! Look in their beds. This comes of
> not tying you up with shorter leashes. But I'll teach you
> now! (p. 179)

And in Act III, when Adela has hanged herself, Bernarda
commands her remaining daughters:

> BERNARDA: And I want no weeping. Death must be
> looked at face to face. Silence!
> [*To one daughter.*]
> Be still, I said!
> [*To another daughter.*]
> Tears when you're alone! We'll drown ourselves in a
> sea of mourning. She, the youngest daughter of Ber-
> narda Alba, died a virgin. Did you hear me? Silence,
> silence, I said. Silence! (p. 201)

It is significant that in Bernarda's closing words there is a clear
echo of her first appearance. Her dialogue reflects, in its
strongly patterned form, Bernarda's own unbending nature.
With neighbours, servants, daughters, she is the same
unyielding figure, belabouring them with her words. But to
see her, as some have done, as a puppet, Punch-like figure,
wielding her stick, is to distort and to diminish her significance
as the principal character of the play.[40] To overact Bernarda
would be, indeed, to make her a comic figure.[41] To strike a
balance between the boldly drawn, one-dimensional character
implicit, perhaps, in the lines themselves and the obsessed
and very human woman who lies behind them is the challenge
for any actress.

The despair of Bernarda's daughters is reflected in the
dialogue of Magdalena and Martirio. Magdalena, at thirty the

second-eldest of Bernarda's children, is resigned to an existence whose hopelessness is encapsulated in the heavy, dragging rhythm of her lines. Thus in Act I:

> . . . I know I'm not going to marry. I'd rather carry sacks to the mill. Anything except sit here day after day in this dark room. (p. 158)

And later in conversation with Amelia:

> AMELIA [to MAGDALENA]: One of your shoelaces has come untied.
> MAGDALENA: What of it?
> AMELIA: You'll step on it and fall.
> MAGDALENA: One less! (p. 163)

Her lines have a regularity, even a monotony of structure and rhythm, which is the essence of the tedium of her life. In this respect Martirio's dialogue is somewhat similar:

> AMELIA: Did you take the medicine?
> MARTIRIO: For all the good it'll do me.
> AMELIA: But you took it?
> MARTIRIO: I do things without any faith, but like clockwork.
> AMELIA: Since the new doctor came you look livelier.
> MARTIRIO: I feel the same. (p. 161)

The enormous contrast between the forceful and aggressive nature of Bernarda's lines and the leaden and lifeless dialogue of Magdalena and Martirio conveys, on the level of the language, the differences between them.[42]

Of all the daughters' dialogue, it is Adela's that, in its force and vigour, is closest to Bernarda's. Thus in Act I she defies Magdalena:

> . . . I will not get used to it! I can't be locked up. I don't want my skin to look like yours. I don't want my skin's whiteness lost in these rooms. Tomorrow I'm going to put on my green dress and go walking in the streets. I want to go out! (p. 165)

Throughout the play the same preponderance of imperatives,

the same sharp, forceful phrases predominate. In its structure and its springy rhythm Adela's dialogue is barely different from Bernarda's. In terms of language, as in other ways, the clash between the mother and her daughters is polarized in the youngest daughter, and any actress playing her would do well to emphasize the linguistic similarity.

Entirely different from Bernarda and her daughters is La Poncia, the old servant, down-to-earth, crafty, worldly-wise and garrulous. While the dialogue of the principal characters reflects their obsessions in its repeated patterns, La Poncia's dialogue is immensely varied, changing constantly in accordance with her circumstances. In the opening conversation with the First Servant Poncia chatters incessantly, revealing on the one hand her bitterness towards Bernarda, on the other her practical common sense: 'I bark when I'm told . . .' (p. 152), and also her humour and enjoyment of the ordinary things of life:

> . . . I certainly like the way our priest sings. In the Pater Noster his voice went up, and up – like a pitcher filling with water little by little. Of course, at the end his voice cracked, but it's glorious to hear it . . . (p. 153)

In Bernarda's presence La Poncia is more inhibited because she is more respectful, even fearful. When provoked, her manner becomes, as befits her crafty nature, quietly insinuating, an attitude caught perfectly in the calculated precision of her every word:

> PONCIA: You should have moved to another town.
> BERNARDA: That's it. To sell them! [*daughters*]
> PONCIA: No Bernarda, to change . . . Of course, any place else, they'd be the poor ones. (pp. 160-61)

If there is a total contrast here and elsewhere in the tone of mistress and servant, it reflects not merely La Poncia's awareness of her place but also her resourcefulness in putting it to her own advantage. On other occasions, dropping her defensive guard in conversation with the girls, she is her normal, humorous, earthy and loquacious self:

> It was very dark. I saw him coming along and as he went

by he said, 'Good evening'. 'Good evening,' I said. Then
we were both silent for more than half an hour. The
sweat poured down my body. Then Evaristo got nearer
and nearer as if he wanted to squeeze in through the bars
and said in a very low voice – 'Come here and let me feel
you!' (p. 171)

But even though La Poncia's dialogue displays a greater
variety than that of the other characters, it is as true of her as of
them that, in terms of the structure, the rhythms and the
intonation of her lines, nothing is wasted. The prose of this
play, deceptively naturalistic, invariably serves a dramatic
end.[43]

Poetry is used in the play on only two occasions, and then
only briefly in the form of songs. But on each occasion it occurs
at key-moments and underlines their highly emotional and
dramatic nature. In Act II, as Bernarda's daughters sit in the
room, burdened by their circumstances and the intolerable
heat, the harvesters pass by singing a song in praise of love:

> The reapers have set out
> Looking for ripe wheat;
> They'll carry off the hearts
> Of any girls they meet. (p. 176)

The song, full of spring and vitality, stands like an oasis in the
surrounding flatness of the dialogue, its vibrant rhythm a
refreshing contrast to the leaden movement of the women's
lines as they lament their fate. Its effectiveness stems from its
very briefness, for it suggests in its few yet evocative lines a
whole world that lies beyond Bernarda's house. Moreover, in
the way the second verse, as it fades away, is taken up by
Martirio and Adela, we see expressed in one heart-rending
moment all their desperate longing:

> MARTIRIO [*with nostalgia*]:
>   Throw wide your doors and windows,
>   you girls who live in the town.
> ADELA [*passionately*]:
>   The reaper asks you for roses
>   With which to deck his crown. (p. 177)

As the harvesters disappear into the distance, it is as though the girls' dreams and illusions themselves slowly fade away and they are left only with their own despair.

In Act III María Josefa sings a lullaby to the lamb she is nursing. The song expresses all her hopes and aspirations, that same yearning felt by Bernarda's daughters:

> Let's go to the shore of the sea,
>
> And on the beach we'll go and hide
> In a little coral cabin. (p. 195)

There is a terrible contrast between the words of the song and the hideous reality of the singer, the old, withered, crazed woman imprisoned in her daughter's house and whose only remaining journey is to the grave. Furthermore, inasmuch as both songs give way to a different reality – the first to the daughters' hopelessness, the second to the older woman's madness – it is a reality that, projecting in the figure of the grandmother the younger women's future, grows increasingly more terrifying. Though poetry is used more sparingly here than in the other tragedies, it is used strikingly and tellingly.

As far as the movements of the characters on the stage are concerned, they are another element in the unified and concentrated vision of the play. From the moment of her first appearance Bernarda's forceful words are accompanied by her vigorous and often violent physical movements, notably by her beating of her cane on the floor. In Act I she harangues her daughters:

BERNARDA [*beating on the floor*]: Don't fool yourselves . . . (p. 167)

In Act II, after a confrontation with the girls, she expresses her frustration: [. . . *Bernarda recovers herself, and beats on the floor.*] (p. 181). There are many occasions when Bernarda's aggression spills over into violence itself. In Act I she strikes Angustias for looking at the men:

BERNARDA: Soft! Honeytongue!
[*She strikes her.*]

At the end of Act I she wipes the powder from Angustias's face

– [*She removes the powder violently with her handkerchief.*] (p. 167)
– and oversees the dragging away of María Josefa (p. 168). In Act II she strikes Martirio with her stick:

> BERNARDA [*advancing on her, beating her with her cane . . .*]
> (p. 180)

At the end of Act III she enters quickly as she hears the quarrel between Adela and Martirio:

> BERNARDA [*going furiously toward* ADELA . . .] (p. 199)

In terms of movement there is, as in the dialogue, a sameness and repetition about the episodes in which Bernarda is involved. The range of movement, from the beating of her stick to physical assaults upon her daughters, is, indeed, limited. But to grasp and express the fact is important, for Bernarda's broad, forceful, repeated gestures and actions, like programmed movements or conditioned responses, should be seized upon to suggest how, as an individual, she is manipulated and dehumanized by her concern with honour.

If Bernarda's presence on the stage is often marked by explosive movement, the scenes involving her daughters have in general a totally different tempo. The beginning of Act II is a good example. La Poncia goes to open the door (p. 169), Amelia goes to the door to see if Bernarda is coming (p. 171), Magdalena goes out to fetch Adela (p. 172), but the predominant feature of the scene is its static quality – of the daughters seated – which evokes the futile inactivity of their lives. It is seen again later:

> ADELA [*sitting down*]: Ay! If only we could go out in the fields too!
> MAGDALENA [*sitting down*]: Each class does what it has to!
> MARTIRIO [*sitting down*]: That's it!
> AMELIA [*sitting down*]: Ay! (pp. 175-76)

Later still, when the harvesters have departed, Martirio is left sitting alone:

> [. . . MARTIRIO *is left sitting on the low chair with her head between her hands.*] (p. 177)

And the same is true of the beginning of Act III where Bernarda and her daughters sit, eating, and the visual effect of the seated group is further reinforced by the seated figure of Prudencia, who sits apart (p. 187). In this sense the play is distinguished by flurries of movement, mainly associated with Bernarda, that punctuate its slow unfolding. But its conclusion is one in which the younger women too, notably Adela and Martirio, are also part of a much more agitated rhythm. Earlier there have been isolated moments when, expressing themselves as much in physical action as in words, Adela and Angustias have broken the bonds of the passivity that is the physical symbol of their emotional prostration. Adela, for example, learns of the marriage of Angustias to Pepe el Romano: ADELA [*bursting out, crying with rage* . . .] (p. 165). Later, Angustias discovers the disappearance of Pepe's portrait: ANGUSTIAS [*she bursts in furiously, in a manner that makes a great contrast with previous silence* . . .] (p. 178). By the end of Act III the sporadic outbursts become the dominant pattern. Adela desperately hugs Martirio and Martirio pushes her away (p. 198). Adela runs to the door and Martirio blocks her path (p. 199). Adela and Martirio struggle, Bernarda rushes in, Adela seizes her cane and breaks it (p. 199), Bernarda rushes out, seizes a gun and fires a shot at Pepe el Romano (p. 200). Adela runs from the room to her bedroom (p. 200). La Poncia tries to break down the locked door. Bernarda hurries forward but is stopped by La Poncia (p. 201). The frenetic movement of the play's finale, like the violent climax of a symphony, is all the more effective for those long, slow sequences that have preceded it.

As for the lighting, it has, like all the other features of the play, that air of naturalness which conceals its artfulness. In Acts I and II there are in the stage-directions no specific references to the lighting of the stage, but the effect, clearly, should be to reinforce the silence and the almost physical weight that oppresses the rooms of Bernarda's house. The shutters are closed, as the dialogue in Act II confirms:

> PONCIA: Be careful not to open the shutter too much . . .
>   (p. 177)

Just before this there is a brief stage-direction: [*Tambourines and carrañacas are heard. Pause. They all listen in the silence cut by the sun.*] (p. 176). We may imagine, then, the sunlight weakly penetrating the cracks of the closed shutters. The effect within the room itself will be one, not of brightness, but of dullness, a faded quality like the skin of the characters themselves; perhaps, indeed, like one of those old pre-colour photographs. Within this general effect of dullness, the occasional brightness will be emphasized all the more. Thus, in Act I the green of Adela's dress is a vivid contrast, an eruption of colour in a scene dominated by the pessimism of her sisters. Similarly, in Act II the whiteness of the lace for the wedding, contrasting with the black of the women's clothes, evokes a world of happiness far from the reality of their lives. And in Act III, enclosed progressively in the blackness of night, the white petticoats of Adela and Martirio suggest the allure and magic of feminine beauty and love in a situation which increasingly denies it.[44] These splashes of light and colour, conjuring up a different kind of world, are repeated, especially in Act I, in the opening and shutting of the doors that lead from the house to the street or the patio. The Beggar Woman and the Mourners come in and leave by the door to the street and Angustias leaves the room by the door that leads to the patio (p. 156). The effect of the light that suddenly floods in as a door is opened and is then gone again is, like those other splashes of colour, not only to suggest a different world outside the house, but, by so doing, to heighten the impression of the total isolation of Bernarda's household from that world.[45] As the play unfolds, of course, the darkness grows, literally as well as metaphorically. In Act II only a window to the outside world is opened, and then but briefly. From the beginning of Act III, lit by a shaded oil-lamp, a glow that comes from the inside of the house, and, to some extent, by moonlight, we move to a point where the darkness is almost complete: [. . . *The stage is left almost dark . . .*] (p. 195). As in *Yerma* the lighting of the stage suggests the movement of the characters into the black world of their own terrible passions and the dark, imcomprehensible forces that, like the night itself, surround them. There is nothing new or startling in the use of lighting but, like the other dramatic elements of the play, it is simply and very strikingly effective.[46]

NOTES

INTRODUCTION

1 For more detailed accounts of Lorca's life see, amongst others, Robert Lima, *The Theater of García Lorca*, New York: Las Americas Publishing Co., 1963, 1-52; José Luis Cano, *García Lorca: biografía ilustrada*, Barcelona: Ediciones Destino, 1962; and, more recently, Mildred Adams, *García Lorca: Playwright and Poet*, New York: George Braziller, 1977.

2 See Ian Gibson, *The Death of Lorca*, London: W. H. Allen, 1973. This is a particularly detailed and well-researched account of the events leading to Lorca's death.

3 For a general survey of twentieth-century Spanish theatre, see, for example, E. Díez-Canedo, 'The Contemporary Spanish Theater', trans. Susan P. Underhill, in *The Theatre in a Changing Europe*, ed., T. H. Dickenson, London, 285-329; G. Torrente Ballester, *Teatro español contemporáneo* (2nd ed.) Madrid: Ediciones Guadarrama, 1968; L. Rodríguez Alcalde, *Teatro español contemporáneo*, Madrid: Epesa, 1973; Victoria Urbano, *El teatro español y sus directrices contemporáneas*, Madrid: Editora Nacional, 1972; and F. Ruiz Ramón, *Historia del teatro español, II: Siglo XX*, Madrid, 1971.

4 There is a very useful study of this particular topic by J. E. Lyon, 'Valle-Inclán and the Art of the Theatre', *Bulletin of Hispanic Studies*, XLVI (1969), pp. 132-52. See too Roberto Sánchez, 'Gordon Craig y Valle-Inclán', *Revista de Occidente*, 4 (1976), pp. 27-37.

5 The translation here and elsewhere is my own unless stated otherwise.

6 There is a useful introduction to the play by William Giuliano in the Harrap edition, London: Harrap, 1952.

7 For an informative account of the period see Max Aub, 'Algunos aspectos del teatro español, de 1920 a 1930', *Revista Hispánica Moderna*, XXXI (1965), pp. 17-28. An interesting account of surrealist plays is given by Barbara Sheklin Davis, 'El teatro surrealista español', *Revista Hispánica Moderna*, XXXIII (1967), pp. 309-29.

8 It is interesting to note that the concept of total theatre taught by Craig and put into practice in Spain by Rivas Cherif and Lorca was also, through Craig's direct influence, a feature of the Irish theatre, notably of W. B. Yeats. If there is a link between the Irish and the Spanish theatre in the first third of this century, as has often been suggested, Craig seems to be an important part of that link.

9 See Suzanne Byrd, *'La Barraca' and the Spanish National Theatre*, New York: Editiones Abra, 1975. This is a fundamental book for a study of the activities of *La Barraca*.

277

10 All page references, unless stated otherwise, are to *Federico García Lorca, Obras completas (Complete Works)*, ed. Arturo del Hoyo, 2nd ed., Madrid: Aguilar, 1955. For this quotation see the 1969 edition, pp.1747-48.
11 The page references to *The Public*, here and elsewhere, are to R. Martínez Nadal's text in *Federico García Lorca, 'El Público' y 'Comedia sin título', Dos obras teatrales póstumas*, Barcelona: Seix Barral, 1978.
12 All translations and page references, unless stated otherwise, are to *Three Tragedies*, trans. James Graham Luján and Richard O'Connell, and *Five Plays*, by the same translators, Harmondsworth: Penguin, 1961 and 1970 respectively.
13 See Suzanne Byrd, *op. cit.*, pp.92-93.

CHAPTER I

1 See Robert Lima, *The Theatre of García Lorca*, pp.56-57.
2 References are, except where stated otherwise, to *Five Plays: Comedies and Tragi-comedies*, translated by James Graham-Luján and Richard L. O'Connell, Harmondsworth: Penguin, 1970.
3 The translations are my own.
4 For studies of *Mariana Pineda* see Robert Lima, *op. cit.*, pp.96-119; Edwin Honig, *García Lorca*, New York: New Directions, 1963, pp.114-123; Virginia Higginbotham, *The Comic Spirit of Federico García Lorca*, Austin: University of Texas Press, 1976, pp.23-28; Sumner M. Greenfield, 'The Problem of *Mariana Pineda*', *Massachusetts Review*, I (1960), pp.751-763; Ricardo Domenech, 'A propósito de *Mariana Pineda*', *Cuadernos Hispanoamericanos*, LXX (1967), pp.608-613.
5 On Lorca's puppet plays see, in particular, Virginia Higginbotham, *op. cit.*, pp.71-88, and William I. Oliver, 'Lorca: The Puppets and the Artist', *Tulane Drama Review*, VII (1962), pp.76-95.
6 The translation is my own.
7 *La Voz*, 19 March, 1935.
8 See M. Fernández Almagro in *El Sol* and M. Nuñez de Arenas in *La Voz*, 6 April, 1933.
9 Lorca called the play a 'farsa violenta', a phrase which refers not to any violence committed by any of the characters but to the speed and vigour with which the play should be performed. There is an excellent introduction to the play by John and Florence Street in their edition of it published by Harrap, London 1962. See too, Robert Lima, *op. cit.*, pp.120-140; Edwin Honig, *op. cit.*, pp.129-131; Virginia Higginbotham, *op. cit.*, pp.28-32; and Carlos Rincón 'La zapatera prodigiosa de Federico García Lorca', *Ibero-Romania*, IV (1970), pp.290-313.
10 On *Don Perlimplín* see Robert Lima, *op. cit.*, pp.141-156; Edwin Honig, *op. cit.*, pp.123-129; Virginia Higginbotham, *op. cit.*, pp.32-40; and Rupert C. Allen, *Psyche and Symbol in the Theater of Federico García Lorca*, Austin: University of Texas Press, 1974.
11 The translations of quotations from the three short plays are my own. Line references are to the Spanish text in *Obras completas*.
12 See especially R. G. Havard, 'Lorca's Buster Keaton', *Bulletin of Hispanic Studies*, LIV (1977), pp.13-20.

13 Only Virginia Higginbotham, of those who have written at any length on these plays, discusses aspects of their staging. She has some interesting comments on *Mariana Pineda* and on the puppet plays in particular.

CHAPTER II

1 See Rafael Martínez Nadal, *Lorca's 'The Public'*, London: Calder and Boyars, 1974, p. 98, and Mildred Adams, *García Lorca: Playwright and Poet*, New York: George Braziller, 1977, p. 196. Nadal observes that there are at least two complete versions of the play, the one which Lorca read at the home of Carlos Morla Lynch in 1930, and one seen by Nadal himself in 1936, the latter the final, revised version. Nadal's copy of the play is, he concludes, 'no doubt the draft for the version I heard him read in 1930 or 1931'. See pp. 19-24.
2 Nadal, *op. cit.*, p. 98.
3 Mildred Adams, *op. cit.*, p. 196.
4 The translation is my own.
5 Nadal, *op. cit.*, p. 20.
6 Mildred Adams, *op. cit.*, p. 198.
7 Nadal, *op. cit.*, p. 73.
8 The page reference is to the Spanish text in *Obras completas*. The English translation is my own.
9 *Ibid.*
10 Nadal, *op. cit.*, p. 73. For a general study of the influence of surrealism on Spanish theatre, see Barbara Sheklin Davis, 'El teatro surrealista español', *Revista Hispánica Moderna*, XXXIII (1967), pp. 309-29.
11 C. B. Morris, *The Dream-House (Silent Films and Spanish Poets)*, University of Hull Publications, 1977, p. 3.
12 For a detailed account of Lorca's screenplay, see C. B. Morris, *op. cit.*, pp. 15-17.
13 Nadal, *op. cit.*, p. 77.
14 The translation is that by James Graham-Luján and Richard L. O'Connell.
15 The translations of quotations from the poems are my own and page references are to *Obras completas*.
16 See Nadal, *op. cit.*, pp. 124-127, for an excellent account of this theme.
17 Any analysis of the themes of *The Public* must begin with Nadal's very detailed, wide-ranging and perceptive study. My debt to this stimulating book is evident throughout this chapter and, indeed, in a more general way, in the other chapters too. All translations into English of lines from the play are my own, while the accompanying page references are to Nadal's text in *Federico García Lorca, 'El público' y 'Comedia sin título', Dos obras teatrales póstumas*, Barcelona: Seix Barral, 1978.
18 The links between individuals and between human beings and the world of Nature are, of course, at the very heart of Lorca's vision of the world, notably in the rural tragedies. In *Blood Wedding*, for example, the Mother who, in Act I, Scene One, laments her dead son, is reflected in the Neighbour, and both of them in another neighbour. Similarly, as the Mother has lost her husband, so the Bride loses hers, and she is echoed too in Leonardo's wife when he is killed. And throughout the play the instincts and passions that dominate the lives of men and women are

T

shown to be part of the natural world to which they live in close proximity.

19 Wilma Newberry, 'Aesthetic Distance in *El Público*', *Hispanic Review*, XXXVII (1969), pp. 276-96, argues that Lorca employs in this play the familiar distancing effects of Pirandello in order to make the point that, by destroying illusion and eliminating the tension between the actor and the spectator, the stage and the audience, such techniques destroyed what he, Lorca, considered to be the essence of the theatre: its appeal to the imagination and its rapport with the audience. My own view is quite the opposite, for what *The Public* undoubtedly does is to make the spectator aware that in the various forms of the characters on the stage he is really seeing himself. The technique is a mirror rather than a distancing technique, and the relationship between actor and public, stage and auditorium is not fundamentally different here from what it is in the later, more 'realistic' plays.

20 It is quite clear at every stage of the play that its themes are those which haunted Lorca throughout his life. The differences between one play and another are differences, more often than not, of technique as Lorca sought continually to find more expressive ways of giving dramatic shape to his ideas.

21 We may compare the incident to what happens in *Blood Wedding*. The Bride and Leonardo escape on a horse only for their love to be destroyed when Leonardo dies. And in *The House of Bernarda Alba* Pepe el Romano gallops off out of Adela's life and she, despairing of finding love and happiness, hangs herself.

22 In this context we recall Lorca's statement to Sebastián Gash in 1928 that the poems he was sending him had an 'absolute poetic logic', a 'very clear awareness' that separated them from true surrealism.

23 In the light of a scene as haunting and evocative as this, it is difficult to understand the criticism of Lorca's surrealist experiments by someone as perceptive as Edwin Honig, *García Lorca*, New York: New Directions, 1963, p. 150: 'Until the appearance of more conclusive evidence, it is perhaps sufficient to say what the facts themselves imply: of the two worlds of dramatic possibility which Lorca was exploring at this time – the folk and the surrealist – it was fortunate that after learning the limitations implicit in the second, he decided to occupy himself exclusively with the first.'

24 Honig suggests, *op. cit.*, p. 150, that the nude figure symbolizes the poet crucified by a merciless public, while Wilma Newberry, *art. cit.*, p. 290, argues that he represents the theatre, or the spirit of the theatre. Virginia Higginbotham, in contrast, sees the dying man as an image of 'Christianity lying moribund and helpless in the face of brutality, hypocrisy and injustice' (*op. cit.*, p. 66). Whatever the interpretation placed on this figure, there can be no doubt that, since he is transformed before us into the First Man, he is intended to be a reflection of other men, of us, and that, as we witness his anguish, we are observing our own.

25 Lorca had, of course, suffered at the hands of an uncomprehending public with his first play, *The Butterfly's Evil Spell*. On the other hand, his plays reveal not so much a fear of the public as a constant desire to eliminate the barrier between stage and audience. See Nadal, *op. cit.*, pp. 225-28.

26 We may compare the circular movement of the play with that of *When Five Years Have Passed*, *Blood Wedding*, and *The House of Bernarda Alba*. In *When Five Years Have Passed*, as in *The Public*, the final setting is a repetition of the first; in *Blood Wedding* the knife dominates the beginning and the ending of

the action and the Mothers's grief for her husband and her elder son becomes her mourning for her younger son; and in *The House of Bernarda Alba* Bernarda's final demand for silence repeats her opening words. The sense of no-escape clearly dominates Lorca's later works, reflecting his growing sense of the futility of things.

27 In her analysis of *The Public* Wilma Newberry suffered from the disadvantage of having to base her interpretation on the two scenes then available, the *Roman Ruin* (Scene Two) and Scene Five. An examination of the play as a whole cannot but lead to the conclusion that, far from being distanced from the action, we, as spectators, are drawn into it.

28 Nadal, *op. cit.*, p. 27.

29 Virginia Higginbotham, *The Comic Spirit of Federico García Lorca*, observes of *When Five Years Have Passed* that 'Lorca uses bizarre costumes, much as Federico Fellini has done in his films, to enhance the fantastic, dreamlike and nightmarish effects of certain characters' (p. 61). All that she says of the play is equally, if not more, applicable to *The Public*.

30 It is an incident like this, when the conflict of the characters is expressed in pure movement, which suggests the influence upon Lorca of the silent films. As far as the visual impact of the play is concerned, and, indeed, the enormous difficulties involved in putting on the stage some of its complex effects, it might be considered as more suited to cinematic techniques in general. On the other hand, the cinema distances its audience in a way which the theatre does not and would destroy the intimacy between the actors and the public which Lorca, in this play above all, wanted.

31 We are reminded here, for example, of Dalí's flat plains with their strange, other-worldly lighting in which figures and objects are placed as though on some vast stage suspended in time and space. The same kind of background can be seen in the pictures of many other surrealist painters – Joan Miró, Max Ernst, Yves Tanguy.

CHAPTER III

1 R. Martínez Nadal is of the opinion that a good deal of the play was written at the Lorca family country house outside Granada. See *Lorca's 'The Public'*, p. 98.

2 *En España con Federico García Lorca*, Madrid: Aguilar, 1958, pp. 105-12.

3 Nadal, *Lorca's 'The Public'*, p. 98.

4 The interview is reproduced in *Federico García Lorca: Obras completas*, pp. 1634-36.

5 *ABC*, September 28, 1978, p. 9. The translation is my own.

6 See C. B. Morris, *The Dream-House (Silent films and Spanish poets)*, pp. 14-15.

7 The point is made by Virginia Higginbotham, *The Comic Spirit of Federico García Lorca*, pp. 61, 63.

8 All translations of quotations, unless stated otherwise, are my own. Line references in these cases are to the equivalent Spanish text in *Obras completas*.

9 The translation is from Rolfe Humphries, *The Gipsy Ballads of Federico García Lorca*, 5th ed., Bloomington, Indiana: Indiana University Press, 1969.

10 See R. Martínez Nadal, *Lorca's 'The Public'*, in particular pp. 82-92 ('Forms –
    metamorphosis – void'), and pp. 155-184 ('Death in the Work of García
    Lorca').
11 Rolfe Humphries, *The Gipsy Ballads of Federico García Lorca*.
12 The translation is my own, the page reference is to the Spanish text in
    Nadal's *Federico García Lorca, 'El público' y 'Comedia sin título', Dos obras
    teatrales póstumas*.
13 For detailed studies of *When Five Years Have Passed* see Edwin Honig, *García
    Lorca*, pp. 135-149; Robert Lima, *The Theatre of García Lorca*, pp. 157-87; R.
    G. Knight, 'Federico García Lorca's *Así que pasen cinco años*', *Bulletin of
    Hispanic Studies*, XLII (1966), pp. 32-46; and Virginia Higginbotham *The
    Comic Spirit of Federico García Lorca*, pp. 55-64.
14 The Old Man is, of course, a form of the Young Man. As R. G. Knight
    suggests, p. 32: 'There is only one real person in the whole play, the Jóven
    (Young Man). All the others either represent the different elements in the
    spiritual struggle, or are projections from the non-human sphere.' See,
    too, Lima, *The Theatre of García Lorca*, pp. 157-58.
15 There is a link here with Doña Rosita, the spinster of the later play. Many
    years after her lover's departure she has a vision of him as he was, or even
    better than he was, at the time of his departure. As in the case of the Young
    Man, it is a dream which is inevitably destroyed by reality.
16 Lima, *The Theatre of García Lorca*, p. 163. Martínez Nadal, *Lorca's 'The
    Public'*, p. 95, makes the point that in Lorca's work grass, and especially
    grass that grows and spreads over stones, is suggestive of death. In this
    sense the Young Man is aware that his dream, symbolized by the quiet of
    the house, is threatened by death.
17 In the sense that this is a scene that is isolated from the surrounding action,
    it is a play-within-a-play, and one of many such scenes in Lorca's drama.
    We can compare it with the second scene of *The Public* in which the
    exchanges between the Figure with Vine Leaves, the Figure with Bells and
    the Roman Emperor, witnessed by the Director and the three men, are
    seen to be a reflection of their relationship, and, beyond them, to con-
    stitute a mirror in which the audience looks upon itself. In the same way
    the Dead Child and the Dead Cat are forms of the Young Man, the Old
    Man, the Friend, and thus of us as we watch the play.
18 Lorca's use of colour has been discussed by various critics. See J. M. Flys,
    El lenguaje poético de Federico García Lorca, Madrid: Gredos, 1955, and, in this
    particular connection, R. G. Knight.
19 Lima, *The Theatre of García Lorca*, pp. 175-76, observes that the repeated
    references to the cat stoned by the children is a Brechtian device used by
    Lorca to remind us that the action is not realistic but is taking place in the
    mind of the Young Man. The illusion of reality is thus shattered from time
    to time. On the other hand, Lorca did not wish, like Brecht, to make his
    audience sit apart from the action so that they would view it intellectually
    rather than respond to it emotionally. His aim was always to involve his
    audience in the stage-action and to break down the barriers between stage
    and auditorium.
20 Although this play is to all appearances so different from *Blood Wedding*,
    the anticipations of the latter occur at almost every stage: the Bride and the
    Father; the Bride's escape with the Rugby Player at the end of Act II; the
    setting of the great wood in Act III, Scene One; the menacing figures of
    Harlequin and the Clown; the suggestion that life is a hunt and that human

beings are the prey of hostile forces. What is so striking, indeed, about
Lorca's plays in general are the links between them, the unified vision
which they present, but equally the varied and vital forms in which that
vision is expressed.

21 Of all the major plays *When Five Years Have Passed, The Public*, and to some
extent *Blood Wedding* in its penultimate scene, most clearly look forward to
the so-called Theatre of the Absurd. Virginia Higginbotham, *The Comic
Spirit of Federico García Lorca*, p. 135, observes that the 'comic violence and
puppet-like characters that Lorca borrowed from ancient farce to dramatize his dark view of life have been similarly adopted, not in Spain, but in
France, by dramatists of the Absurd, such as Eugène Ionesco, Jean Genet
and Fernando Arrabal.'

22 *Lorca's 'The Public'*, p. 99.

23 Like *The Public, When Five Years Have Passed* is a good example of Lorca's
championing of a theatrical style in which all the different dramatic elements have their part to play and which, put to good effect in his own
plays, he was to put into practice at this time in the productions of *La
Barraca*.

24 Robert Lima, *The Theatre of García Lorca*, p. 157, suggests that this is Lorca's
most intellectual play, though he does not take *The Public* into account, and
María Teresa Babín in *García Lorca, vida y obra*, New York: Las Américas,
1955, speaks of the play's dialogue 'lacking the flexibility and the grace
evident in Lorca's other plays, for its essence is the discussion of a
subjective idea . . .'

25 Estimates of Lorca's achievement in this play vary considerably. Nadal and
Robert Lima, rightly in my view, see it as an original, successful and
influential work, and Lima, *The Theatre of García Lorca*, p. 186, suggests that
'although it has only received grudging attention in the past, the modern
theatre may soon adopt it as the earliest example of the "theatre of the
absurd", placing it alongside the already accepted works of Beckett,
Pinter, Ionesco and Genet.' In contrast, R. G. Knight considers that it is 'an
unsatisfactory play because of its unfinished condition, and the fact that
the dramatist is working in an unfamiliar style . . .' (see p. 46). And Edwin
Honig, *García Lorca*, p. 136, argues that in *When Five Years Have Passed* Lorca
'became for the first time creatively conscious of his dramatic limitations'.
Lorca's critics have not until now had the opportunity of seeing the play on
the stage and therefore of experiencing the full impact of the play's fusion
of the different dramatic elements. It is to be hoped that the recent Madrid
performance will be followed by others that will finally establish the true
stature of this unusual play.

CHAPTER IV

1 See Carlos Morla Lynch, *En España con Federico García Lorca*, pp. 285-87,
329-35.

2 See Robert Lima, *The Theatre of García Lorca*, pp. 32-33.

3 *La noce meurtriere*, tr. Marcel Auclair and Jean Prevost, *La Nouvelle Revue
Française*, Paris, 1938, No. 295-97. The play was performed with the title of
Noces de sang. The American translation by José Weissberger has the rather
curious title of *Bitter Oleander*.

4 See Robert Lima, *op. cit.*, pp. 34-35, and Morla Lynch, *op. cit.*, pp. 368-71, 380-81.

5 'From Granada to Bleeker Street', *The New York Times* (30 January, 1949), p. 1.

6 See the introduction to *Three Tragedies: Blood Wedding, Yerma, Bernarda Alba* tr. James Graham-Luján and Richard L. O'Connell, Harmondsworth: Penguin, 1961, pp. 24-25. All quotations in this chapter, unless stated otherwise, are from this translation.

7 The translation is my own.

8 See in this respect Alfredo de la Guardia, *García Lorca: persona y creación*, 4th ed., Buenos Aires: Editorial Schapire, 1961, pp. 330-31.

9 'Introduction to *The Gipsy Ballads of Federico García Lorca*, tr. Rolfe Humphries, p. 16.

10 See Robert Lima, *op. cit.*, pp. 30-32.

11 The quotation is taken from *Lope de Vega, Five Plays*, tr. Jill Booty, New York: Hill and Wang, 1961.

12 The translation is my own.

13 Much has been made of these influences by Alfredo de la Guardia, *op. cit.*, pp. 335-38.

14 See, for example, Charles Lloyd Halliburton, 'García Lorca, the Tragedian: An Aristotelian Analysis of *Bodas de sangre*', *Revista de Estudios Hispánicos*, 2 (1968), pp. 35-40; and especially Luis González del Valle, *La tragedia en el teatro de Unamuno, Valle-Inclán y García Lorca*, New York: Eliseo Torres and Sons, 1975, pp. 101-35. Most critics, on the other hand, while acknowledging the existence and the importance of many of the traditional tragic elements in *Blood Wedding*, would not draw such a rigid comparison with Greek tragedy. Indeed, in the character and traditions of Andalusia itself, so heavily impregnated with Arabic and gipsy influence, there is much to do with sorrow, fate and death which Lorca expressed in his writings and which can be explained without reference to other sources.

15 Morla Lynch, *op. cit.*, pp. 285-86, found the title too melodramatic and sensational for a work of such beauty. Gustavo Correa, on the other hand, discusses very perceptively its various implications. See *La poesía mítica de Federico García Lorca*, Madrid: Gredos, 1975, 2nd ed., pp. 82-116, especially pp. 103-106.

16 On this particular point William I. Oliver has observed that, as a consequence of the close identification between Man and Nature, Lorca's rural tragedies, especially *Blood Wedding* and *Yerma*, are alien to the way of thinking and feeling of modern, technological man, and he sees this as a reason for the failure of American audiences, in particular, to respond to Lorca's plays. See 'The Trouble with Lorca', *Modern Drama*, 7 (1964), pp. 2-15. In her recent book, *García Lorca: Playwright and Poet*, Mildred Adams observes of the first New York performance of the play: 'From time to time the audience, never really caught by the play's dramatic texture, laughed at an inept phrase. They found the mother's passionate way of addressing her beloved son as "my carnation" merely funny' (p. 172). To accept such arguments would clearly exclude the plays of many other dramatists, not least Shakespeare, from the appreciation of a modern audience.

17 For a detailed examination of the relationships between Man and Nature and of the force of inclination and instinct in human lives, see Gustavo Correa, *op. cit.*, pp. 82-116. The themes of the play have also been studied

by Ronald Gaskell, 'Theme and Form: Lorca's *Blood Wedding'*, *Modern Drama*, 5 (1963), pp. 431-39; Eva K. Touster, 'Thematic Patterns in Lorca's *Blood Wedding'*, *Modern Drama*, 7 (1964), pp. 16-27; and R. A. Zimbardo, 'The Mythic Pattern in Lorca's *Blood Wedding'*, *Modern Drama*, 10 (1968) pp. 364-71.

18 If in the second Scene rose suggests not only the bloodshed associated with Leonardo's family but also his passion for the Bride, here it hints at her passion for him, while white is symbolic of her virginity.

19 Correa, *op. cit.*, pp. 87-89, draws attention to those positive and constructive forces in the play that seek to control the anarchy of passion.

20 We can compare the allusions to the heat with those in *The House of Bernarda Alba*. See, for example, the beginning of Act II.

21 See Correa, *op. cit.*, pp. 88, 112-16.

22 Correa, *op. cit.*, pp. 103-106, is again particularly perceptive regarding the various meanings of 'blood' in the play. On the one hand there is good blood, equivalent to good seed and good stock, which assures the continuity of families, while on the other there is bad blood which corrupts and infects families and, in consequence, can have disastrous consequences for other families. For the Mother her son exemplifies the former, Leonardo and the Félix line the latter. On this point see, too, Eva K. Touster, *art. cit.*, pp. 19-22.

23 For some critics the symbolism of the last Act is a discordant element in the play. William I. Oliver observes, *art. cit.*, p. 6: 'Lorca in no way justifies a departure from the heightened realism of the first two acts of the play. His figures and his "basic" plot are capable of forcefully expressing everything encompassed in this play without aid of such allegorical beings as the Moon and Death. I must admit, however, that the ironic dilemma of any critic dealing with this play is that any one passage is theatrically brilliant in its own right. The Moon, the Weavers' song, the dialogue with Death all play beautifully as separate entities. The trouble is that they do not fuse naturally with the rest of the play – they refuse to take on an esthetic homogeneity.' For my own part, I do not feel that the different elements do not fuse successfully. Lorca, indeed, had already written another final Act in which supernatural or symbolic figures appear and manipulate the lives of human beings, for the three Card Players of *When Five Years Have Passed* anticipate, and with equal success, the characters of the Moon and Death in *Blood Wedding*.

24 We may compare the particular and the more general significance of their song with others in the play, notably the lullaby in Act I, Scene Two, and the Servant's song at the beginning of Act II, Scene Two.

25 Correa, *op. cit.*, pp. 93-94, points out that in the play there is a close identification between women and the earth. The Mother has already produced her harvest while the Bride is fertile soil ready to be sown. Men, on the other hand, are equated with the seed and the power to make the land fertile.

26 There have been differences of opinion about the ending of the play. William I. Oliver, *art. cit.*, pp. 13-15, is particularly harsh in his comments on the lament of the women:

'. . . having ended *Blood Wedding* with the mother's moving and shocking confession, her surrender of pride, Lorca gave in to the suggestion of Margarita Xirgu and added the sensational but thematically misleading section about 'With a knife, a little knife . . .' etc. This last section shows us a group of women sitting and making great noises of agony. How unlike a similar ending in *Riders to the Sea* in which the endless struggle of life is actually affirmed. Life is inescapable and, therefore, not bad, in spite of its pain. However, this is not the way with Lorcan tragic endings. They all end in a great clap of negative despair'.

Morla Lynch, much more attuned to the depth of feeling in Lorca's work, had been deeply moved by the ending, as indeed, had the Spanish audience at the play's Madrid première. In purely artistic terms the lament seems to me entirely appropriate, for it is the logical conclusion of the Mother's initial fears: the insistence on the knife, echoing the play's first Scene, brings it full circle; and, finally, it is linked too with the lullaby of Act I, Scene Two, for the lament is the realization of all the lullaby's ominous implications.

27 K. M. Cameron and T. J. C. Hoffman, *A Guide to Theatre Study*, 2nd ed., New York: Macmillan, 1974, p. 158.

28 The point is well made by Angel del Río, 'Lorca's Theater', in *Lorca: A Collection of Critical Essays*, ed., Manuel Durán, Englewood Cliffs, N. J.: Prentice-Hall, 1962, p. 149: 'The tiniest slip in the handling of any . . . elements of the play would have reduced it to a melodrama of local color...'

29 It is important to bear in mind that Lorca wrote the play for the traditional type of theatre with a picture-frame stage such as the Beatriz in which it had its première. This is not to say that performances in other kinds of theatres do not work, but a performance 'in the round', for example, loses something in the sense that the stage-settings cannot form a background to the words and movements of the characters.

30 Robert Lima, *op. cit.*, p. 191, refers to the room as being in 'a pale yellow color' but also concludes that the general effect is one of bareness and starkness. Robert Barnes, 'The Fusion of Poetry and Drama in *Blood Wedding*', *Modern Drama*, 2 (1960), relates the yellow of the room to the wheat and thus to the virility of the Bridegroom. It seems more likely here that, since the Mother is the dominant figure in the scene, the colour is associated with her.

31 Robert Lima, *op. cit.*, p. 195, observes that 'the various gradations of red in the house – the rose of the walls, the reds in the flowers, the tinted glow reflected in the copperware – are symbolic of the Félix name. The blood in the lullaby completes the tonality representing the household.' In general this point is a valid one, but the initial effect of the setting should clearly be one of tranquillity.

32 There are several very useful studies concerned with drama in performance, though none of them refer to Lorca. See, for example, Raymond Williams, *Drama in Performance*, Harmondsworth: Penguin 1972; John Fernald, *The Play Produced*, London: Kenyon-Deane, 1933; Ronald Hayman, *Techniques of Acting*, London: Methuen, 1969, *How to Read a Play*, London: Eyre Methuen, 1977; J. L. Styan, *The Elements of Drama*, Cambridge: Cambridge Univeristy Press, 1960; Harley Granville-Barker, *Prefaces to Shakespeare*, London: Sidgwick and Jackson, 1927-47.

33 In this context it is interesting to note the discussion of characterization by some of the writers mentioned in n. 32. Ronald Hayman, for example, makes this comment: 'When we read a play, the only evidence we have about a character is the stage directions and the dialogue – what he says

and does and what other people say about him and do to him during two
hours (or so) of stage action. This is quite enough evidence for constructing
an idea of what the play would be like in performance, but not nearly
enough evidence – and not the right sort – for constructing an idea of an
individual human being whose behaviour can be explained in terms of
motivations and psychological patterns.' (*How to Read a Play*, p. 50). The
psychological approach to characters in plays, whether we are reading or
seeing them is, therefore, a trap to be avoided. As far as Lorca is concerned, this suggests in turn that those who have faulted his 'characterization' have adopted mistaken criteria in approaching his plays.

34 It is difficult for an English audience not familiar with Spanish poetry and
drama to appreciate the impact of such passages in Spanish and the effect
that should, therefore, be aimed at in a performance in English. Records of
Lorca's plays and poetry are very useful in this respect. On the particular
question of lullabies Lorca himself wrote: 'I wanted to know how the
women of my country put their children to sleep and, after a certain time, I
got the impression that Spain makes use of its melodies of most marked
sadness and its texts of most melancholy expression to tinge the first sleep
of their children. This does not only concern a model or an isolated song in
some region, by any means; all regions accentuate their poetic character
and background of sadness in this type of song . . .' ('Childen's Cradle
Songs', *Zero Anthology No. 8*, New York: Zero Press, 1956, pp. 64-65,
tr. R. Artesani-Lyons).

35 Carlos Morla Lynch, having heard Lorca read the play aloud, refers to its
'musical' character, *op. cit.*, p. 286. Angel del Río observes that Lorca
'makes use with admirable economy of all the known devices of his art.
Music has a role, together with folk poetry, in the lullabies and wedding
songs, and in the rhythm which envelops the action . . .' (*art. cit., op. cit.*,
p. 149). It is no coincidence that the play has been adapted as a ballet nor
that in performance individual scenes lend themselves to a ballet-like
treatment.

36 Carlos Morla Lynch, *op. cit.*, p. 287, describes Lorca's own reading of these
lines and his own reaction to them: 'there is not a heart in the world that
would not bleed before the elegy, so disconsolate, . . . of the weeping
mother overcome by grief . . .
. . . Federico has recited it magically . . .'
Of the same passage in the first stage performance Morla Lynch, p. 334,
suggests clearly the tone – a lament, a supplication, a litany. The non-
Hispanist should listen to a record of the play or to Lorca's magnificent
Lament for the Death of a Bullfighter (Llanto por Ignacio Sánchez Mejías).

37 I have been helped greatly in the writing of this chapter by having the
opportunity of attending both the rehearsals and an excellent performance
of the play, staged in April 1978 by the students of the Drama Department
of the University College of Wales, Aberystwyth. I wish to thank their
director, Mrs. Emily Davies, for her very helpful comments.

CHAPTER V

1 Carlos Morla Lynch, *op. cit.*, pp. 426-29.
2 See pp. 432-36. The reviews of the Madrid newspapers were, as indicated,
extremely enthusiastic, and there was only an occasional censure – as in

ABC – of 'unnecessary crudities' in the mouths of some characters. In the light of this, the statement by Mildred Adams is very strange and, it would appear, at odds with the truth of the matter: 'It got critical praise, but in the hands of actors who were sometimes less than subtle its underlying beauties failed to move the audience. Even though played at home in the language in which Federico had written it, the production won no more than a pale acclaim.' See *García Lorca: Playwright and Poet*, p. 172.

3 Morla Lynch, *op. cit.*, pp. 436-37.

4 The translations of the poems, except where indicated, are my own.

5 The translation is taken from Rolfe Humphries, *The Gipsy Ballads of Federico García Lorca*, pp. 28-29.

6 *Ibid.*, pp. 32-33.

7 The translations of the plays, except where indicated, are those by James Graham-Luján and Richard L. O'Connell.

8 The translation is my own. The page reference is to the Spanish text in *Obras completas*.

9 *Ibid.*

10 See R. Martínez Nadal, *op. cit.*, p. 115. Nadal has an equally illuminating section on Lorca's treatment of the theme of frustrated love in men. See pp. 124-27.

11 Most critics mention the significance of honour for Yerma, though they do not all form the same conclusion. See, for example, Robert Lima, *op. cit.*, pp. 220, 232-35, whose views are similar to my own. It is a view expressed too by Alfredo de la Guardia, *op. cit.*, p. 350, and Edwin Honig, *op. cit.*, pp. 172-3. L. González del Valle, on the other hand, *op. cit.*, p. 142, argues that Yerma uses the argument of honour merely as an excuse to preserve her own barrenness.

12 See Virginia Higginbotham, *op. cit.*, p. 39.

13 The point has been made by Alfredo de la Guardia, *op. cit.*, pp. 350-51, and also by Edwin Honig, *op. cit.*, p. 163: 'While *Bodas de Sangre* follows in the tradition of Lope de Vega, who insisted on the spectacular and collective conception of tragic action, *Yerma* follows in the tradition of Calderón de la Barca, who insisted on the individual conception of tragedy . . .'

14 Several critics have discussed the significance of Yerma's name. The most perceptive on this particular point is Rupert Allen, *Psyche and Symbol in the Theater of Federico García Lorca*, Austin: University of Texas Press, 1974. He observes that ' "Yerma" as a name will not bear analysis . . . For *yermo*, after all, is a descriptive adjective, and when it is applied to the protagonist of this play, it functions primarily as an epithet . . . after five years of childless marriage she has earned an epithet . . .' (pp. 154-55).

15 The figure of the shepherd evokes Victor on the one hand, but on the other is reminiscent of Yerma's father, Enrique the shepherd (see the beginning of Act I, Scene Two), also a strong, physical man, enjoying all the masculine attraction that her husband so clearly lacks, at least in her own eyes. See Robert E. Lott, 'Yerma: The Tragedy of Unjust Barrenness', *Modern Drama*, 8 (1965), pp. 20-27.

16 The controversies about Juan's part in Yerma's barrenness are many and varied. Robert Lima, *op. cit.*, p. 238, observes: 'There is a curious state which remains mysterious: whether Juan is impotent or whether his selfishness commands his abstention.' He is neither impotent nor totally abstinent, however, and Rupert Allen, *op. cit.*, pp. 127-30, has rightly taken to task those critics who see him as such. Brian Morris refers to Juan's

'emotional stiffness', 'his monumental incomprehension of his wife', and his commitment 'to the narrow principles of hard work and material success, which take no account of deep human wants'. The differences between them are, therefore, predominantly psychological and are accentuated by a loveless marriage. See 'Lorca's Yerma: Wife without an Anchor', *Neophilologus*, LVI (1972), pp. 285-97.

17 We may validly compare Yerma's domestic tasks, particularly sewing, with the monotonous and equally unproductive tasks of the spinster daughters of Bernarda Alba.

18 Rupert Allen, focusing too much on Yerma's psychological deficiencies, fails to do justice to her virtues and thus to the unfairness and the pity of her lot. Morris, Lima and Honig present a much more balanced view both of her and of the pathos of her situation.

19 Honig, *op. cit.*, p. 168, observes that 'Victor . . . is Yerma's natural mate', Lima, *op. cit.*, p. 227, that 'there is an unmistakeable recognition by Victor and Yerma that it is they who should have been joined in marriage', Robert Lott, *art. cit.*, p. 21, that 'Victor, the only man who ever appealed to her physically, is a strong vital shepherd', and Cedric Busette, *op. cit.*, p. 48, that the only man who really awakens Yerma's passions is Victor. Rupert Allen, arguing that Yerma is sexually repressed, would clearly take the view that she would be unable to respond to Victor or any other man.

20 Rupert Allen contrasts what he considers to be Yerma's sexually repressed nature with the sexual enjoyment experienced by the other women in the play and gives little importance to the fact that Yerma admits to having trembled at Victor's touch as does María at her husband's. I would suggest that Yerma's inability to respond to her husband is due very largely to the simple fact that their marriage was imposed on her, that she does not love him, and that she does not find him in any way attractive. While it is impossible to prove that things would have been different had she married Victor, there is much in the play to suggest it and her tragedy is, of course, that she is married to a man so different from herself in every way.

21 Brian Morris, *art. cit.*, p. 287, notes that here 'Yerma expresses her subconscious desire for Victor . . .' Her desire for water, symbolic of her longing for a child, is, of course, unsatisfied, her thirst unquenched, but this is not to say that in different circumstances it could not be quenched.

22 We may compare the cleaning of the house by Juan's sisters to the cleaning of Bernarda Alba's house by the servants, just as earlier Yerma's sewing, symbolic of her repetitive and meaningless domestic tasks, parallels the sewing of Bernarda's daughters.

23 For a general discussion of honour in the play, see Cedric Busette, *op. cit.*, pp. 53-54, 65-66, 69, and especially Gustavo Correa, *op. cit.*, pp. 121-127. Correa distinguishes quite rightly between Yerma's sense of honour as virtue and integrity and Juan's conception of honour as public reputation, though it would be wrong to assume that a belief in the one entirely excludes a belief in the other.

24 For a study of *Yerma* in terms of fertility rite and, beyond that, of myth, Correa, *op. cit.*, pp. 117-143, is particularly interesting. See too the detailed analysis by Patricia L. Sullivan, 'The Mythic Tragedy of *Yerma*', *Bulletin of Hispanic Studies*, XLIX (1972), pp. 265-78.

25 We are reminded here of similar passages in Luis de Góngora's *Solitudes (Las soledades)* where women kneel on the banks of streams, their hands in the water, and relationships between the creativity of Nature and the

beauty and perfection of human beings are constantly suggested. It should
not be forgotten that Góngora's poetry was the subject of one of Lorca's
famous lectures, *The Poetic Image in Don Luis de Góngora (La imagen poética de
Don Luis de Góngora)*, and that the seventeenth-century poet was, therefore, another of those key Golden Age influences on Lorca. On this point
see Edwin Honig, *op. cit.*, pp. 31-36.

26 The question of the conflicting aims of Yerma and Juan is the central one in
the play, stemming from their incompatibility and exacerbated from the
very moment of their marriage. Brian Morris, *art. cit.*, p. 286, has put the
point well: 'Both Yerma and Juan are stubbornly committed to opposing
ideals . . . Their stubborn commitment to two incompatible, irreconcilable
ideals guarantees a perpetual collision and the climactic explosion . . .
Yerma and Juan are searching for something the other cannot – or will not –
provide . . .'

27 See L. González del Valle, *op. cit.*, pp. 136-37; Brian Morris, *art. cit.*, p. 289.

28 There is an anticipation here of *The House of Bernarda Alba* where the old,
crazed figure of María Josefa, Bernarda's mother, is a living reminder to
Bernarda's spinster daughters of the fate that awaits them.

29 Some critics have, of course, used the First Old Woman's words to
strengthen their argument concerning Juan's inadequacy, be it impotence
or emotional coldness. What matters here is not whether her statement
is true or not but its effect on Yerma at this particular moment in time.

30 Rupert Allen suggests that throughout the play sexual passion is equated
with 'singing' and that Juan, inasmuch as at the end of the play he makes
sexual advances to Yerma, 'sings' to her. She, unable to 'sing', is 'confronted by an erotic challenge, and this quite unhinges her . . . That
strangling is the mode of execution called for ought to be explained within
the context of the play; and can there really be any doubt that the way Juan
dies is a retaliatory punishment for his "singing", a punishment by talion?
The pick-pocket gets a hand lopped off, the Peeping Tom is blinded – and
the singer is strangled' (p. 151). It is an ingenious explanation but it does
not, of course, exclude the others I am suggesting.

31 See the introduction to *Three Tragedies . . .*, p. 25.

32 *Ibid.*, p. 25.

33 *Op. cit.*, pp. 198-99.

34 There is no suggestion that, as Mildred Adams implies, *Yerma* was played
entirely realistically in its first Madrid performance in 1934. The critics
praised the sets by Fontanals, suggesting that they were entirely in keep-
ing with the 'poetic' character of the work, while Díez-Canedo, writing in
La Voz, spoke of their lack of fussiness. In the Madrid production of Luis
Escobar in the early sixties the sets were certainly stripped of realistic
detail, as the photographs of each of the Acts prove. The sets of José
Caballero sought a balance between naturalism and abstraction, attempting to avoid simultaneously the coldness of too great an austerity and the
provincialism of too much local colour. The controversial production by
Víctor García for the company of Nuria Espert took place at the Teatro de la
Comedia in Madrid and was performed afterwards in London, Berlin,
Belgrade, Venice and the United States. The director's aim in this production was to get rid of any suggestion of realism and to create, by means of a
vast, suspended canvas, a timeless, undefined space in which the characters act out their lives.

35 In this sense we can compare the function and character of the dialogue

with that of *Blood Wedding*. In both plays hardly a word is wasted.

36 For a study of the songs see Gustavo Correa, *op. cit.*, pp. 134-43. As well as emphasizing particularly dramatic moments, the effect of song and poetry, as in *Blood Wedding*, is to universalize the particular, to make an identification between Yerma and ourselves and between her and the broader context of Nature, of which we are all part.

37 Correa makes the valid point that this song, through its sheer concentration of emotion, expresses more effectively than the ensuing dialogue both the longing and the isolation of Yerma and Juan.

38 In the sense that these songs focus on Yerma herself and her growing anguish, revealing so powerfully each stage in her emotional disintegration, they establish in the structure of the play that very strong sense of a relentless, unswerving advance towards catastrophe which must be part of the movement of tragedy.

39 Correa notes perceptively, pp. 137-40, that the song of the Laundresses traces the entire process of childbirth from the sexual act to the birth of the child and the joy of the parents. Together with the ritual songs of the last Act, it establishes a sense of the urgent, vital rhythms of life, of a collective energy in the context of which the anguished songs of Yerma, a single, isolated voice, seem more pitiful. If drama is itself a ritual, giving men an insight into the nature of things, the ritualistic element of Lorca's plays immeasurably enhances that effect, especially in *Blood Wedding* and *Yerma*. Martin Esslin, *An Anatomy of Drama*, London: Abacus, 1978, has a very relevant section on the relationship between drama and ritual. See pp. 23-32.

40 The point has already been made (see note 38) that the songs sung by Yerma are like sign-posts marking out the stages in her emotional journey. The effect of repeated movements is much the same, suggesting the enormous concentration in this play.

CHAPTER VI

1 Carlos Morla Lynch, *op. cit.*, pp. 462-64.
2 *El Sol*, 15 December, 1935, p. 4.
3 *La Vanguardia*, 14 December, 1935, p. 9.
4 See Robert Lima, *op. cit.*, p. 243.
5 See the introduction to the Penguin translation of the three tragedies, pp. 22-23.
6 Alfredo de la Guardia, *op. cit.*, pp. 365-66.
7 The translations, except where indicated, are my own. Page references in the case of my own translations are to the *Obras completas*. All quotations from the play are from the translation of James Graham-Luján and Richard L. O'Connell.
8 The bitter sweetness of the play has been commented on by most critics. Morla Lynch, listening to it being read, observed that it was 'a human story, sweetly sad or painfully pleasant' (p. 463). But, as we have seen, this was nothing new in Lorca's theatre, for in many of his plays he is constantly preoccupied with the juxtaposition of opposites in the lives of his characters.
9 R. Martínez Nadal, *Lorca's 'The Public'* . . . has an interesting section on Rosita's frustration as well as very useful observations throughout the

book on Rosita in relation to some of Lorca's other female characters. See, in particular, pp. 121-24.

10 There is a similar scene in *Mariana Pineda*, the comic counterparts there being Amparo and Clavela. For a study of the comic elements in *Doña Rosita*, see Virginia Higginbotham, *op. cit.*, pp. 102-11.

11 There is a clear parallel between the silent opening of the third Act here and the beginning of Acts I and III of *The House of Bernarda Alba*, especially the former where the stage is empty and the only sound is the tolling of bells.

12 The links between *Doña Rosita* and Chekhov's *The Cherry Orchard*, of which the desolate ending of both plays is only one example, have often been suggested. See, for example, Ángel del Río, *Vida y obras de Federico García Lorca*, Zaragoza: Heraldo de Aragón, 1952, p. 127; and Virginia Higginbotham, *op. cit.*, pp. 109-11.

CHAPTER VII

1 Carlos Morla Lynch, *op. cit.*, pp. 483-88. Lorca gave another private reading of the play at the home of Eusebio Oliver in Madrid in the presence of his fellow poets – Dámaso Alonso, Jorge Guillén and Guillermo de Torre.

2 See Carlos Morla Lynch, *op. cit.*, pp. 488-89. The translation is my own.

3 Robert Lima, *op. cit.*, p. 265, cites the opinion of the reporter, Claude Couffon, who obtained much of his information from Lorca's cousin, María.

4 The translations of the poems, except where indicated, are my own.

5 All quotations from the plays, unless stated otherwise, are taken from the translations already cited.

6 Many critics have noted the relationship between the two dramatists and even between the two plays, but none have examined it in any detail. See, for example, Alfredo de la Guardia, *op. cit.*, p. 380, and D. Pérez Minik in the introduction to *La casa de Bernarda Alba*, 5th ed., Barcelona: Aymá, 1974, pp. 27-28.

7 The translations are my own. Line references are to the Spanish text in the edition of the play by C. A. Jones, Oxford: Oxford University Press, 1961.

8 See Alfredo de la Guardia, *op. cit.*, pp. 380-81, D. Pérez Minik, *op. cit.*, p. 29, and Francisco García Lorca in the introduction to the Penguin translation of the play, p. 29.

9 The point is made by Victoria Urbano, *El teatro español y sus directrices contemporáneas*, Madrid: Editora Nacional, 1972, p. 109. Another, more general influence which should be mentioned here, as well as in relation to the other rural tragedies, is that of Benavente. Victoria Urbano, pp. 125-28, sees the influence of his rural dramas as decisive upon the development of modern Spanish tragedy and upon Lorca in particular. D. Pérez Minik, *op. cit.*, pp. 24-26, acknowledges Benavente's influence, as well as that of Dicenta, Guimerá and Valle-Inclán, but sees these earlier plays as merely transposing to the countryside, especially in Benevente's case, tragedies thought up in a Madrid flat and which might equally have a middle-class setting.

10 Allardyce Nicoll, *World Drama*, 9th ed., London: Harrap, 1966, p. 57.

11 *Ibid.* p. 76.

12 See the earlier discussions of *Blood Wedding* in terms of Aristotelian tragedy.

13 The *Obras completas* text does not contain Lorca's subtitle for the play: *A play about women in the villages of Spain*. With regard to the main title, the symbolism of Alba, 'dawn', has often been mentioned. See, for example, L. González del Valle, *op. cit.*, p. 163: '. . . the whiteness in her name and the association between this colour and her obsession with purity.' There is also, of course, the irony that the action of the play presents not the dawn or beginning but the extinction of a household in the sense that no child will be born to any of the women.

14 The subtitle is significant in this sense. For many critics the play is both a comment on the Spain of the 1930s and an image of the clash between the individual and society on a more general level. See J. Rubia Barcia, 'El realismo "mágico" de *La casa de Bernarda Alba*', *Revista Hispánica Moderna*, XXXI (1965), pp. 385-98; Sumner Greenfield, 'Poetry and Stagecraft in *La casa de Bernarda Alba*', *Hispania*, 38 (1955), pp. 456-61; Roberto Sánchez, 'La última manera dramática de García Lorca', *Papeles de son Armadans*, 60 (1971), pp. 83-102.

15 See note 35.

16 On the question of honour see Robert Lima, *op. cit.*, pp. 270, 280-81, 286-7; D. Pérez Minik, *op. cit.*, pp. 26-28; Roberto Sánchez, *art. cit.*, pp. 92, 96, 98-100; L. González del Valle, *op. cit.*, pp. 153-55.

17 Thus Robert Lima, *op. cit.*, p. 268: 'La Poncia and La Criada both decry the injustices of Bernarda, but they, in turn, assume similar attitudes towards others.'

18 L. González del Valle, *op. cit.*, p. 160, suggests that María Josefa's name, evoking the parents of Christ, indicates that she is symbolic of the creative forces in life, of everything that in Bernarda assumes its negative form.

19 The most detailed study of the symbolism of the horse in Lorca's work is that by R. M. Nadal in *Lorca's 'The Public'* . . .

20 On the symbolism of the names, see J. Rubia Barcia, *art. cit.*, pp. 388-89; L. González del Valle, *op. cit.*, p. 163; and Robert Lima, *op. cit.*, p. 271. The folly of attempting to read too much into some of the names is clear in the differing interpretations arrived at by these critics. González del Valle, for example, takes 'Adela' to be a shortened form of 'adelante', 'forward', and thus to symbolize Adela's striving. In contrast, Rubia Barcia states that the name is of Germanic origin and signifies to be 'of a noble nature'.

21 For the symbolism of green, see Thomas F. Sharp, 'The Mechanics of Lorca's Drama in *La casa de Bernarda Alba*', *Hispania*, 46 (1961), pp. 231-33. There is also the point, of course, that, as in the ballad 'Somnambulistic Ballad' *(Romance sonámbulo)*, green suggests death and anticipates here Adela's suicide.

22 The relationship between Man and Nature and the theme of the force of inclination and instinct in human lives are essentially the same in this play as in *Blood Wedding* and *Yerma*, but the fact that the action of the play takes place not in Nature's setting but within the confines of a house does not allow for the development of those ideas in quite the same detailed and direct manner. On the other hand, Gustavo Correa, *La poesía mítica de Federico García Lorca*, suggests that the patterns which he traces in *Blood Wedding* and *Yerma* may equally be found in *The House of Bernarda Alba*.

23 For a study of the importance of determinism in the play, see C. Busette, *Obra dramática de García Lorca: Estudio de su configuración*, New York: Las Americas Publishing Co., 1971, pp. 78-111.

24 On this point, see C. Busette, *op. cit.*, p. 90. There is a clear parallel here with the cyclic movements and the oppression of Nature suggested in *Blood Wedding* and *Yerma*.

25 In the way in which within a play one episode is reminiscent of another, characters act out similar roles, and the whole becomes suggestive both of life's unchanging patterns and of the subjection of individuals to those patterns, there is a remarkable similarity to certain plays of Calderón. See in this respect my own study of Calderón: *The Prison and the Labyrinth: Studies in Calderonian Tragedy*, Cardiff: University of Wales Press, 1978.

26 L. González del Valle, *op. cit.*, pp. 152-53, argues that only Adela can be regarded as tragic since only she suffers on account of her actions. In my view it goes without saying that Bernarda brings upon herself the consequences of her tyranny and achieves, in a sense, the opposite of what she seeks. She is no less the victim of society's tyranny than is Adela the victim of her mother's. Lorca was too sensitive and understanding a dramatist to focus the tragedy on only the youngest daughter, even though he may have sympathized with her most.

27 J. Rubia Barcia, *art. cit.*, p. 389, considers that Prudencia, as her name indicates, symbolizes resignation and the wisdom of old age. In this sense she represents a tolerance towards her daughter's error that is a contrast to Bernarda's lack of charity.

28 We have in Martirio's allusion to a well of poison the source of Bardem's inspired idea that the walls of the house should in their height and their bareness suggest a well from whose depths escape is increasingly impossible.

29 L. González del Valle, *op. cit.*, p. 162, sees María Josefa's allusions to whiteness and foam as symbolizing sperm and the creative processes of Nature. The sea, in any case, is an old-established symbol of creativity and continuity.

30 Francisco García Lorca, introduction to *Three Tragedies* . . . , p. 28.

31 Many critics discuss the 'realism' of the play. L. Rodríguez Alcalde, for example, *Teatro español contemporáneo*, Madrid: Epesa, 1973, observes that here 'the poet has stripped himself of all superficial adornment in order to penetrate to the heart of the tragedy . . .; the language of *The House of Bernarda Alba* is bare, wonderfully realistic, just as the extremely accurate portrayal of each of those women, each different from the other, is realistic . . . In *Bernarda* we find Lorca the dramatist rooted in reality, at the end of a conscious evolution . . .' (pp. 141-42). See too, in this connection, Alberto del Monte, 'Il realismo di *La casa de Bernarda Alba*', *Belfagor*, 20 (1965), pp. 130-48; and R. A. Young, 'García Lorca's *Bernarda Alba*: A Microcosm of Spanish Culture', *Modern Languages*, 50 (1969), pp. 66-72. Detailed studies of the play's mixture of realism and symbolism include Sumner M. Greenfield, *art. cit.*, pp. 456-61; J. Rubia Barcia, *art. cit.*, pp. 385-98; and Luis González del Valle, *op. cit.*, pp. 148-68. A particularly interesting study of the realism of the play in terms of its social criticism is offered by Roberto G. Sánchez, *art. cit.*, pp. 83-102.

32 The Aymá edition of the play, Barcelona, 1974, contains production notes made by Juan Antonio Bardem for the Madrid performance of the play in 1964. They are extremely useful in a consideration of the play in performance. The translations of Bardem's observations are my own.

33 Bardem, considering the amount of detail required in his sets, opted for a further simplification of what is suggested by Lorca's stage-directions: 'if

one wishes to retain only what is necessary and sufficient, then the *"jute curtains tied back with tassels and ruffles"* and the *"pictures of unlikely landscapes full of nymphs or legendary kings"* will disappear. What do we have left? Some white walls, some doorways . . . and some objects. What are they? Wicker chairs. How many? A cupboard. A mirror. Sewing baskets. A lamp.' (p. 109).

34 Bardem has a very perceptive observation on the presentation of the walls and the doors: '. . . Let us place these women at the bottom of this well of bitterness. Some high walls, very high, as high as possible . . . And let us have doorways higher than their normal height. Thick walls, high, white walls bare, and high doorways' (p. 111). It is a set which emphasizes, even more than Lorca's own stage-directions, the idea of imprisonment and no-escape.

35 See J. Rubia Barcia, *art. cit.*, p. 390. Robert Lima merely suggests that 'the baroque paintings . . . are obsolete against the mass of white' (*op. cit.*, p. 267). L. González del Valle makes the unlikely suggestion that the pictures are 'another example of the lack of reality that dominates everything in this household . . .' (*op. cit.*, pp. 158-59).

36 Sumner M. Greenfield interprets the photographic effect more in terms of Lorca's intention to create a realistic setting: 'Lorca augments the illusion of concrete reality not only by dint of the restraints placed on his poetic inclinations but in a positive way, through his theatrical vision of the play as the reproduction of a photograph, not in its details but in its color: black and white.' (*art. cit.*, p. 456).

37 The English translation does not contain what is clearly an important stage-direction and which is given in both the *Obras completas* and the text of the Buenos Aires first performance: [*The setting should be one of absolute simplicity*] (p. 1416).

38 Bardem, pp. 110-11, makes the important point that in a physical as well as in an emotional sense there is a progressive inward movement in the play. In Act I the world outside Bernarda's house seems near enough. Act II removes the action a stage further to an inner room, while in the patio of Act III the very centre of the house, isolated from the outside world, has been reached. As for the patio-setting, Bardem observes that the sky should not be seen. It is far away and out of reach. The walls of the patio should be very high, enclosing the women totally.

39 L. González del Valle, *op. cit.*, pp. 165-66, makes the rather strange observation that in the white of the walls there is symbolized Bernarda's concern with the purity of her daughters and in the blue the 'devotion' or 'constancy' with which Adela and Martirio pursue Pepe el Romano.

40 See Virginia Higginbotham, *op. cit.*, pp. 113-14, 132-33: '. . . Bernarda resembles the villain of a puppet farce, whose body jerks into stiff but automatic poses . . . Bernarda conveys her anger with gestures much like those of the mock-ferocious puppet Cristóbal . . .' And: 'Bernarda . . . shouts or speaks loudly more often than she participates in normal conversation . . .'

41 Bardem, p. 118, makes the crucial point, in discussing how Bernarda should be played, that 'her voice should be raised only when necessary...'

42 See Bardem, pp. 119-22, for the need to distinguish in performance between Bernarda and her daughters and between one daughter and another.

43 Especially interesting in Bardem's observations on the role of La Poncia is

u

the point that the actress playing her should avoid gestures: 'No gestures. The peasant community, expecially women, do not wave their arms about, or they do so awkwardly in moments of extreme joy or sorrow'.

44 Bardem felt that in the last Act only Adela should be dressed totally in white: 'How should we see those women – Bernarda and the other girls? Should they wear petticoats and wrap themselves in shawls? No. Impossible. Bernarda must always be in black. She *is* black . . . Martirio . . . *is* black too. For the other three sisters one can look for something between black (Bernarda – Martirio) and white (Adela). So they can appear with a single bit of white – the bodice – but with black skirts and shawls.' (pp. 114-15).

45 Bardem, pp. 112-14, was greatly preoccupied with the lighting and draws several important conclusions. He insists that the lighting of the stage should never change within an Act. It should be constant, suggesting that nothing changes within Bernarda's household. Changes in the lighting should always come from outside, by means of the doorways. In this way we are made aware of the world outside the house and, in consequence, of the isolation of the house itself. In general terms the lighting should never be used merely to create a 'pretty effect'.

46 L. Rodríguez Alcalde, *op. cit.*, p. 136, makes the point that 'if we consider the works performed in Lorca's lifetime, their technical or formal innovation was not very great . . .'

SELECT BIBLIOGRAPHY

ENGLISH TRANSLATIONS

Three Tragedies, trans. James Graham Luján and Richard O'Connell, Harmondsworth: Penguin, 1961.

Five Plays: Comedies and Tragi-comedies, trans. James Graham Luján and Richard O'Connell, Harmondsworth: Penguin, 1970.

The Gipsy Ballads of Federico García Lorca, trans. Rolfe Humphries, Bloomington and London: Indiana University Press, 5th ed., 1969.

CRITICISM

Adams, Mildred. *García Lorca: Playwright and Poet*, New York: George Braziller, 1977.

Aguirre, J. M. 'El sonambulismo de Federico García Lorca', *Bulletin of Hispanic Studies*, XL (1967), pp. 267-285.

Alberich, J. 'El erotismo femenino en el teatro de García Lorca', *Papeles de Son Armadans*, XXXIX (1965), pp. 9-36.

Allen, Rupert. *Psyche and Symbol in the Theater of Federico García Lorca*, Austin and London: University of Texas Press, 1974.
The Symbolic World of Federico García Lorca, Albuquerque: University of New Mexico Press, 1972.

Babín, María Teresa. 'García Lorca, poeta del teatro', *Asomante*, IV (1948), pp. 48-57).
García Lorca, vida y obra, New York: Las Américas, 1955.
Estudios lorquianos, Puerto Rico: Editorial Universitaria, 1976.

Barea, Arturo. 'El lenguaje poético de Federico García Lorca', *Bulletin of Hispanic Studies*, XXXI (1944), pp. 3-15.
Lorca: The Poet and His People, New York: Grove Press, 1949.

Barnes, Robert. 'The Fusion of Poetry and Drama in *Blood Wedding*', *Modern Drama*, II (1960), pp. 395-402.

Berenguer Carisomo, Arturo. *Las máscaras de Federico García Lorca*, Buenos Aires: Ed. Universitaria de Buenos Aires, 1969.

Blanco-González, Manuel. 'Lorca: The Tragic Trilogy', *Drama Critique*, LX (1966), pp. 91-97.

Borel, Jean-Paul. *El teatro de lo imposible*, Madrid: Ediciones Guadarrama, 1966.

Buero Vallejo, Antonio. 'García Lorca ante el esperpento'. In *Tres maestros ante el público*, Madrid: Alianza, 1973.

Bull, Judith M. 'Santa Bárbara and *La Casa de Bernarda Alba*', *Bulletin of Hispanic Studies*, XLVII (1970), pp. 117-123.

Burton, Julianne. 'Society and the Tragic Vision in Federico García Lorca', *Dissertation Abstracts International*, XXXIII (1972), p. 2362A.

Busette, Cedric. *Obra dramática de García Lorca: Estudio de su configuración*, New York: Las Américas Publishing Co., 1971.

Byrd, Suzanne. *'La Barraca' and the Spanish ·National Theatre*, New York: Ediciones Abra, 1975.

Cangiotti, Gualtiero. 'Federico García Lorca, poeta del 'desengaño', *Litteratura Moderni*, II (1961), pp. 34-55.

Cannon, Calvin. 'The Imagery of Lorca's *Yerma*', *Modern Language Quarterly*, XXI (1960), pp. 122-130.

'*Yerma* as Tragedy', *Symposium*, XVI (1962), pp. 82-93.

Cano, José Luis. 'De *El Maleficio* a *Mariana Pineda*', *Cuadernos Americanos*, XXIII (1962), pp. 201-213.

García Lorca: biografía ilustrada, Barcelona: Ediciones Destino, 1962.

Carrier, Warren. 'Poetry in the Drama of Lorca', *Drama Survey*, II (1963), pp. 297-304.

Colecchia, Frances. 'Doña Rosita – una heroina aparte', *Duquesne Hispanic Review*, II (1967), pp. 37-43.

Correa, Gustavo. 'Honor, Blood and Poetry in *Yerma*', *Tulane Drama Review*, VII (1962), pp. 96-110.

La poesía mítica de Federico García Lorca, 2nd ed., Madrid: Gredos, 1975.

'El simbolismo del sol en la poesía de Federico García Lorca', *Nueva Revista de Filología Hispánica*, XIV (1960), pp. 110-119.

Crow, John A. *Federico García Lorca*, Los Angeles: University of California Press, 1945.

Cuadra Pinto, Fernando. 'Para un análisis de *Bodas de sangre*', *Revista Signos de Valparaiso*, III (1969), pp. 97-115.

Devoto, Daniel. '*Doña Rosita la soltera*: estructura y fuentes', *Bulletin Hispanique*, LXIX (1967), pp. 407-440.

Díaz-Plaja, Guillermo. *Federico García Lorca*, Buenos Aires: Espasa-Calpe, 1954.

Doménech, Ricardo. '*La casa de Bernarda Alba*.' *Primer Acto*, L (1963), pp. 14-16.

'A propósito de *Mariana Pineda*', *Cuadernos Hispanoamericanos*, LXX (1967), pp. 608-613.

Durán, Manuel. 'El surrealismo en el teatro de Lorca y Alberti', *Hispanófila*, (1957), pp. 61-66.

Lorca: A Collection of Critical Essays, ed. Manuel Durán, Englewood Cliffs, N. J.: Prentice-Hall, 1962.

Eich, Christoph. *Federico García Lorca: Poeta de la intensidad*, Madrid: Gredos, 1958.

Falconieri, John V. 'Tragic Hero in Search of a Role: Yerma's Juan.' *Revista de Estudios Hispánicos*, I (1967), pp. 17-33.

Flecniakoska, Jean-Louis. *L'Universe poétique de Federico García Lorca*, Paris: Bière, 1952.

Flys, Jonathan M. *El lenguaje poético de Federico García Lorca*, Madrid: Gredos, 1955.

Frazier, Brenda. *La mujer en el teatro de Federico García Lorca*, Madrid: Ed. Plaza Mayor, 1973.

García Lorca, Federico. *Cartas a sus amigos*, Preface by Sebastián Gasch, Barcelona: Ed. Cobalto, 1950.

Gaskell, Ronald. 'Theme and Form: Lorca's *Blood Wedding*', *Modern Drama*, V (1963), pp. 431-439.

Gibson, Ian. *The Death of Lorca*, London: W. H. Allen, 1973.

González Guzmán, Pascual. 'Los dos mundos de don Perlimplín', *Revista do livro*, IV (1959), pp. 39-60.

Greenfield, Sumner M. 'Poetry and Stagecraft in *La casa de Bernarda Alba*', *Hispania*, XXXVIII (1955), pp. 456-461.

'The Problem of *Mariana Pineda*', *Massachusetts Review*, I (1960), pp. 751-763.

Guardia, Alfredo de la. *García Lorca: Persona y creación*, Buenos Aires: Editorial Schapire, 1944.

Guillén, Jorge. *Federico en persona: Semblanza y epistolario*, Buenos Aires: Editorial Emecé, 1959.

Halliburton, Charles Lloyd. 'García Lorca, the Tragedian: An Aristotelian Analysis of *Bodas de sangre*', *Revista de Estudios Hispánicos*, II (1968), pp. 35-40.

Higginbotham, Virginia. 'Bernarda Alba – A Comic Character?' *Drama Survey*, VI (1968), pp. 258-265.

'Lorca and Twentieth-Century Spanish Theater: Three Precursors', *Modern Drama*, XV (1972), pp. 164-174.

'Lorca's Apprenticeship in Surrealism', *Romanic Review*, LXI (1970), pp. 109-122.

The Comic Spirit of Federico García Lorca, Austin and London: University of Texas Press, 1976.

Honig, Edwin. *García Lorca*, New York: New Directions, 1963.

'Lorca to Date', *Tulane Drama Review*, VII (1962), pp. 120-126.

Knight, R. G. 'Federico García Lorca's *Así que pasen cinco años*.' *Bulletin of Hispanic Studies*, XLIII (1966), pp. 32-46.

Laffranque, Marie. *Federico García Lorca*, Paris: Seghers, 1966.

Lázaro Carreter, F. 'Apuntes sobre el teatro de García Lorca', *Papeles de Son Armadans*, XVIII (1960), pp. 9-33.

Lima, Robert. *The Theater of García Lorca*, New York: Las Americas Publishing Co., 1963.

Lott, Robert. 'Tragedy of Unjust Barrenness', *Modern Drama*, VIII (1965), pp. 20-27.

Machado Bonet, Ofelia. *Federico García Lorca: Su producción dramática*, Montevideo: Imprenta Rosgal, 1951.

Martínez, Miguel. 'Realidad y símbolo en *La casa de Bernarda Alba*.' *Revista de Estudios Hispánicos*, IV (1970), pp. 55-66.

Miralles, Enrique. 'Concentración dramática en el teatro de Lorca', *Archivum*, XXI (1971), pp. 77-94.

Monte, Alverto del. 'Il realismo di *La casa de Bernarda Alba*', *Belfagor*, XX (1965), pp. 130-148.

Mora Guarnido, José. *Federico García Lorca y su mundo*, Buenos Aires: Losada, 1958.

Morla Lynch, Carlos. *En España con Federico García Lorca: Páginas de un diario íntimo, 1928-36*, Madrid: Aguilar, 1958.

Morris C. B. 'Lorca's Yerma: Wife without an Anchor', *Neophilologus*, LVI (1972), pp. 285-297.

Nadal, Rafael Martínez. *Federico García Lorca, 'El público' y 'Comedia título', Dos obras teatrales póstumas*, Barcelona: Seix Barral, 1978.
Lorca's 'The Public', London: Calder and Boyars, 1974.

Newberry, Wilma. 'Aesthetic Distance in *El público*', *Hispanic Review*, XXXVII (1969), pp. 276-296.

Nonoyama, Minako. 'Vida y muerte en *Bodas de sangre*', *Arbor*, LXXXIII (1972), pp. 307-315.

Nourissier, François. *Federico García Lorca: Dramaturge*, Paris: L'Arche, 1955.

Oliver, William I. 'Lorca: The Puppets and the Artist', *Tulane Drama Review*, VII (1962), pp. 76-96.
'The Trouble with Lorca', *Modern Drama*, VII (1964), pp. 2-15.

Olmos, Francisco. 'García Lorca, el teatro clásico, y Lope de Vega', *Primer Acto*, XXXVII (1962), pp. 15-27.

Palley, Julian. 'Archetypal Symbols in *Bodas de sangre*,' *Hispania*, L (1967), pp. 74-79.

Pérez Marchand, Monalisa Lina. 'Apuntes sobre el concepto de la tragedia en la obra dramática de García Lorca', *Asomante*, IV (1948), pp. 86-96.

Riley, Edward C. 'Sobre *Bodas de sangre*', *Clavileño*, VII (1951), pp. 8-12.

Rincón, Carlos. '*Yerma* de Federico García Lorca: Ensayo de interpretación', *Beiträge zur Romanischen Philologie*, V (1966), pp. 66-99.
'*La zapatera prodigiosa* de Federico García Lorca', *Ibero-Romania*, IV (1970), pp. 290-313.

Río, Angel del. *Vida y obras de Federico García Lorca*, Zaragoza: Heraldo de Aragón, 1952.

Rubia Barcia, J. 'El realismo "mágico" de *La casa de Bernarda Alba'*, *Revista Hispánica Moderna*, XXXI (1965), pp. 385-398.

Rodrigo, Antonina. *Margarita Xirgu y su teatro*, Barcelona: Editorial Planeta, 1974.

Ruiz Ramón, Francisco. *Historia del teatro español*, 2: Siglo XX., Madrid: Alianza, 1971.

Sánchez, Roberto G. *García Lorca: Estudio sobre su teatro*, Madrid: Ed. Jura, 1950.

'La última manera dramática de García Lorca', *Papeles de Son Armadans*, LX (1971), pp. 83-102.

Sapojnikoff, Victor K. 'La estructura temática de *Así que pasen cinco años'*, *Romance Notes*, XII (1970), pp. 11-20.

Scarpa, Roque Estéban. *El dramatismo de Federico García Lorca*, Santiago: Ed. Universitaria, 1961.

Sharp, Thomas F. 'The Mechanics of Lorca's Drama in *La casa de Bernarda Alba'*, *Hispania*, XLIV (1961), pp. 230-233.

Skloot, Robert. 'Theme and Image in Lorca's *Yerma'*, *Drama Survey*, V (1966), pp. 151-161.

Smoot, Jean J. *A Comparison of Plays by John Millington Synge and Federico García Lorca: The Poets and Time*, Madrid: Ediciones José Porrúa Turanzas, 1978.

Sullivan, Patricia L. 'The Mythic Tragedy of *Yerma'*, *Bulletin of Hispanic Studies*, LXIX (1972), pp. 265-278.

Touster, Eva K. 'Thematic Patterns in Lorca's *Blood Wedding'*, *Modern Drama*, VII (1964), pp. 16-27.

Valle, Luis González del. *La tragedia en el teatro de Unamuno, Valle-Inclán y García Lorca*, New York: Eliseo Torres and Sons, 1975.

Wells, C. Michael. 'The Natural Norm in the Plays of Federico García Lorca', *Hispanic Review*, XXXVIII (1970), pp. 299-313.

Young, Raymond A. 'García Lorca's *Bernarda Alba*: A Microcosm of Spanish Culture', *Modern Languages*, L (1969), pp. 66-72.

Zdenek, Joseph M. 'La mujer y la frustración en las comedias de García Lorca', *Hispania*, XXXVIII (1955), pp. 67-69.

Zimbardo, R. A. 'The Mythic Pattern in Lorca's *Blood Wedding'*, *Modern Drama*, X (1968), pp. 364-371.

Ziomeck, Henryk. 'El simbolismo del blanco en *La casa de Bernarda Alba* y en *La Dama del alba'*, *Symposium*, XXIV (1970), pp. 81-85.

Zuleta, Emilia de. 'Relación entre la poesía y el teatro de Lorca', in *Cinco poetas españoles* (Salinas, Guillén, Lorca, Alberti, Cernuda), by Emilia de Zuleta, Madrid: Gredos, 1971.

INDEX

308 LORCA